beyond
essence

new recipes from
le champignon sauvage
david everitt-matthias

foreword by
pierre koffmann

photography by lisa barber

To Helen, my wonderful staff and the customers that have kept me going for the last 25 years.

beyond *essence*

new recipes from
le champignon sauvage

david everitt-matthias

foreword by pierre koffmann

photography by lisa barber

Absolute Press

First published in Great Britain
in 2013 by Absolute Press,
an imprint of
Bloomsbury Publishing Plc

Absolute Press
Scarborough House
29 James Street West
Bath BA1 2BT
Phone 44 (0) 1225 316013
Fax 44 (0) 1225 445836
E-mail info@absolutepress.co.uk
Website www.absolutepress.co.uk

Publisher
Jon Croft
Commissioning Editor
Meg Avent
Editor
Norma MacMillan
Art Director
Matt Inwood
Photographer
Lisa Barber
Photography Assistant
Rachelle Cousineau

A catalogue record of this book is
available from the British Library

ISBN 13: 9781906650780

Printed and bound by
Printer Trento, Italy

Bloomsbury Publishing Plc
50 Bedford Square,
London WC1B 3DP
www.bloomsbury.com

A note about the text
This book is set in Sabon MT.
Sabon was designed by Jan
Tschichold in 1964. The roman
design is based on type by Claude
Garamond, whereas the italic
design is based on types by Robert
Granjon.

contents

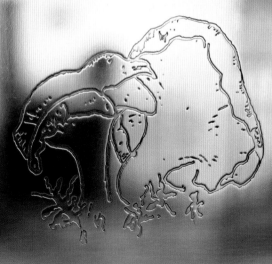

foreword by pierre koffmann

It is a real honour and a pleasure to have been asked to contribute a foreword to David's latest collection of recipes, a collection that clearly demonstrates why he is one of the most respected chefs working in Britain today.

I first met David when he came for a brief *stage* at my restaurant, La Tante Claire, many years ago, just prior to him opening his own restaurant in Cheltenham. My memory of him is of a young man eager to learn all that he could about how serious kitchens worked, fascinated by the process of cooking food full of flavour and integrity and desperate to absorb all that he could about the process of running a Michelin-starred restaurant.

Now over 25 years later his own restaurant, Le Champignon Sauvage, has become a legendary destination for diners from all over the world. He has held 2 Michelin stars for over 10 years and his cookbooks have been sold worldwide to great acclaim. He has famously never missed a service in the 25 years since first opening and he and his lovely wife Helen, who is the charming front of house face of Le Champignon Sauvage, have created a unique restaurant that exemplifies the culinary ideals and ambitions that David has espoused all his professional life.

I, along with a number of other chefs, was recently invited down to Le Champignon Sauvage for a lunch to celebrate the 25th anniversary of its first opening. The lunch overall was, of course, wonderful, but the striking memory that stays with me – and for a French man this is hard to say – is that the brandade that David cooked for us, was one of the finest that I have ever eaten. I can think of no greater compliment to pay him!

This latest collection of recipes shows the development in David's cooking since the publication of his first book, *Essence*, in 2006 and is, I suspect, destined to become an essential addition to the cookery shelves of both dedicated amateur cooks and professional chefs of all levels.

The first 25 years of Le Champignon Sauvage have proved to be a journey of culinary adventure and excellence – I am sure the next 25 years will prove to be just as exciting and influential. I wish David and Helen and their new book all the best in the world.

Pierre Koffmann, London, December 2012

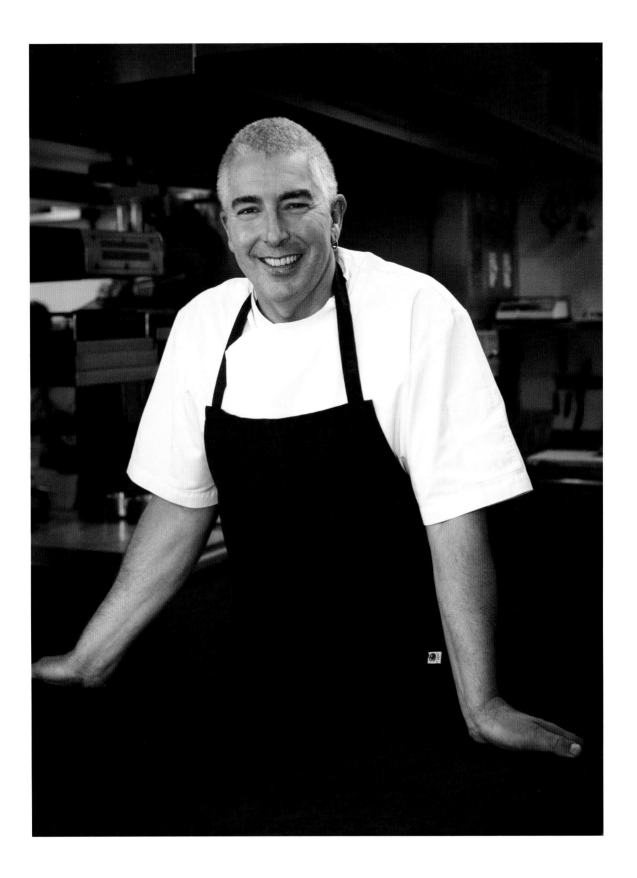

introduction

It is now 25 years since Helen and I opened the doors for the first service at Le Champignon Sauvage.

Looking back at it now, I realise that I had the passion and the skill for the job in hand but I was a little naïve on the business side, which a lot of fellow chefs – if they are being honest – will agree with. If you are investor- or partner-free, running a restaurant is something you are not taught but have to learn as you go along, and it is a big learning curve. Economic pressures outside become a factor beyond your control and when recession hits, boy, do you need to be sure of what you are doing. It is no good at all chopping and changing every week. You need to have an idea and then to stick with it. In my first book, *Essence*, I talked about cooking for the guides. This is my one regret. I should have just cooked with my heart because once I did that the customers increased, and returned, and the awards started to come our way.

Making use of the humblest ingredients due to economic necessity has stayed with me over the 25 years: using all the parts of an animal, marrying rich and poor, and then, about 10 years ago, the emergence of the foraging that has become recognisable as a feature of my food. This, of course, is only one part of my style, as there are also the spicings, the use of ingredients like pig's head and cockscombs, and, more recently, my take on desserts.

So, why a third book? Well, this one is 6 years on from *Essence* and it shows a progression in techniques and finesse. There are more outside influences, learnt from talking to chef friends like Eric Chavot, Brett Graham and Phil Howard; from eating out in different countries; and from my insatiable desire to read any new and half decent cookbook out there. As my knowledge has increased, this in turn sparks off some new and exciting ideas and combinations. I now have a tasting menu, which has created more freedom in plating with smaller cuts of meat and fish, and the presentation of our food now can match its textures and flavours.

I mentioned finesse. Well, a good example of this is a recipe that appeared in *Dessert*: a salted chicory parfait with vanilla rice pudding and bitter chocolate sorbet. This has undergone a 'tweak' and I wanted to put it in this book to show that you can never stop improving things. We tweaked the sorbet to be a little more bitter; the parfait has become a salted chicory mousse and the vanilla rice pudding a vanilla cheesecake, the whole being topped with chicory glaze. The transformation of the flavours is wonderful and the presentation cleaner with a finer line (see for yourself on page 162).

Seasonality has just as big a part to play in my food – the first partridge heralding the game that I use when the season is in full swing, the first wild garlic leaves a sign that spring is on its way with such wonderful bounty. When seasonal produce is at its prime, it tastes at its best and is usually well priced – British strawberries in the summer are the best in the world; Evesham asparagus is fantastic, you can't get better. At the moment the seasons seem to be getting muddled up, with wild garlic appearing earlier than it used to, wild mushrooms too. So the weather has to play a massive part in the choice for a menu. It is our job as chefs to keep a close eye on the seasons to gather and use the best produce.

While my cooking has evolved with all the new techniques and ingredients that have come to light in the last 6 years, I have not forgotten my past, the roots of my basic style. I have just added another string to my bow. I still have no preconceptions about what I am doing and have an open mind to learning. A good example of that being I shop in the local Asian store, walking around the shelves looking for new ingredients and asking questions. It was there that I spotted lotus seeds, something I had never seen or used before. I bought them and, in a moment of madness, decided to roast them and make ice cream. Luckily this worked out perfectly, making an ice cream with an enchanting flavour.

Chefs gain knowledge from so many sources today. For example, just sitting in an armchair with their laptop they can be whisked off to any country in the world and in turn virtually dine in nearly every restaurant, gaining inspiration and useful information. I think the thing I would pass on to a young chef now would be that you will never know everything in this trade so don't ever think you do. Be humble about learning, because it is only through this that you can actually become better.

David Everitt-Matthias, Cheltenham, December 2012

The team who have been with me during the creation of this book:
This page, top, left to right: Sue Ellis; Matthew Worswick. Bottom, left to right: Mark Stinchcombe; Keiron Stevens.
Opposite page, top, left to right: George Blogg; Justyna Juszczuk and Eva Worswick. Bottom: myself and Helen with our wonderful team.

how to use my book

As with my first two books, *Essence* and *Dessert* (both Absolute Press), most of the dishes are made up of several separate components, each of which has its own heading in the ingredients list and the method. That way, if you want to skip a particular element in a recipe, or prepare parts of it in advance, it is very easy to do.

an important note on measurements

All the measurements in this book are metric. It is a very wise investment to get yourself a good set of scales that will measure accurately down to the very last gram. To this end, I have decided to give the liquid measures in this book in grams and kilograms. You can obtain such great precision with digital scales and I urge you to gain optimum enjoyment from these recipes by weighing all your liquid measures. If you don't own a pair of digital scales or if this method simply isn't for you, then millilitres and grams (and litres and kilograms) are interchangeable when it comes to liquids, so you can just as easily choose to measure by volume if you wish.

a note on ingredients

I prefer to use unsalted butter, as it enables you to be more precise when it comes to seasoning. I buy my butter from a small dairy in Stow-on-the-Wold.

Lecithin is invaluable for helping foams become more stable. I get it from my local healthfood shop in the form of soya lecithin granules, which I then grind to a powder in a spice mill. It can be stored like this and used when needed.

I use cold pressed virgin rapeseed oil from a local supplier (see page 182). Hamish's oil has a wonderful nuttiness to it and is a lovely light amber colour.

Salt and pepper for general seasoning have not been included in ingredients lists in this book. I recommend using table salt and freshly ground black pepper unless otherwise stated.

To add texture to a dish I use Maldon salt, which I consider to be the best in the world. It comes from the east coast of England and its fine, delicate crystals give a wonderful finish to terrines and fish dishes.

13 beyond *essence*   *how to use my book*

storecupboard

Below are some of the standbys we use in the restaurant kitchen. It certainly makes life easier to have them on hand and you'll find they appear in a lot of the recipes in this book. As I stressed in my first book, *Essence*, if you build up a storecupboard according to your own preferences, it makes cooking for friends who just drop round much less of a hassle. Choose dishes that have a good shelf life or that you know you will use quickly because they are your favourites.

salted oranges

These came about through my use of salted lemons, one of the Middle Eastern flavours and spices I like, so I thought why not try oranges? I added juniper and sage because they complement the flavour of the orange, as would cardamom or coriander – or indeed both. The salted oranges are wonderful with fish, and their saltiness also goes very well with desserts that are rich, like chocolate or caramel.

8 oranges, washed
250g Maldon salt
4 sage leaves
5 juniper berries, crushed
100g lemon juice
about 200g orange juice
200g olive oil

Cut each orange into 6 wedges, but not quite all the way through. Sprinkle the inside of the oranges with salt. Pack 2 of them in a sterilised large, wide-mouthed jar, add a sage leaf and 2 crushed junipers, and sprinkle with a little more salt. Push down well to release the juices.

Repeat with another 2 oranges, pushing them down well. Add the final 2 oranges, then pour in the lemon and orange juices.

The fruit should be covered with juice, so add a little more if needed. Pour in the olive oil; this will form a seal that air cannot penetrate. Wipe the mouth of the jar and seal it with a tight-fitting lid.

Leave at least 1 month before using – the peel needs to soften. To use the peel, scrape off the pulp and quickly rinse the peel under cold running water.

Note: Don't throw away the pulp – both it and the juice can be used, for example in small amounts to flavour a light broth or a tagine, or even to flavour a dark chocolate fudge.

salted wild garlic buds

These wonderful little buds appear after the flowers of the wild garlic have gone. Keep your eye on them as they grow; they will slowly increase in size over a few weeks. Pick them when they are at their biggest. They could be pickled, as in the green elderberry recipe (see page 14), but I prefer just to salt them. A great addition to salads, they just explode with garlicky flavour and add another texture to any dish they are in. They will also hold their own against many of the more powerful flavours in the kitchen.

40g salt
200g water
250g wild garlic buds

Combine the salt and water in a small saucepan and bring to the boil. Remove from the heat and leave to cool.

Make sure the garlic buds are free of stalks, then rinse thoroughly. Place them in a sterilised jar, pour over the brine solution and cover. Keep in a cool, dark place for

2–3 weeks before using. If you want to keep them longer than this, drain the buds, place in another sterilised jar and cover with olive oil. Keep in the fridge until needed.

pickled green elderberries

I first read about these 'elderberry capers' in a book called *The Wildfoods Cookbook* by Joy O. I. Spoczynska and immediately felt an urge to give them a go. Well, I thought, I use ripe elderberries and the flowers, so why not the green berries? These have a lovely little bite to them and we use them frequently now in our corned beef and with our Witchill potato dish (see page 74). They provide saltiness, sweetness and sourness all in one go, as well as a nice textural crunch. This is my version of the book's recipe, using white balsamic vinegar for its sweetness and allowing the elderberries much longer in the initial brine to develop their saltiness. The best way to remove the berries from the elderberry heads is to pull the heads through a fork – the prongs will pull off the berries quickly.

75g salt
350g water
500g green elderberries
400g white balsamic vinegar

Put the salt and water in a medium saucepan and bring to the boil to dissolve the salt. Place to one side to cool.

Check the elderberries for any bugs, then put them in a sterilised container that has a tight-fitting lid. Pour in the brine. Cover the container and keep in a cool place or the fridge for 2–3 weeks. Keep an eye on the berries; you don't want them to shrivel. If they start to look a bit too wrinkled, drain and quickly rinse under cold running water.

Once the salting period is over, drain the brine from the berries and put them into a clean, sterilised, warm jar. Bring the vinegar to the boil, then pour over the berries to cover them completely. Immediately cover with a tight-fitting lid and leave to cool. Keep in the refrigerator (they can be stored for 6–8 months).

pickled peaches

Pickling fruits when they are at their prime is a great way to enjoy their flavour out of season. They can help lift a heavy winter dish, introducing a freshness by helping to cut through fat. This pickling liquor also works well with cherries, apples and damsons. You can of course change the spicing in the liquor – alexander seeds or lovage seeds can be used to give a celery-like flavour; Indian or Moroccan spicing will give a more exotic base. Good with fish, shellfish and game dishes, a little of the pickled fruit could also be added to a peach dessert for a different flavour. I've used them in this book with stuffed goose neck.

8 slightly under-ripe peaches, peeled by blanching

for the pickling liquor
600g granulated sugar
400g cider or white balsamic vinegar
400g white wine
5 allspice berries, crushed slightly
6 cloves
6cm piece cinnamon stick
30g peeled fresh ginger
20 black peppercorns
zest of 1 lemon, peeled in strips

Bring all the ingredients for the pickling liquor to the boil in a large saucepan. Simmer for 20 minutes to infuse the liquid with the flavour from the spices.

Cut the peeled peaches in half and remove the stones (they could be cut into sixths if you prefer). Poach the peaches gently in the liquor until tender; they must still hold their shape. Remove the peaches from the pan and leave to cool. Cool the pickling juices too.

Pack the peaches into a sterilised, warm Kilner jar, pour the pickling juices over and cover. Store in the fridge. The peaches will keep for 2–3 months.

spiced bread

I have carried this recipe over from my first book, *Essence*, because I use the bread in several recipes in this book, both dessert and savoury. The bread complements many different flavours as any of its ingredients – orange, lemon, ginger, aniseed or cinnamon – can echo the main flavouring of the dish it is served with. Wonderful with rich pâtés and shellfish dishes too. It is better made a few days ahead so it can mature and develop the flavours.

Makes 1 loaf

100g milk
200g chestnut honey
150g rye flour
150g plain white flour
75g demerara sugar
25g baking powder
75g unsalted butter, diced
2 eggs
grated zest of 1 orange
grated zest of 1/2 lemon
5g ground ginger
5g ground green aniseed
3g ground cinnamon
2g ground nutmeg
1g ground cloves

Warm the milk and dissolve the honey in it, then leave to cool. Place both the flours, the demerara sugar, baking powder and diced butter in the bowl of a freestanding electric mixer. Mix on a low speed until the texture resembles breadcrumbs, then add the eggs and the honey mixture and beat until smooth. Add all the remaining ingredients and mix well.

Pour into a greased and lined loaf tin, about 20 x 7.5 x 7.5cm. Place in an oven preheated to 160°C/Gas Mark 3 and bake for 45–50 minutes, until deep golden and firm to the touch. Leave to cool in the tin for 20 minutes, then turn out on to a wire rack to cool completely.

marinated prunes in jasmine tea and rum

Prunes are perfect with so many things, from the humblest rice pudding to a more sophisticated parfait, and they work with myriad unusual flavours – burdock, liquorice and the more pronounced yuzu, even smoke (in fact, there is a Chinese smoked plum). This recipe makes a great syrup for use with desserts involving plums, going so well with their acidity. The prunes are a useful addition to game and guinea fowl dishes and a must with chestnuts in a Christmas stuffing for turkey. Combined with figs, both fresh and dried, they also make a wonderful preserve to serve with terrines.

1 orange
800g water
200g caster sugar
10cm piece cinnamon stick
1kg Agen prunes
6 jasmine tea bags
200g dark rum

Peel the zest off the orange in long strips, then squeeze out the juice. Place the zest and juice, water, sugar and cinnamon in a pan large enough to hold all the prunes. Bring to the boil, stirring to dissolve the sugar. Simmer for 5 minutes. Add the prunes and place the tea bags on top. Remove from the heat and leave to macerate overnight.

The next day, remove the tea bags from the mixture. Pour in the rum and stir carefully to distribute the rum evenly. Store in a sterilised Kilner jar for 1 month before use.

honeyed mustard seeds

These little mustard-seed jewels are so shiny because they release pectin as they simmer with honey and vinegar. They give a pleasing flavour and texture to cold meats and fish dishes – in the book they're used with our pig's cheek and smoked ham hock terrine (see page 61). Great with fruits used in savoury recipes too. You could use black mustard seeds instead of yellow ones, although I find them a touch more bitter. If you wish, add crushed and toasted coriander seeds to the base or even a little chilli.

350g yellow mustard seeds
325g cider vinegar
325g water
300g chestnut honey
4g salt

Put the mustard seeds in a medium saucepan and cover with water. Bring to the boil, then remove from the heat, drain in a sieve and rinse well under cold running water. Repeat this process two more times.

Place the drained mustard seeds back in the pan and add the vinegar, measured water and honey. Bring to the boil, then simmer

for 50 minutes to 1 hour, until al dente; add the salt halfway through the cooking. When cooked, the seeds should be shiny and the liquor thickened. If they are getting too dry during cooking, add more water to the pan.

Remove from the heat and leave to cool. Place in a sterilised jar, cover and keep in the fridge until needed (up to one month).

leek ash

Leek ash is very simple to make and is the ideal way to use the green top of the leek when you only want the white bottom part for another recipe. It gives a wonderful smokiness to a dish, although you need to use it sparingly as too much leads to bitterness. Try adding leek ash to a mayonnaise to make a creamy sauce that will go well with salsify, oysters and, of course, poached leeks and onions.

3 leeks (the part from the middle up the green end)

Set a large pan of salted water on the heat and bring up to the boil. Meanwhile, cut the leeks in half lengthways, separate the layers and wash well, removing any grit. Drain. Blanch the leeks in the boiling water, then drain and refresh. Place on a cloth to dry.

Spread out a batch of leeks, in a single layer, on a baking tray and grill until black and dry. Repeat until all the leek layers have been grilled. Place the blackened, dried leeks in a blender, or a clean spice mill or coffee grinder, and blend to a powder. Pass the powder through a fine sieve, to end up with a uniform fine powder with no big bits in it. Store in an airtight container until needed (up to one month).

elderberry vinegar

This is a lovely vinegar to have in your storecupboard to make dressings for salads and to use to deglaze the juices from roast game (I use it with grouse). It has the right amount of sweet and sour so cuts through fat perfectly. The vinegar could also be made with bullaces (a variety of wild plum), sloes for a more tannic and less sweet vinegar, and blackcurrants, although the sugar content might need to be changed, depending on the ripeness of the fruit.

Makes 1.5–2 litres

1kg ripe elderberries
1.2kg cider or white wine vinegar
1.1kg caster sugar

Pick through the elderberries, discarding any that are not perfect, then place in a tub or a bowl. Pour the vinegar over and cover with muslin. Leave in a warm (but not too warm) place for 6 days. Stir each day with a clean spoon and re-cover.

After the 6 days, strain off the liquid (discard the fruit) and place in a stainless steel saucepan with the sugar. Bring up to the boil, stirring until the sugar has dissolved. Turn the heat down and simmer for 15 minutes. Strain through muslin and pour into warm sterilised bottles, using a sterilised jug. Put the tops on immediately, then allow to cool. Leave in a cool place for a week before using (can be kept for 4–6 months).

pickled shimeji

A good addition to salads and terrine dishes, these mushrooms could also be used with a fresh tagliatelle or scattered over a risotto. The same technique can be applied to other mushrooms too. The pickled shimeji must be used fairly quickly. If you need them to last longer, you'll need to boil them in some of the vinegar first to kill any bacteria present. This will change the flavour, which is why I think this version that needs to be used up quickly is better.

1kg shimeji mushrooms
400g olive oil
100g chopped onions
2 garlic cloves, finely chopped
200g white wine
50g white wine vinegar
15g soft brown sugar
10 black peppercorns, crushed
10 coriander seeds, crushed
3 sprigs of thyme
3g salt

Trim the shimeji mushrooms so you only have the top 1cm. Put to one side. Place a medium saucepan on the heat and add the olive oil, onions and garlic. Sweat without colouring for 3–4 minutes. Deglaze with the white wine, then boil for 1 minute. Add all the other ingredients, apart from the mushrooms. Boil for 2 minutes.

While the pickling liquor is boiling, wash the mushrooms well. Drain and place in a sterilised Kilner jar. Pour the boiling liquor over the mushrooms. Leave to cool, then cover and keep in the refrigerator for up to 2 weeks (if boiled in the vinegar they can be kept for 2–3 months).

elderflower cordial

This is one of the freshest-tasting cordials you can have. I've included it in the book because the elderflower season is so short and it deserves to be prolonged a bit. This cordial helps do just that. It tastes wonderful topped up with Champagne or Crémant de Bourgogne, and it's a useful ingredient for mousses and ice creams as well as fish dishes. The recipe would work well with meadowsweet blossom too.

2 lemons
1 orange
1.2kg water
950g caster sugar
15 elderflower heads
40g citric acid

Peel the zest from the lemons and orange in wide strips. Set the fruit aside. Place the lemon and orange zests in a large saucepan with the water and sugar. Bring to the boil, stirring to dissolve the sugar.

While this is coming up to the boil, check over the elderflower heads for bugs. Remove the flowers, making sure there are no leaves in with them, and put them in a bowl.

Leave the syrup to cool for 10 minutes, then pour over the elderflowers. Add the citric acid. Juice the orange and lemons and add the juice to the elderflowers. Stir well, then cover and leave to infuse overnight.

Strain the cordial through muslin, then taste to check if it is the flavour you want. If it is too sweet, add a little citric acid; if it is not sweet enough, boil a little of the cordial with a little more sugar, then cool. Pour into sterilised warm bottles and cover. Keep in the fridge until needed (4–6 weeks).

elderflower vinegar

To make elderflower vinegar, put the flowers from 20 elderflower heads, picked and checked for bugs, in 1kg of white wine or cider vinegar and leave in a cool place for 2–4 weeks. Strain through muslin and keep in corked bottles in a cool place for 6–12 months.

pickled walnuts

Walnuts for pickling are picked when they are green and the nuts haven't hardened inside. At this stage they are called 'wet' walnuts and it is best to pick them before July (June is the best time). It's so good to have a jar of pickled walnuts in the fridge to have with some of our country's wonderful Cheddar, as part of a salad. They have a rich deep flavour, quite unlike anything else. Paired with sweet fruit, like a pear or a ripe peach, they complete the sweet and sour flavour that works perfectly with game and beef dishes. Tip: Always wear rubber gloves when picking and pricking the fresh green walnuts because they can stain your hands. The pickling does take 4–6 months, but they are well worth the wait. I love them with my Boxing Day turkey.

Makes 2 x 1.4kg jars

2kg fresh green walnuts

for the brine
250g salt
2kg water

for the pickling liquor
1.2kg malt vinegar
600g soft brown sugar
2 split red chillies
3g juniper berries

3g allspice berries
2g cloves
5g yellow mustard seeds
5cm piece cinnamon stick

brine

Dissolve the salt in the water by bringing to the boil in a pan. Put to one side to cool. Carefully prick the walnuts all over with a thick needle or a small roasting fork, remembering to wear your gloves. Place in a container just slightly larger than the space the walnuts take. Cover with the cooled brine. There will be a lot of brine left – keep it. Leave the nuts in the brine in the fridge for 24 hours.

Remove the walnuts from the brine and drain. Put them back in the container and top up with some more of the reserved brine. Again leave them in the brine in the fridge for 24 hours. Repeat a third time, then remove the nuts from the brine and spread out on a tray. Leave out at room temperature for half a day. The walnuts should go black.

pickling liquor

Combine all the pickling liquor ingredients in a pan, bring to the boil and simmer for 15 minutes. Remove from the heat. Pack the walnuts into warm sterilised jars and pour the pickling liquor over. Cover and leave to mature in a cool, dark place for 4–6 months, so they are ready for late autumn/winter. They can be kept for 1^1/$_2$–2 years.

granola

This is one of those recipes that can be used for both a savoury and a sweet alike, so it is a really useful addition to the storecupboard. Granola will add texture to desserts such as mousses or can be sprinkled on game to add a sweetness that enhances the game's flavour (I have used it with venison in the past). A little on the plate under an ice cream will stop it rolling around. The spices can be changed to suit your taste or the recipe you want to add it to – perhaps coriander seeds and orange zest, or some shaved nuts.

35g maple syrup
35g honey
40g unsalted butter
75g caster sugar
seeds from 1 vanilla pod
3g ground cinnamon
2g ground nutmeg
2g ground ginger
4 dried tonka beans, ground to a powder
2.5g salt
200g jumbo oats

Heat the maple syrup, honey, butter and caster sugar in a medium saucepan over a low heat, stirring until the sugar has dissolved and the mixture is smooth. In a bowl, mix all the spices and salt with the oats, then pour the syrup over. Mix well. Spread out on a non-stick baking sheet. Place in an oven preheated to 160°C/ Gas Mark 3 and bake, stirring every 3–4 minutes, for 30–35 minutes, until a deep golden brown.

Remove from the oven and give the mixture a final stir, then leave to cool. When completely cold, store in an airtight container. Keep in a cool place for no longer than a week.

foundations

I hope owners of my first book, *Essence*, will forgive me reiterating my words from there, but the same advice and many of the same foundation recipes remain appropriate for this book: good cooking depends on good foundation recipes – for stocks, pasta dough, pastry and so on. Master these and you have a sound basis for a whole repertoire of different dishes.

Making stock is quite a personal thing, with as many different recipes as there are chefs. Chefs with a subtle touch go for a lighter stock, often preferring to use chicken stock rather than veal or beef, while chefs such as myself prefer a purer, more meaty flavour, with few vegetables, if any, added. It's always worth taking care when making stock. If you have a weak stock, lacking in flavour, how will you ever achieve a great sauce?

Although I encourage you throughout this book to use my recipes as a guideline, pastry recipes are the one exception to the rule. Quantities matter, so do follow them to the letter. Having said that, it's perfectly okay to vary the flavourings, as long as the proportions stay the same.

white chicken stock

This is a good, light stock that can be made stronger by either halving the amount of water or substituting chicken stock for the water, thus giving a double-concentrated stock.

Makes 2kg

30g olive oil
1 large onion, finely sliced
1 large celery stick, sliced
2kg chicken bones (a mixture of wings and carcasses)
100g white wine
10 black peppercorns, crushed
1 bay leaf
$^1/_2$ sprig of thyme
3kg water

Heat the oil in a large saucepan, add the onion and celery and cook without colouring for 2–3 minutes. Add the chicken bones and cook for 5 minutes without letting them colour. Pour in the white wine and simmer until reduced by half. Add the peppercorns, herbs and water and bring to the boil. Reduce the heat and simmer for 2–2$^1/_2$ hours, regularly skimming the froth from the top.

Remove from the heat and leave to stand for 15–20 minutes; this allows the particles to settle. Strain through a fine sieve and leave to cool.

brown chicken stock

Makes 2kg

30g olive oil
2kg chicken bones (half wings, half carcasses)
1 large onion, finely sliced
1 large celery stick, sliced
75g fresh tomato pulp
100g red wine
10 black peppercorns, crushed
1 bay leaf
$^1/_2$ sprig of thyme
3kg water

Heat half of the oil in a large saucepan. When hot, add the chicken bones and cook until a deep golden brown. Add the onion and celery and cook for a further 5 minutes. Pour off the fat from the pan, then add the tomato pulp and deglaze with the red wine. Reduce by half. Add the peppercorns, herbs and water and bring to the boil. Simmer for 2–2$^1/_2$ hours, skimming regularly. Remove from the heat and leave to stand for 15–20 minutes (this allows the particles to settle). Strain through a fine sieve and cool if not needed immediately.

fish stock

Makes 2kg

1.5kg fish bones and heads (turbot, brill, sole, skate)
50g olive oil
white of 1 leek, finely sliced
1 onion, finely sliced
250g white wine
10 black peppercorns
2.5kg water

Remove any gills and eyes from the fish heads you may have. Chop the bones roughly and rinse under cold running water for 2–3 minutes.

Heat the oil in a large saucepan. When hot, add the leek and onion and cook without colouring for 2–3 minutes. Add the fish bones and heads and cook for a further 5 minutes without colouring. Pour in the white wine and reduce by half. Add the peppercorns and water, bring back to the boil and simmer for 20–30 minutes, skimming regularly.

Remove from the heat and leave to stand for 15–20 minutes (this allows the particles to settle). Strain the stock through a fine sieve and cool if not using right away.

Note: Sometimes if I am doing a meaty fish dish such as monkfish, bass or skate, I use chicken stock as a base for the fish stock instead of water.

lamb stock

Makes 2kg

75g olive oil
2kg lamb bones, chopped up into small
  pieces
3 garlic cloves, crushed
1 large onion, finely sliced
100g Madeira
200g red wine
10 black peppercorns, crushed
1 bay leaf
1/2 sprig of rosemary
3kg water

Heat the oil in a large saucepan. When hot, add the lamb bones and cook to a deep golden colour, which will take about 10 minutes. Add the garlic and onion and cook for a further 2–3 minutes. Pour in the Madeira and cook until evaporated, then add the red wine and reduce by half. Add the peppercorns, herbs and water. Bring back to the boil and simmer for 2–2 1/2 hours, skimming regularly to remove excess fat.

Remove from the heat and leave to stand for 15–20 minutes (this allows the particles to settle). Strain through a fine sieve and cool if not needed immediately.

Note: If you want to make this a stronger stock, substitute chicken stock or even veal stock for the water. You could also add 3–4 tablespoons of fresh tomato pulp, as long as the tomatoes are ripe.

dashi

I have started using this as a base for some of the lighter dishes we serve on the tasting menu. Dashi is both light and savoury at the same time. The idea for adding chrysanthemum came about while I was looking through an Asian supermarket. Seeing that dried chrysanthemum was used as a tea, I thought it might complement the broth. In the past I've given this a Thai influence with a little lemongrass and lime leaf added to the base stock.

Makes about 1.5kg

2kg water
40g piece kombu seaweed
40g finest quality bonito flakes
10g dried chrysanthemum flowers
2g fresh chrysanthemum petals (these will
  be added to the finished broth when used
  in a recipe)

Pour the water into a large saucepan and set on a medium heat. Add the kombu seaweed and cook at 60°C for about 1 hour. It is imperative that the water does not boil.

Remove the kombu. Bring the temperature of the liquid up to 80°C, then add the bonito flakes and dried chrysanthemum flowers. Remove from the heat. When the bonito and chrysanthemum flowers have sunk to the bottom of the dashi, leave for 2 minutes, then strain the dashi through muslin; do not squeeze. Cool and keep in the fridge until needed.

brown beef stock

Makes 2kg

100g olive oil
3kg beef bones, chopped
1 veal trotter or 2 pig's trotters, chopped
200g Madeira
200g red wine
1 large onion, finely sliced
3 garlic cloves, crushed
1 bay leaf
a sprig of thyme
300g fresh tomato pulp (optional)
4kg water

Heat half of the olive oil in a roasting tray in an oven preheated to 240°C/Gas Mark 9. Add all the bones and brown for 30 minutes. Remove the bones from the tray, pour off the fat and deglaze with the Madeira and then the red wine. Set aside. Heat the remaining oil in a large saucepan. When hot, add the onion and cook until golden, then add the garlic, herbs and tomato pulp, if using. Add the browned bones, the juices from the roasting tray and the water. Bring to the boil and skim, then simmer for 3–3 1/2 hours.

Remove the bones and strain the liquid through a fine sieve into another saucepan. Reduce to 2 kilograms, skimming occasionally. Strain through a fine sieve again and cool. Any fat that forms on the surface can easily be removed when set.

white beef stock

Follow the recipe for Brown Beef Stock, above, but sweat the bones without browning them; use white port instead of Madeira and white wine instead of red wine; and omit the optional tomato pulp.

vegetable stock

Makes 1kg

50g olive oil
200g chopped onion
200g chopped carrot
200g sliced leek
150g sliced celery
25g sliced fennel
2 garlic cloves, crushed
100g white port
100g white wine
10 white peppercorns
2 sprigs of thyme
2 bay leaves
2 sprigs of chervil
1.2kg water

Heat the oil in a large saucepan and, when hot, add the vegetables and garlic and cook without colouring for 2–3 minutes. Pour in the white port and reduce by half, then add the white wine and reduce by half. Add the peppercorns, herbs and water. Bring to the boil, then simmer for 15–20 minutes, skimming regularly.

Remove from the heat and leave to stand for 15–20 minutes (this allows the particles to settle). Strain through a fine sieve and cool if not needed immediately.

malt pasta dough

When raw, this dough has a colour almost like squid ink, then turns the deepest brown chocolate shade when cooked. It has a nutty taste that complements powerful flavours like wood pigeon or hare, and teamed with peas and broad beans it's absolutely fantastic. Rye flour could be substituted for the malt flour, giving a different flavour. You may need a touch of water if you do this, as I have always found rye to be drier than malt flour.

Makes about 600g

400g type '00' pasta flour
50g black malt flour
50g nut brown malt flour
25g spray malt flour
3 eggs
3 egg yolks

Place all the flours in a food processor, add the eggs and yolks and pulse until the mixture forms a loose ball. Tip out on to a lightly floured work surface and knead well until smooth. Divide in half and wrap each portion in cling film. Leave to rest for at least 2 hours before using (longer than this, keep in the fridge).

Note: The dough can be frozen. Simply wrap tightly in cling film and place in a polythene bag. Store in the freezer for 1–2 weeks. Thaw completely in the fridge before using.

sweet pastry

Makes enough for a 29cm tart

270g plain flour
150g cold unsalted butter, diced
50g ground almonds
grated zest of 1 lemon or orange
seeds from 1 vanilla pod
100g icing sugar
1 egg
1 egg yolk

Place the flour, butter, almonds, lemon or orange zest, vanilla seeds and sugar in a food processor and pulse until the texture resembles breadcrumbs. Add the egg and egg yolk and pulse until the mixture starts to form a ball.

Turn out on to a lightly floured surface and work together as little as possible until the dough is smooth. Form into a ball and flatten, then wrap in cling film and chill for at least 3 hours before using.

Note: This can be made well in advance, wrapped in cling film and frozen. Thaw in the fridge for 24 hours.

almond craquant

A must for the foundations section. It is used in so many dessert recipes in different forms. I have also started to use it in a number of savoury dishes, in particular the duck egg dish in this book and as a coating for bon bons (see page 66). The almonds can be replaced with desiccated coconut, cooked and crumbled shortcrust pastry, roasted beechnuts, crumbs of spiced bread (see page 15) and cocoa nibs. Spices could be added at the powder stage to complement the main ingredient of the dish.

400g glucose syrup
400g caster sugar
100g water
200g flaked almonds, toasted until golden

Place the glucose syrup, caster sugar and water in a heavy-based saucepan and dissolve on a gentle heat, then bring up to the boil and cook until caramelised to a golden amber colour. Immediately pour on to an oiled lipped baking tray and sprinkle over the almonds. Put to one side until cold and set hard.

Break up the caramel and place in a food processor, then pulse to a coarse powder. Store in an airtight container until needed (up to a week).

miso glaze

Miso is made with fermented soya beans and is very salty, with red miso being even more savoury than white. It pairs well with sesame, ginger and roasted peanuts. I've used white miso for ice creams and brûlées, to which it gives a unique taste. This glaze has a sweet-sour flavour and is intensely savoury, good with grilled fish or meats. I use it particularly with scallops and mackerel.

Makes 300–350g

250g sake
250g mirin
115g granulated sugar
100g white miso

Combine the ingredients in a medium saucepan and whisk well. Place on the heat and bring to the boil, whisking. Reduce by at least half to a syrupy consistency. Pass through a fine chinois. Cool and keep in a squeezy bottle until needed (for 1–2 weeks in the fridge). To glaze fish, drizzle over cooked fish, then flash under the grill for a few seconds.

confit of duck leg

I have carried this recipe, and the one following, over from my first book, *Essence*, as I use confit in some of the recipes in this book too.

Serves 6

6 plump duck legs
2 sprigs of thyme, chopped
2 bay leaves, chopped
2 teaspoons juniper berries, crushed
1 teaspoon white peppercorns, crushed
2 strips of orange zest, finely chopped
3 garlic cloves, roughly chopped
50g sel gris (grey sea salt)
750g duck fat

Make sure the duck legs are thoroughly trimmed and that any feather stubble is removed. Combine the herbs and aromatics with the salt. Rub the mixture into the duck legs, then cover and leave in the fridge for 24 hours.

Remove the salt mixture by rubbing the duck legs with kitchen paper, or quickly rinsing them under cold running water and patting dry. In a heavy-based flameproof casserole or other pot large enough to fit the legs snugly, melt the duck fat over a low heat. Add the legs, which should be completely covered with fat. Cover with foil and transfer to an oven preheated to 150°C/Gas Mark 2. Simmer gently for about 3 hours, until fully cooked. To test, the meat should come away from the bones; if pricked with a fork the juices should be clear.

Place the confit legs in a container. Strain the duck fat through a fine sieve into a tallish jug. Leave the juices to separate from the fat, then carefully ladle the fat only over the confit until covered. Cover with a lid and store in the fridge until needed (up to a week).

When you want to serve the confit, heat an ovenproof frying pan large enough to take the duck legs in one layer. Remove them from the fat and place, skin side down, in the pan. Cook for 2–3 minutes, then transfer the pan to an oven preheated to 220°C/Gas Mark 7. Cook for a further 20–25 minutes, until the skin is thoroughly crisp and golden and the meat is heated all the way through.

duck gizzard confit

Serves 6–8

450g cleaned duck gizzards
2 garlic cloves, chopped
1 bay leaf
a sprig of thyme
1 teaspoon white peppercorns, crushed
30g sel gris (grey sea salt)
500g duck fat

The technique for this recipe is the same as for the duck legs (right), except only salt the gizzards for 8–10 hours as they are much smaller than the legs – any longer and they would be too salty. Also reduce the cooking time to 2 hours, or 2½ hours if they are large gizzards. Store the same way.

To serve, remove the gizzards from the fat and cut each into 4–5 slices. Heat a little of the duck fat in a frying pan and fry the gizzards until golden, then season lightly.

breads

brioche

I have included this recipe, carried over from my first book, *Essence*, because we have recipes requiring brioche in this book too. We use this as our basic brioche, sometimes adding a bacon and shallot mixture to it.

Makes 2 loaves

50g warm water
20g fresh yeast
40g caster sugar
500g strong white flour
5 eggs, whisked to mix and strained
  through a sieve
10g salt
300g unsalted butter, softened and diced
a little milk, for brushing

Put the warm water in a small bowl and mix in the yeast and sugar until dissolved. Leave for 2–3 minutes, until frothy.

Place the flour in the bowl of a freestanding electric mixer fitted with the dough hook and add the yeast mixture. Slowly pour in the eggs, adding the salt too, beating on a low speed. Continue beating for 2 minutes. Add the butter bit by bit, waiting until each piece has been incorporated before adding the next. Continue beating/kneading until the dough is smooth and elastic.

Divide the dough in half. Butter 2 loaf tins, each about 18 x 11 x 7cm, and line the bottom with baking parchment. Place the dough in the tins. Cover with a damp cloth and leave to prove at fairly warm room temperature (26°C) for 45–60 minutes, until doubled in size.

Lightly brush the top of the loaves with a little milk, then place in an oven preheated to 180°C/Gas Mark 4. Bake for 45 minutes, until the brioche is golden and sounds hollow when tapped on the base. Leave to cool in the tins for 5 minutes, then turn out on to a wire rack to cool completely.

Note: You could keep one loaf, well wrapped, in the freezer if it is to be used for toast.

chestnut bread rolls

We put these on the menu now and again during the autumn months – a welcome addition to our bread basket. They have a slight sweetness due to the use of chestnut flour and chestnut honey and a wonderful nutty scent.

Makes about 30 rolls

30g fresh yeast
700g warm water
30g chestnut honey
1kg strong white flour, plus extra for dusting
300g chestnut flour
20g salt
beaten egg, to glaze

starter
Crumble the yeast into a smallish bowl, add 100g of the warm water and the chestnut honey, and mix well. Whisk in 150g of the white flour, mixing until a loose paste has formed. Keep in a warm place for 10 minutes, until frothy.

dough
Put the remaining white flour and the chestnut flour in the bowl of a freestanding electric mixer fitted with the dough hook. Add the contents of the starter bowl and the remaining water and mix on a medium speed for 5–8 minutes to make a soft, sticky dough; halfway through this time, add the salt.

Turn out on to a floured work surface. Knead the dough by pulling, stretching and hitting it on the work surface until it is perfectly smooth, adding more flour if it is too sticky. Put the dough in a large bowl, cover with cling film and leave to prove at fairly warm room temperature (26°C) for 50–60 minutes, until doubled in size.

shaping and baking rolls
Turn the dough on to the floured work surface and knead well (this is called knocking back). Divide into 30 portions, each weighing 70g, and roll into smooth balls. Arrange, spaced apart, on baking sheets. Lightly egg wash the dough balls and dust heavily with white flour. Leave to prove at 26°C again for 20 minutes, until doubled in size.

Slash the top of each roll once or twice. Place in an oven preheated to 220°C/Gas Mark 7, with a tray of hot water in the bottom of the oven. Bake for 10–14 minutes, until deep golden brown and crisp. To check if the rolls are cooked, remove from the oven and tap the bases; the rolls should sound hollow. If not, bake a little longer. Cool on a wire rack.

duck confit and wild garlic focaccia

This is a bread that we occasionally make in the spring when the first wild garlic shoots, or ramsons, appear. With the duck confit these give the focaccia a wonderful flavour that is just so moreish. There is also hedge garlic or 'jack-by-the-hedge' that could replace the wild garlic. Or you can use normal garlic, although the quantity would need to be drastically reduced. This bread is great with chorizo and olives.

Makes 1 loaf

for the dough
650g warm water
20g fresh yeast
10g caster sugar
500g strong white flour
500g type '00' pasta flour
35g duck fat from Duck Confit (see page 22), melted and warm
17g salt
250g meat from the confit, chopped
150g wild garlic, finely chopped

for the salt wash and to finish
100g olive oil, plus extra for drizzling
100g water
15g salt
100g Parmesan cheese, grated
Maldon salt, for sprinkling

dough
Put 50g of the warm water in a small bowl with the yeast, half of the sugar and 2 tablespoons of the strong flour. Whisk well to form a light paste, then set aside in a warm place until frothy and doubled in size.

Combine the remaining strong flour with the pasta flour in the bowl of a freestanding electric mixer fitted with the dough hook. Add the duck fat and mix for 2–3 minutes. Add the yeast mixture to the bowl together with the remaining water and mix on a medium speed for 5–8 minutes to make a soft, sticky dough; halfway through this time, add the salt and remaining sugar.

Turn out on to a floured work surface. Knead the dough by pulling, stretching and hitting it on the work surface until it is perfectly smooth, adding more flour if it is too sticky. Finally, add the duck confit and wild garlic, and mix in well. Place the dough in a large bowl, cover with cling film and leave to prove at a fairly warm room temperature (26°C) for 50–60 minutes, until doubled in size.

Line a baking tray, measuring 40 x 30cm or near to this, with baking parchment. Carefully remove the dough to a floured surface and stretch into an oblong shape. Place in the tray. Cover and leave to prove for a further 10 minutes.

salt wash and baking
Put the oil, water and salt in a blender and blend until emulsified. Brush the dough with this mixture, then sprinkle with the Parmesan and a little grain salt. Stab your fingers into the dough all over to create little pockets that will catch the oil. Bake in an oven preheated to 220°C/Gas Mark 7 for 20–25 minutes, until golden.

Remove from the oven and leave to cool for 5 minutes, then drizzle over a little extra olive oil. Serve straight away.

sweet potato and red onion loaf

This bread is made in the style of a ciabatta, so the dough will be wetter than a normal bread dough. At the restaurant, we make smallish loaves that we serve in our bread basket. I love this bread, especially cracking open the very crisp crust to release the wonderful bread scent and to see all those holes that have developed. The crisper the crust, the better. I also like the caramelisation of the red onions, giving a wonderful aroma as the bread bakes and a lovely, sweet taste. You can use roasted pumpkin purée instead of sweet potato, if you prefer.

Makes 2 loaves

30g fresh yeast
550g warm water
30g honey
1kg strong white flour
300g sweet potato purée (cooked weight)
30g salt
200g red onions, very finely sliced
30g olive oil
Maldon salt, for sprinkling

starter
Crumble the yeast into a small bowl, add 75g of the warm water and the honey, and mix well. Whisk in 50g of the flour and mix until a loose paste has formed. Leave in a warm place for 10 minutes, until frothy.

dough
Put the remaining flour in the bowl of a freestanding electric mixer fitted with the dough hook and add the sweet potato purée, half of the remaining water and the yeast starter. Mix for 2–3 minutes to break the purée down. Add the remaining water and mix on a medium speed for 5–8 minutes to make a soft, sticky dough; add the salt after 3 minutes.

Turn out on to a floured work surface. Knead the dough by pulling, stretching and hitting it on the work surface until it is perfectly smooth, adding more flour if it is too sticky. Place the dough in a large bowl, cover with cling film and leave to prove at fairly warm room temperature (26°C) for 50–60 minutes, until doubled in size.

shaping
Tip the dough on to the work surface. Oil your hands, then knead the dough (to knock it back) and divide in half. Take one portion and form a ball, then stretch it out into an oblong and fold one end carefully over the other. Repeat with the other portion of dough.

Stretch out each piece of dough again to an oblong 30 x 10cm and repeat the folding, trying to trap as much air in the dough as possible. Repeat the process a third time, then place each piece on a baking sheet lined with baking parchment. Cover and leave in a warm place to prove for a 20–30 minutes, until doubled in size.

to finish
Quickly toss the sliced onions in the olive oil, then scatter over the two loaves. Sprinkle with Maldon salt. Bake in an oven preheated to 220°C/Gas Mark 7 for 30 minutes. The loaves should be evenly coloured with the onions a darkish brown. Remove from the oven and leave to cool on a wire rack.

soda bread

This is without doubt the easiest of breads to make as it doesn't require much kneading and no proving. It has a wonderful crisp crust and a great depth of flavour – lovely as a picnic bread and goes so well with cheese. We also make a Guinness bread using this as a base, and this is then turned into Guinness bread porridge, served with a rich milk foam as a pre-dessert. Nuts and dried fruit can be added to the dough for a different flavour.

Makes 2 loaves

500g plain white flour, plus extra for
  dusting
500g plain wholemeal flour
20g bicarbonate of soda
12g salt
30g black treacle
30g malt extract
80g unsalted butter, melted
800g buttermilk

Place both of the flours, the bicarbonate of soda and salt in a mixing bowl. Lightly warm the treacle with the malt extract, then add the butter and half of the buttermilk and stir until the butter has melted. Add to the flour mixture. Mix together slowly, then add the rest of the buttermilk. The dough will be quite sticky.

Tip the dough out on to a floured work surface and work for a good 1–2 minutes, adding a little more flour if needed. Divide the dough in half and knead each portion into a ball. Flatten slightly, then place on 2 parchment-lined and floured baking trays. Cut a cross on the top of each loaf, or use the handle of a wooden spoon to make a deep impression in the bread. Dust with flour and place in an oven preheated to 200°C/Gas Mark 6. Bake for 30–45 minutes, until deep golden brown. Transfer to a wire rack and leave to cool (you will probably want a slice while it is still warm).

Note: This is quite a dense loaf. If you want to lighten it a touch you could add 30g fresh yeast. To do this, mix the yeast with a little warm treacle and 50g warm milk, then leave in a warm place to froth before adding to the dough with the second addition of buttermilk.

starters

deep-fried sand eels with a borage cacik

Johnny, our fishmonger, has become a firm friend of mine and he constantly looks out for things for me. I asked him if he could get me some sand eels for a dish I wanted to try and – hey presto! – they appeared the very next day. Whitebait can be substituted if you don't have such an accommodating friend. Sand eels are best between April and September.

The borage cacik is a play on a dish I've had in Turkey. It is sort of similar to Greek tzatziki. I replaced the cucumber with borage, which has a cucumber taste to it, and created a smooth dip for the sand eels. A little grated cucumber could be added for texture. As it is a nibble, I've allowed 4–5 sand eels per person.

Serves 6

for the sand eels
24–30 small sand eels
500g milk
grated zest of 1 lemon
10 mint leaves, finely chopped
vegetable oil, for deep-frying
100g plain flour
100g cornflour
*pinch of cayenne pepper or medium chilli
   powder*

for the borage cacik
250g Greek yoghurt
1/2 garlic clove, peeled
50g borage
4 mint leaves
20g olive oil

sand eels
Make sure the sand eels are of the freshest quality. Wash them to remove any sand, then pat dry with kitchen paper. Soak in the milk for 2 hours. Drain, discarding the milk. Toss the soaked sand eels with the lemon zest and mint. Cover and place in the fridge for 2 hours.

borage cacik
Wrap the Greek yoghurt in a piece of muslin, hang and leave to drain to remove excess water. Transfer the drained yoghurt to a blender. Finely grate the garlic directly into the blender to release the juices. Add the borage and mint, and blend until the mixture is smooth and all the borage has broken down and become amalgamated. Season. Divide among 6 little pots and drizzle over the olive oil.

frying the eels
Fill a deep-fat fryer or a large, deep, heavy-based pan two-thirds full with vegetable oil. Heat the oil to 190°C.

Mix together the flour, cornflour, cayenne pepper and salt. Dredge the eels in the mixture, shaking off the excess. Deep-fry the eels, in batches, for 2–3 minutes, until golden in colour; stir them during frying so they don't stick together. Drain on kitchen paper. Season with a little salt and freshly ground black pepper, then serve hot with the little pots of borage cacik.

curried popcorn

This is a quick little snack that can be served to accompany a drink, or used as a garnish for a soup – spiced chickpea, for example. I have left the spices for you to tailor to your own taste, but I like to use cumin, coriander, chilli and ajowan seeds, all freshly roasted and ground to create the most amazing perfume. I do like very spicy food, and have been known to put a little chopped, fresh naga chilli in with the mixture too.

Serves 4

50g sunflower oil
30g popcorn kernels
30g maple syrup
30g unsalted butter
5g curry spices (see recipe introduction)
1g salt

Heat the oil in a large saucepan over medium high heat, add a few kernels of popcorn and cover with a lid. When you hear the popping start, add the rest of the kernels together with the other ingredients and quickly put the lid back on. Gently shake the pan from side to side while the kernels pop. When the popping stops, the popcorn is ready.

Tip on to a tray lined with kitchen paper to soak up any excess oil. Taste and add a little more salt if needed. Serve immediately.

sweetcorn and smoked bacon muffins

These are lovely little, moist muffins that pack a punch of flavour, great for a cocktail party at home. The base mix can be changed in so many ways. For example, you could switch peas for the sweetcorn, and add some herbs, garlic or chilli. For convenience, the mixture can be made in advance and put in the moulds, ready to bake at the last minute. We use a silicone baby canelé mould, to give them a more distinctive shape.

Makes about 40 little muffins

25g duck fat
100g smoked bacon, finely diced
50g chopped onion
60g cooked fresh sweetcorn kernels
15g dried shallots
175g milk
65g unsalted butter, melted
1 egg
115g yellow cornmeal or fine polenta
75g plain flour
17g caster sugar
6g baking powder
3g salt

Melt the duck fat in a large frying pan, add the chopped bacon and cook until the bacon fat is rendered and the bacon is golden. Add the onion and sweetcorn and cook for a further 4–5 minutes. Remove from the heat and stir in the dried shallots to absorb any juices. Leave to cool.

Meanwhile, put the milk, melted butter and egg in a mixing bowl and mix well. Add all the remaining dry ingredients and mix to obtain a smooth paste. Stir in the bacon mixture. Keep in the fridge until needed.

Divide the mixture among the muffin moulds – 20g of mix for each mould. The silicone moulds we use measure 30 x 30mm. You could also use petit four cases in a mini muffin tin. Bake in an oven preheated to 180°C/Gas Mark 4 for 10–12 minutes, until golden brown. Leave to cool in the moulds for 2 minutes, then remove and serve.

parmesan custard with chorizo crumbs

These little cheese canapés can be varied in lots of ways. The recipe uses a dried chorizo coating, but you could also coat them in dried and powdered bacon, powdered roasted hazelnuts or chopped fresh herbs. You could change the cheese, maybe for a blue cheese or a good fresh goat's cheese. Whatever you choose, you need to make sure the flavour is intense as these are to go with drinks. This is a scaled-down recipe but it still makes quite a lot, so it will be best used for a cocktail party.

Makes about 100 cubes

for the parmesan custard
300g double cream
125g Parmesan cheese, grated
2g English mustard powder
2 eggs, lightly whisked to mix

for the chorizo crumbs
750g chorizo picante

parmesan custard

Bring the cream to the boil in a saucepan, then add the Parmesan and stir until dissolved. Remove from the heat and add the mustard, then whisk in the eggs. Return to the heat and cook for 1–2 minutes, to raise the temperature.

Pass through a sieve into a baking tray measuring 24 x 18 x 4cm. Bake in an oven preheated to 120°C/Gas Mark $\frac{1}{2}$ for about 20 minutes. The custard should just be set. Remove from the oven and leave to cool, then cover and keep in the fridge overnight.

chorizo crumbs

Slice the chorizo finely (best to ask the deli to do this for you), then put it through a very fine mincer (or you could mince it with a food processor as long as the blade is very sharp). Roll out a little of the minced chorizo very thinly between 2 sheets of baking parchment. Microwave on full/high (100%) power for 40–100 seconds, depending on the wattage of your microwave. The chorizo needs to dry out without burning. Test by touching it: it should not feel moist. Break up the chorizo and place on a tray. Repeat until all the chorizo has been dried.

Leave to cool and dry out further, until it is almost hard, then blitz in a clean spice grinder until very fine. Store in an airtight container until needed.

serving

Remove the custard from the fridge and cut into cubes about 2cm in size. Coat in powdered chorizo on all sides.

poppy seed and goat's cheese cookies

I warn you: these little cookies are so moreish, they will be eaten very quickly! The saltiness of the goat's cheese and the texture of the cheesy biscuits make them an ideal snack to accompany an aperitif. You can change the cheese on the top of the cookies – perhaps a good, aged Beaufort or Gouda – and of course the goat's cheese in the filling could be replaced by a blue cheese such as Roquefort or Stilton. It's best to fill and sandwich the cookies near to serving time so they don't soften.

Makes 35 cookies

for the cookies
125g Parmesan cheese, grated
100g cold unsalted butter, diced
120g plain flour, plus extra for dusting
3g salt
1g caster sugar
2g baking powder
4 egg yolks

for sprinkling
30g poppy seeds
100g Mimolette or Parmesan cheese, finely grated
1 egg and 1 tablespoon milk, whisked together, for egg wash

for the goat's cheese cream
250g goat's cheese
40g mascarpone
175g cream cheese

cookies
Combine the Parmesan and butter in the bowl of a freestanding electric mixer and mix together. Add all the remaining dry ingredients and mix, then add the egg yolks and mix. Bring together into a ball, with as little working as possible. Cover with cling film and leave to rest in the fridge for at least 4 hours.

Lightly dust a work surface with flour and roll out the dough to a thickness of 2mm. Using a 5cm round cutter, cut out the cookies – the dough should make around 70 cookies. Arrange on a baking tray lined with baking parchment, then place in the fridge to relax for 30 minutes.

sprinkling and baking
Lightly mix the poppy seeds with the cheese. Brush the egg wash over the cookies, then sprinkle with the seed and cheese mixture. Place in an oven preheated to 180°C/Gas Mark 4 and bake for 7–8 minutes, until golden brown. Transfer to a wire rack to cool.

goat's cheese cream
Place the goat's cheese in a mixing bowl and beat until smooth. Add the mascarpone and cream cheese and beat in until well mixed. Pass through a fine drum sieve. Check the seasoning – it will depend on the saltiness of the goat's cheese. Keep, covered, in the fridge. When needed, beat well and place in a piping bag fitted with a fine nozzle.

serving
Turn one cookie upside down so the seeds are on the bottom. Pipe a spiral of the cheese cream on the cookie. Place another cookie on top, seeds uppermost, to make a cookie sandwich. Repeat until the cheese mixture and cookies are all used up.

brandade

This is my reworking of the famous salt cod dish from the south of France. I have used the ingredients from the original dish, but presented them in a different form. The freshly salted cod is cut into small dice and poached in olive oil, thus giving it a little texture; the potatoes are turned into a loose purée and the garlic into a froth; and the onions are fried slowly until they are very crisp. All the elements are arranged in layers so you can plunge your spoon through them, taking a little of each to get the true brandade taste.

Serves 10

for the salt cod
1 garlic clove, finely chopped
35g Maldon salt
1 juniper berry, crushed
a sprig of thyme
450g skinless tail fillet of cod
75g olive oil

for the crisp-fried onions
500g vegetable oil
2 large onions, finely diced

for the potato foam
500g Desiree potatoes, peeled
100g milk
200g double cream
50g unsalted butter

for the garlic froth
250g milk
150g fish stock (see page 19)
100g double cream
5 garlic cloves, sliced
3g lecithin powder

salt cod
Combine the chopped garlic, salt, juniper and thyme. Sprinkle half of this mixture on to a small tray and place the cod fillet on top. Sprinkle with the remaining salt mixture. Cover and keep in the fridge for 4–6 hours.

Quickly rinse the cod under cold running water to remove the salt, then press dry with kitchen paper. Cut into small dice, about 5mm. Pour the olive oil into a small saucepan and add the diced cod. Bring up to heat and cook until the cod turns opaque (this won't take long at all), then cover and remove from the heat. Keep warm until needed.

crisp-fried onions
Warm the vegetable oil in a cast-iron pan. Add the onions and turn the heat to medium low – you want the onions to colour slowly to a nice deep golden, which will take 5–10 minutes. It is important not to do this too quickly because you want to drive all the moisture from the onions. Remove the onions from the oil using a slotted spoon and drain on kitchen paper to remove excess oil. Season and keep warm on some fresh kitchen paper.

potato foam
Cut the potatoes into even pieces and place in a saucepan of salted water. Bring to the boil and cook until tender, then drain, keeping 75g of the cooking water. Combine the milk, cream and reserved potato cooking water in a small saucepan and bring to the boil. Remove from the heat. Place the drained potatoes in a blender with the milk mixture and blend until smooth, adding the butter bit by bit until it is all incorporated. Season, then pour into a 1 litre iSi gun (see Note), charge with 2 cartridges, and keep warm.

garlic froth
Put the liquids and sliced garlic in a small saucepan and bring to the boil. Cook for 3 minutes to soften the garlic. Pour the mixture into a blender and blend until smooth, then add the lecithin and blend again. Strain into a saucepan and season. Keep warm.

serving
Drain the cod and divide among 10 serving glasses of about 200ml capacity. Cover with a good amount of potato foam, then sprinkle with the fried onions. Froth the garlic mixture with a hand blender and spoon on top.

Note: Isi cream whippers are little stainless steel containers that have a gas cylinder injected into them for making whipped cream. Ferran Adrià, from El Bulli restaurant in Spain, has made these famous for many other uses, including foams and fruit and vegetable mousses, and they are now an essential part of the professional kitchen. They can be obtained from online suppliers.

parsley panna cotta, white onion purée, smoked bacon foam

This dish has been created by Keiron Stephens, a young man who came to stay during his school holidays some years ago. He showed such passion that I created a position for him as an apprentice. Now, a few years on, he is a commis chef and a valued member of my brigade. He is developing his palate and, with guidance, his ideas are starting to take shape. In this dish, the parsley could be replaced with watercress for a more peppery flavour and the smoked bacon with smoked haddock. Sometimes we also substitute powdered crisp bacon for the powdered cep.

Serves 8–10

for the parsley panna cotta
80g milk
225g double cream
3.5g bronze gelatine leaves
30g flat-leaf parsley leaves
3g salt

for the white onion purée
40g unsalted butter
500g white onions, finely sliced
50g double cream
2g salt

for the smoked bacon foam
25g vegetable oil
200g smoked bacon, diced
175g milk
175g double cream

cep powder, for dusting

parsley panna cotta
Combine the milk and cream in a heavy-based saucepan and bring to the boil. Meanwhile, soften the gelatine in cold water; when it is soft, squeeze out the excess water and add to the cream mixture. Stir until completely melted. Add the parsley leaves and pour into a blender. Blend until smooth and the parsley has been thoroughly puréed, then add the salt. Pass the mixture through a fine sieve into a jug. Pour into 8–10 serving glasses (about 125ml capacity) to half fill. Cover them and place in a flat area in the fridge. Leave to set for at least 12 hours.

white onion purée
Heat the butter in a heavy-based saucepan; when foaming, add the sliced onions. Cook over a low heat, without colouring, for about 1 hour, until translucent and soft and the liquid has disappeared. Add the double cream and bring to the boil, then remove from the heat and pour into a blender. Blend until smooth. Add the salt, then pass through a fine sieve into a bowl and leave to cool. When cold, spoon an even layer on top of the parsley panna cotta, tapping the glasses gently on the work surface to make sure the onion purée layer is flat. Keep in the fridge until needed. Remove 30 minutes before serving.

smoked bacon foam
Heat the oil in a heavy-based saucepan, add the bacon and cook until golden and the fat is rendered. Add the milk and cream and bring to the boil. Pour into a blender and blend until smooth. Pass through a fine sieve into a jug and allow to cool. When cool, pour into a 500ml iSi gun and charge with one cartridge. Keep in the fridge until needed.

serving
Squirt some smoked bacon foam on top of the onion purée and sprinkle with cep powder.

chicken mushi, broccoli cream, crisp chicken skin

This is my nod to mushi, a Japanese savoury egg custard. These are made with stock as a base, not milk or cream, and as a result their flavour is more intense and pure. I have used a powerful chicken stock flavoured with miso, but you could change the chicken stock to lobster stock, beef tea or a good powerful fish stock. A parsnip or cauliflower cream or a chervil tuber purée (see page 128) could replace the broccoli cream. The custards are served with crisp chicken skin for added texture.

Serves 8

for the chicken stock base
50g vegetable oil
1kg chicken bones, chopped
100g chopped onion
5 garlic cloves, sliced
20g dried shiitake mushrooms
150g white wine
1kg water
65g white miso paste
35g kecap manis
3 eggs

for the crisp chicken skin
skin from 8 chicken legs
sashimi togarashi

for the broccoli cream
2 large heads of broccoli, about 600g each
40g double cream
40g unsalted butter
2.5g xanthan gum

chicken stock base
Heat the oil in a large saucepan, add the chicken bones and colour until golden. Add the onion and garlic and cook for 2 minutes, then add the shiitake and deglaze with the white wine. Reduce by half. Add the water, miso paste and kecap manis and bring to the boil, then simmer for 1½ hours, skimming occasionally.

Remove from the heat and pass through a fine chinois while the mixture is still warm. Measure out 400g of stock and reserve. Any remaining stock can be measured into 400g amounts and kept frozen for other uses.

crisp chicken skin
Line a heavy lipped baking tray with baking parchment. Arrange the chicken skins on the tray, not touching each other. Season, then sprinkle lightly with sashimi togarashi. Place another sheet of baking parchment on top and then another heavy baking tray on top of that. Press down well. Add a weight (it needs to be ovenproof) if your baking tray isn't heavy enough. Cook in an oven preheated to 200°C/Gas Mark 6 for 10–15 minutes, until golden and crisp. Drain on kitchen paper to remove excess grease. Serve while still crisp.

broccoli cream
Trim off the greenest, very top parts of the broccoli; you need about 400g. Bring a large pan of salted water to the boil, add the broccoli and cook for 1 minute. Immediately remove from the heat, refresh and drain.

Combine the cream and butter in a small saucepan and bring to the boil. Put the broccoli into a blender and pour on the cream mixture. Blend until smooth, adding the xanthan gum halfway through. Pass through a fine chinois and season, then place in an iSi gun, charge with 2 cartridges and keep warm until needed.

finishing the mushi and serving
Whisk the eggs in a bowl and pour on the chicken stock. Season. Pour into heatproof serving bowls (135ml capacity), cover tightly with cling film and steam for about 13 minutes, until the mushi has just set – the residual heat of the bowls will finish the cooking. Top the mushi with broccoli cream and sprinkle with sashimi togarashi. Serve with the crisp chicken skin on the side.

From left: *Brandade (page 32)*
Parsley Panna Cotta, White Onion Purée, Smoked Bacon Foam (page 33)
Chicken Mushi, Broccoli Cream, Crisp Chicken Skin (opposite)

'blancmange' of lovage, chilled pea, apple and mint

This is a lovely little *amuse-bouche* with flavours that creates a fresh-tasting dish with texture and balance. It is a great summer appetiser served chilled.
The blancmange is set here with carrageen moss, a seaweed with great gelling properties. The elements could be altered to suit the seasons – perhaps wild garlic taking the place of the lovage in spring, and morels taking the place of the peas.

Serves 15

for the lovage blancmange
600g milk
150g double cream
6g carrageen moss, soaked in cold water
  for 5 minutes
100g green of leek, chopped
75g lovage
1 egg
a pinch of caster sugar

for the dressing
1 egg yolk
10g cider vinegar
a pinch of caster sugar
120g olive oil
20g water

for the peas
150g podded peas, blanched
1 Granny Smith apple, peeled, cored and
  finely diced
8 mint leaves
8 pea tendrils (shoots)

lovage blancmange
Put the milk and cream in a saucepan and bring to the boil. Squeeze excess water from the moss and add the moss to the saucepan. Stir, then simmer for 6–8 minutes, stirring occasionally. Add the leek and lovage and cook rapidly for 1–2 minutes.

Pour into a blender and blend until smooth, adding the egg and sugar halfway through. Season. Pass through a fine sieve into a measuring jug, then divide among 15 individual serving bowls – I use 6.5cm-wide and 5cm-deep bowls for this. Leave to cool.

dressing
Put the egg yolk in a bowl and whisk in the vinegar followed by the sugar. Gradually whisk in the olive oil, then finish with the water. Taste and season. Keep in the fridge until needed.

peas
Mix the peas with the diced apple. Chop the mint at the last minute and add to the pea mixture. Mix with a little of the dressing and season, then spoon on to the blancmange. Add the pea tendrils and serve.

cream of cauliflower and cherry kernel soup

Cauliflower has a great flavour of its own, but it is also a perfect foil for other strong flavours, for example cheese, curry spices and nuts. Here kernels from cherry stones provide a complementary almond flavour. The stones are slightly more bitter than almonds, which gives a nice balance to the soup. You could garnish this with some deep-fried cauliflower florets added at the last minute, or perhaps a cheese and almond biscotti. If you don't want an almond flavour, then use truffle, which also goes well with cauliflower and gives a touch of luxury (just omit the cherry stones and instead garnish the soup with fine slices of black truffle).

Serves 4–6

100g unsalted butter
100g chopped onions
750g cauliflower florets
500g vegetable stock (see page 20)
500g milk
about 20 cherry stones
200g double cream

Melt 75g butter in a heavy-based saucepan, add the onions and sweat for 5 minutes without colouring. Add the cauliflower florets and cook for 2 minutes, again without colouring, then add the vegetable stock and milk.

Crack the cherry stones, remove the kernels and crush them. Add the kernels to the soup and cook for 30 minutes, until the cauliflower is soft. Taste the soup: if the almond flavour is a bit weak, add a few more cherry kernels and cook for a little longer.

Blend the soup, then pass through a fine sieve into a clean pan. Bring to the boil. Whisk in the cream and remaining butter, season and serve.

crown prince pumpkin soup, sauté of rabbit kidneys, fried sage breadcrumbs

When I see the first of the pumpkins outside the Over Farm shop, I know that autumn has truly arrived. Anyone who has read either of my other books will know that I have a great fondness for the Crown Prince variety of pumpkin. It is sweet, less starchy and less fibrous than many other varieties, and the flavour – wow! As far as I'm concerned, it is the best.

Here, it is served with sautéed rabbit kidneys and sprinkled with crisp-fried breadcrumbs with sage running through them. It is the perfect warming soup for a chilly autumn day. You could roast the pumpkin for a different flavour, or give a different depth to the soup by sprinkling with pickled wild garlic buds (see recipe on page 14).

Serves 6

for the pumpkin soup
50g duck fat
50g smoked bacon, chopped
120g chopped onions
125g chopped carrots
2 garlic cloves, smashed
4 sage leaves
1kg pumpkin flesh, ideally Crown Prince, chopped
25g cider vinegar
1.25kg chicken or vegetable stock (see pages 19 and 20)
250g milk
100g chilled unsalted butter, diced

for the fried sage breadcrumbs
20g olive oil
30g unsalted butter
125g fresh white breadcrumbs
6 sage leaves, chopped

for the sauté of rabbit kidneys
24 rabbit kidneys
40g duck fat
4 sage leaves
25g unsalted butter

pumpkin soup
Melt the duck fat in a heavy-based saucepan and heat until hot. Add the bacon and cook until its fat is rendered a little, but it hasn't started to colour. Add the onions, carrots and garlic and cook with the lid on for 3–4 minutes, so the vegetables begin to soften but not colour.

Add the sage and pumpkin, stir to mix and cook for 5 minutes, with the pan still covered. Add the vinegar and cook uncovered until it has evaporated, then add the stock and milk and cook for 30–45 minutes on a slow simmer.

Pour the soup into a blender and blend until smooth, then pass through a fine sieve into another saucepan. Whisk in the butter and season to taste. If the soup is a bit too thin, reduce it a little; if it is too thick, add a little more milk or stock.

fried sage breadcrumbs
Heat the olive oil in a large frying pan. When hot, add the butter and heat until foaming. Add the breadcrumbs with the chopped sage and cook until golden and crisp, stirring all the time so they don't burn. Season and turn out on to a tray lined with kitchen paper to absorb any excess fat.

sauté of rabbit kidneys
Remove the outer membranes from the kidneys and trim off any tubes. Heat a large frying pan and, when hot, add the duck fat and then the kidneys. Sauté for 1–1¹/₂ minutes, tossing the kidneys in the pan, adding the sage leaves halfway through. Add the butter, toss the kidneys around a little and season. Drain on kitchen paper, reserving the cooking juices in the pan. Keep warm.

serving
Reheat the soup if necessary, then ladle into 6 soup plates – shallow ones are ideal. Add the sautéed rabbit kidneys and drizzle a little of their cooking juices over the top. Finally, sprinkle with the fried sage breadcrumbs.

fermented rye flour soup, fried smoked bacon and curd cheese

Some time ago we had a Polish chef named Agnieszka do a few *stages* with us and she introduced us to this wonderful soup. One staff dinner it was served to us in a mug with piroshky (little fried ravioli filled with curd cheese, bacon and onion). The flavour was beautiful although the presentation left a little to be desired. So we worked on it for her and came up with a dish that was just as tasty but more suited to a fine dining restaurant. Here, I've used the elements of the piroshky filling to garnish the soup. If you wish, you could make piroshky and then put them in the middle of the bowl, sitting on top of some fried onions and bacon, or even a sauerkraut of white cabbage.

Serves 8

for the **kwas** *(ferment)*
300g rye flour
500g boiled water, cooled until warm
4 garlic cloves, lightly crushed
3 rye bread crusts
a pinch of salt

for the soup
30g duck fat
125g smoked bacon
125g finely chopped onions
1 garlic clove, chopped
a sprig of thyme
40g dried ceps (porcini), soaked in warm water for 1 hour
450g kwas (ferment), strained through a fine sieve
1kg beef or vegetable stock (see pages 20–21 – I prefer the depth of the beef stock)
200g single cream
100g soured cream

for the garnish
30g duck fat
250g smoked bacon, cut into small lardons
200g curd cheese
50g soured cream

kwas *(ferment)*

Place the rye flour in a Kilner jar and mix with a third of the warm water to make a paste. Pour on the remaining warm water, but do not mix. Add the garlic cloves, rye bread crusts and salt, then cover the jar with a piece of muslin. Leave in a warmish place, such as an airing cupboard, for 4 days. After this time, the mixture should have started to ferment and be giving off a pleasant sour smell.

soup

Set a large, heavy-based saucepan on a moderate heat, add the duck fat and the smoked bacon, and render the fat from the bacon a little without colouring. Add the onions and sweat for 2–3 minutes, then add the garlic and thyme.

Drain the ceps in a sieve set over a bowl. Add them to the pan and strain in their soaking water. Add the strained *kwas* and the stock. Bring to the boil, stirring to make sure it doesn't catch (the flour in the *kwas* will thicken the liquid). Simmer for 30 minutes, stirring occasionally.

Stir in the single cream and soured cream. Simmer for a further 5 minutes. Pass through a fine chinois and season. Keep warm.

garnish

Melt the duck fat in a frying pan, add the smoked bacon lardons and cook on a moderate heat until golden brown. Drain off the fat and spread the bacon on kitchen paper to absorb any excess fat. Break the curd cheese into 1cm pieces.

serving

Scatter the curd cheese in the soup bowls, then carefully ladle in the soup. Sprinkle over the smoked bacon lardons and drizzle with soured cream.

velouté of *new season's asparagus, ground ivy*

I am lucky living in Cheltenham because there is an abundance of wonderful foods available to me. And not too far away is the Vale of Evesham, where some of the best asparagus in the world is found. It is not in season very long, but while it is here I make the most of it. Anyone who uses asparagus knows there is a reasonable amount of wastage. Well, this velouté addresses that problem by using the stalks and the trimmings as well as the 'best parts'. I've partnered it with ground ivy, a little wild plant with a pretty bluish-violet flower. It has a mild mint taste, which adds a freshness to the soup. If you can't find this plant then a little wild mint can be used instead. The soup is lovely chilled, and can be garnished with some asparagus spears wrapped in slices of British cured ham and grilled.

Serves 4–6

750g Evesham asparagus
100g unsalted butter
50g finely sliced white of leek
125g peeled potatoes, sliced
400g milk
750g good-quality vegetable or chicken
  stock (see page 19 and 20)
125g spinach
75g finely sliced green of leek
50g ground ivy
50g double cream

Carefully bend the asparagus spears – they will snap just at the right point where the bottoms become tough. Keep the tops and bottoms separate, and finely slice them both.

Heat half of the butter in a heavy-based saucepan. When melted, add the white of leek with the sliced asparagus bottoms and cook for 5 minutes without colouring. Add the potatoes, milk and stock and bring to the boil, then simmer for 20 minutes. Add the spinach, green of leek, ground ivy and the asparagus tops and cook for a further 2 minutes.

Pour into a blender and blend to a smooth, fine purée. Push through a fine sieve into another saucepan. Add the cream, then whisk in the remaining butter. Bring up to heat again and season. Serve immediately.

Note: If you want to prepare the soup in advance, cool and chill as quickly as possible to keep the freshness of taste and colour. Keep in the fridge, then reheat gently but briefly before serving.

white borscht

This is a little play on the traditional borscht and never fails to get a response from customers when they are expecting a deep purple soup. You can, of course, use traditional deep red beetroot or golden beetroot, if you prefer. I love to top the borscht with a horseradish cream, or foam. This soup is just as good cold as it is hot, although if serving cold you may need to thin it slightly, perhaps with a little soured cream or buttermilk. Then drizzle with a little good balsamic vinegar or sprinkle with a little grated horseradish.

Serves 8

50g duck fat or vegetable oil
75g smoked bacon, chopped
250g chopped onions
50g finely chopped celery
1.5kg white beetroot, peeled and sliced
350g white cabbage, finely sliced
30g white wine vinegar
2 garlic cloves, finely sliced
15g dried ceps (porcini)
1kg white beef stock (see page 20)
30g unsalted butter

Melt the duck fat in a heavy-based saucepan, then add the smoked bacon and cook until it is starting to get a little colour. Add the onions, celery, beetroot and cabbage and sweat for 5 minutes without colouring. Add the white wine vinegar, garlic and dried ceps and cook for a further 2 minutes. Pour in the beef stock and bring to the boil, then lower the heat to a simmer and cook for 20–30 minutes, until all the vegetables are soft.

Pour into a blender and blend until smooth, then pass through a fine sieve into another pan. Reheat gently. Season, then whisk in the butter and serve.

seared scallops, *miso glaze,* sesame purée, turnip and verjus cream

We are lucky enough to get some wonderful scallops and langoustines from Island Divers in Kyle of Lochalsh, Scotland. The seafood has a wonderful sweetness to it. This dish is a sort of play on sweet, sour and bitter – the sweetness coming from the scallops, the sweet-sour from the miso glaze and the bitter from the turnips. They all complement each other to create a wonderful rounded dish. A white balsamic glaze would work with the scallops, instead of the miso, and a walnut purée could add the bitterness.

Serves 6

for the scallops
9 extra-large hand-dived scallops
50g olive oil
50g unsalted butter
50g Miso Glaze (see page 22)

for the sesame purée
50g water
40g dark soy sauce
20g sake
100g mirin
50g toasted sesame seeds
8g lecithin powder
50g vegetable oil
30g toasted sesame oil

for the caramelised turnips
4 turnips
50g unsalted butter
20g honey
5g verjus

for the sesame caramel
200g caster sugar
30g water
5g white balsamic vinegar
25g sesame seeds

for the turnip and verjus cream
400g peeled turnips
50g unsalted butter
40g verjus
125g double cream

wood sorrel or red-veined sorrel, to garnish

scallops
Remove the skirt and the orange roe, leaving only the pure white part of the scallop. Remove any grit with a damp cloth. Cut each scallop horizontally in half to give you 18 discs. Place on a damp cloth on a tray, then cover and keep in the fridge until needed.

sesame purée
Place the water, soy sauce, sake and mirin in a small saucepan and bring to the boil. Pour into a blender and add the sesame seeds. Turn on the blender and add the lecithin to the vortex in the middle. Blend until smooth. Drizzle in the vegetable oil in a slow steady stream, followed by the sesame oil, again in a steady stream. You want the mixture to emulsify and become thick. Place in a squeezy bottle and set aside until needed.

caramelised turnips
Cut each turnip into 6 segments, then with a small knife turn each segment into a small turnip shape. Bring a medium saucepan of water to the boil. Season with salt. Add the turnips and cook for 2 minutes, then drain and place on a cloth-lined tray. Leave to cool.

sesame caramel
Combine the sugar, water and white balsamic vinegar in a small heavy-based saucepan. Cook slowly, stirring, until the sugar has dissolved, then raise the heat and cook to a golden caramel. Meanwhile, line a baking tray with baking parchment and set on the work surface with a rolling pin and another sheet of baking parchment.

When the caramel is the correct colour, stir in the sesame seeds, then immediately pour on to the lined tray. Place the other sheet of baking parchment on top and carefully roll out until very thin. Leave to set hard before breaking into shards.

turnip and verjus cream
Cut the turnips in half, then slice them finely. Set a medium heavy-based saucepan on a medium heat and add the butter. Add the turnips and cook for 2 minutes without colouring, stirring all the time. Deglaze with the verjus and cook until it has all evaporated. Pour in the cream and bring to the boil, then reduce the heat to a low simmer and cook for about 5 minutes, until the turnip slices are tender.

Transfer to a blender and blend to a smooth, velvety purée, adding seasoning towards the end. Keep warm.

finishing the caramelised turnips
Heat a large pan and add the butter followed by the turnips and cook until golden and tender. Add the honey and verjus and continue to cook, rolling the turnips around in the pan until they are evenly coated and starting to take on a golden glaze. Season. Remove from the pan and keep warm.

searing the scallops
Heat a large, heavy-based frying pan. When you feel the heat coming off it, add half the olive oil, then place half of the scallops in the hot pan. Cook for 30 seconds, then add half the butter and cook for a further 30–60 seconds. Turn the scallops and cook for a further 1 minute, adding the miso glaze halfway through. Remove to a warm plate and keep warm. Wipe the pan and repeat to cook the other scallops. When they are all cooked, season.

serving
For each serving, make a little streak of turnip and verjus cream down both sides of an oval plate, then place 3 scallop halves on the plate. Arrange 4 pieces of caramelised turnip, then dot the plate with sesame purée. Finally, garnish with the caramel shards and the wood sorrel.

scallops, *maple-glazed chicken wings, sweetcorn custard, sea aster*

When I eat out if I see scallops on the menu I order them as one of my courses. I love their meatiness and sweetness and that lovely caramelised taste when they are cooked. Shellfish goes extremely well with sweetcorn so here I've used that to make a custard – and quite simply by using the starch in the sweetcorn as the thickening. Chicken wings glazed with maple syrup and sea aster, a wonderful salty fleshy leaf, add complementary flavours, with the sheep's sorrel garnish giving a little acidity to match the sweetness of the scallops and wings.

Serves 4

for the chicken wings
8 chicken wings
10g Maldon salt, plus extra for seasoning
1 garlic clove, finely chopped
200g duck fat
25g unsalted butter
50g maple syrup

for the scallops
6 extra-large hand-dived scallops
50g olive oil
50g unsalted butter

for the sweetcorn custard
5 large, compact ears of sweetcorn
40g unsalted butter
a few drops of lemon juice

for the sea aster
50g unsalted butter
50g water
20 nice long sea aster leaves

sheep's sorrel, to garnish

chicken wings
Joint the chicken wings, chopping both end bits of knuckle off the middle section; discard these knuckles. Sprinkle the middle sections with the sea salt and garlic, then cover and keep in the fridge for 6–8 hours.

Heat the duck fat in a flameproof casserole and add the chicken wings. Place in an oven preheated to 140°C/Gas Mark 1 and cook for 2 hours. The wings should be very tender. Remove from the fat (reserve the fat) and leave to cool a little, then push out the two bones in the wings. Keep in a cool place until needed.

scallops
Remove the 'skirt' and orange roe from each scallop, leaving only the pure white part. Remove any grit with a damp cloth. Cut each scallop horizontally in half. Place on a damp cloth on a tray, cover and keep in the fridge. Remove 5 minutes before needed.

sweetcorn custard
Shuck the sweetcorn, removing all the 'silk'. Shave the kernels off the cob without taking any of the white husk. Place the kernels in a juicer and extract as much juice as you can – you will have 400–450g. Place the juice in a saucepan and bring to the boil, stirring constantly. Simmer gently for 3–4 minutes, until thickened, being careful it doesn't catch. It is the starch present in the sweetcorn that will thicken the juice, giving it the consistency of custard. The longer you simmer it, the thicker it will get, even to a purée consistency.

Remove from the heat and whisk in the butter. Season, adding a little lemon juice to balance the sweetness of the sweetcorn. The custard should be the consistency of thick pouring cream. If it is a bit too thick, add a little water and heat up. Strain through a sieve into a clean pan and cover the surface with cling film to prevent a skin from forming. Reheat when needed.

sea aster
Place a large sauteuse on the heat, add the butter and water, and bring to the boil. Add the sea aster leaves and cook for 1–2 minutes, until just wilted. Season. Drain and keep warm.

glazing the wings
Heat a little of the reserved duck fat in a frying pan and cook the wings until golden on both sides. Add the butter and maple syrup and cook until glazed and sticky. Season with Maldon salt and place on a tray. Keep warm.

finishing the scallops
Heat a large heavy-based frying pan. When you feel the heat coming off it, add half of the olive oil and then half of the scallops. Cook for 30 seconds, then add half of the butter and cook for a further 30–60 seconds. Turn over and cook for about 1 minute. Remove to a warm plate. Wipe the pan and repeat with the remaining scallops. When all are cooked, season. Keep warm.

serving
Lay out 3 of the sea aster leaves on each plate, topping and tailing them. Drizzle a little of the sweetcorn custard in lines on the plate, over and around the sea aster. Place 2 pieces of scallop and 2 chicken wings at different places on the plate. Arrange the other 2 leaves of sea aster in rough piles, then garnish with the sheep's sorrel. Place a little Maldon salt on the scallops and serve.

pan-seared langoustines, ajo blanco, watermelon

Ajo blanco is a white gazpacho, normally served with grapes from the Andalusia region of Spain. I am serving it with watermelon, warmed through to enhance the sweetness. With some seared juicy langoustines and a little wild rocket, you have a lovely light and refreshing starter for summer. This would also work with scallops or a little crab salad in the middle of the soup. The langoustines are seared at the last minute, so you can get the contrasting temperatures of chilled soup, warm melon and hot langoustine.

Serves 6

for the ajo blanco
200g stale bread, crusts removed
1kg water
200g freshly blanched almonds
3 garlic cloves, peeled and green core
  removed
120g extra virgin olive oil
40g sherry vinegar

for the watermelon
1 medium seedless watermelon, about
  1.5kg
50g extra virgin olive oil
50g olive oil

for the langoustines
18 large raw langoustine tails, peeled
100g olive oil
50g unsalted butter

to serve
50g baby wild rocket leaves
Maldon salt

ajo blanco
Soak the bread in a little of the water, covered, for 2 hours, until softened. Transfer to a blender, add the almonds and garlic, and blend until smooth. With the machine running, slowly add the olive oil in a steady stream, followed by the sherry vinegar. Finally, add the remaining water in a steady stream and blend well to create an emulsion. Pass through a sieve and season. Cover and keep in the fridge until needed.

watermelon
Cut the watermelon into slices 2.5cm thick. Cut some rectangles of flesh 10 x 4cm; set these aside. Remove any seeds from the trimmings of watermelon flesh. Blend the trimmings with the extra virgin olive oil until smooth, then season with a little salt. Place in a squeezy bottle.

Heat the olive oil in a medium frying pan, add the watermelon rectangles and season, then quickly and gently just warm through. You don't want them to be hot. Remove from the pan and keep warm.

langoustines
Season the langoustine tails. Heat the olive oil in a large frying pan. When you can feel the heat coming off the pan, quickly sauté the langoustine tails for 30 seconds on one side. Add the butter and flip over the langoustine tails, then remove the pan from the heat and allow the langoustines to finish cooking in the residual heat of the pan. Remove from the pan when golden and pink, then season again. Drain on kitchen paper or a J-cloth. Serve while still hot.

serving
Place some watermelon rectangles in the middle of each shallow soup plate. Pour in the ajo blanco to come halfway up, then quickly arrange the hot langoustines along the top of the watermelon. Dress with baby wild rocket leaves, drizzle the watermelon olive oil around, and sprinkle a little Maldon salt over the melon and langoustines.

sauté of langoustines, roasted heritage carrots, carrot purée, buttermilk

Seafood loves sweetness, which I think is because much of it has a slight sweetness of its own. There are many things that can be used to enhance the sweetness, such as pumpkin, parsnip, chervil tuber, peas and, as here, carrots. The langoustines are seared quickly to give a lovely caramelised exterior. I've put them with buttermilk in two different forms – a purée and a foam – to balance the dish with a slight acid note. Finally, there is a seasoning of spiced bread that has been powdered into crumbs.

Serves 6

for the langoustines
12 extra-large raw langoustines
100g olive oil
50g unsalted butter
juice of 1/4 lemon

for the buttermilk purée
1kg buttermilk
500g double cream
5g agar agar
5g xanthan gum
3.5g lemon juice
2.5g lecithin powder

for the roasted heritage carrots
6 baby purple heritage carrots with tops
6 baby yellow heritage carrots with tops
6 baby orange heritage carrots with tops
100g duck fat
30g unsalted butter

for the carrot purée
100g unsalted butter
500g carrots, peeled and finely sliced
100g double cream
100g milk

for the buttermilk froth
50g milk
50g double cream
400g buttermilk
squeeze of lemon juice
1.5g xanthan gum

4g lecithin powder

100g Spiced Bread (see page 15), made into fine breadcrumbs, to garnish

langoustines
Bring a large pan of water to the boil, then blanch the langoustines for about 1 minute. Drain. While still slightly warm, shell the tails. Then, using nutcrackers, remove the meat from the claws (keep for another dish, such as tortellini, or serve with this dish for a slightly larger portion). Keep the langoustine tails and claw meat in the fridge until needed (or wrap and freeze the claw meat).

buttermilk purée
Place the buttermilk and cream in a large saucepan, bring to the boil and simmer, stirring occasionally, to reduce to 500g, being careful it doesn't catch. Pour into a blender, add the other ingredients and blend for 2 minutes. Pour into a clean pan. Place back on the heat and bring up to just below boiling, then cook for 2 minutes. Pass through a sieve into a container and cool, then leave in the fridge for at least 4 hours, preferably overnight, to set.

Put the set buttermilk in a blender and blend until smooth. Place in a squeezy bottle and set aside in a cool place until needed.

roasted heritage carrots
Scrub the carrots carefully and cut each stem to 1cm long. Keep some of the better leaves; wash and keep in a container in the fridge until needed.

Set a roasting tray with the duck fat on a high heat, add the carrots and cook for 2 minutes, tossing them around in the pan to make sure they are coated in the fat. Season and place in an oven preheated to 180°C/Gas Mark 4. Cook for 10 minutes, adding the butter after 3 minutes and

mixing it in. Remove the carrots from the tray and season again. Keep warm.

carrot purée
Heat 50g butter in a saucepan, add the carrots and cook for 5 minutes without colouring. Add the cream and milk and cook for a further 15 minutes. The carrots should be very tender. Transfer to a blender and blend to a smooth purée, adding the remaining butter while still hot. Season and keep warm.

buttermilk froth
Combine the milk and cream in a medium saucepan and bring to the boil. Add the buttermilk and lower the heat to a simmer. Squeeze in the lemon juice. Pour into a blender and turn on at a medium speed. Remove the central lid and add the xanthan gum and lecithin to the vortex in the centre of the machine. Blend for 2 minutes. Pass through a sieve into a saucepan and season. Keep warm.

sautéeing the langoustines
Season the langoustine tails. Heat the olive oil in a large frying pan and, when you can feel the heat coming off the pan, quickly sauté the langoustine tails for 30 seconds on one side. Add the butter and flip over the langoustine tails, then remove the pan from the heat and allow the residual heat from the pan to cook the other side. Remove the langoustines from the pan when they are golden and pink, then season with the lemon juice. Drain and keep hot.

serving
Make 2 swipes of carrot purée across each plate at different angles followed by a line of the powdered spiced bread, then place 2 langoustines on each plate. Arrange the caramelised carrots and carrot leaves. Pipe little mounds of the buttermilk purée from the squeezy bottle. Finally, use a stick blender to froth the buttermilk sauce and spoon over the langoustines.

native lobster with wilted cos lettuce,
peas and pistachios

Shellfish and peas have a natural affinity, and with this country having some of the best native lobsters in the world, why wouldn't you put them together? I first had a pistachio and pea combination in a soup at a private Sunday lunch with Claude Bosi from Hibiscus, who was then in Ludlow. It was so nice that it has stuck in my mind for years. So here it is, in a different form, with cos lettuce, sometimes now called romaine. Good King Henry or spearhead orache could replace the cos, and peanuts replace the pistachios.

Serves 6

for the lobsters
3 live native lobsters, 600–800g each
50g olive oil
30g unsalted butter
juice of 1/2 lemon

for the charred button onions
12 button onions, peeled
50g unsalted butter
olive oil

for the pistachio oil
75g toasted peeled pistachios
75g pistachio oil

for the pea purée
500g podded fresh peas or thawed frozen peas
50g water
75g unsalted butter
25g peeled pistachios

for the wilted lettuce
2 small cos lettuces
25g unsalted butter
40g water

for the peas
100g podded fresh peas or frozen peas
30g unsalted butter
10g water

lobsters
Bring a large pan of salted water to the boil. Hold each lobster, stomach down, on a board. On the top of the head you will see a cross. Quickly push the tip of a large chopping knife into it; this will kill the lobster instantly. Put the lobsters into the boiling water and cook for 4 minutes, then immediately transfer to iced water to stop the cooking. Drain.

Pull the head away from the body and put the tail to one side. Remove the claws and put to one side. Split the head and remove the stomach sac and intestine, then remove the liver and the coral (you can make a butter with these for use in sauces). Remove the meat from the claws and knuckles. Remove the tail meat in one piece by snapping the shell on each side of the tail and pulling the meat out. Keep all the lobster meat in the fridge until needed.

charred button onions
Put the onions in a medium frying pan and add enough water to half cover them. Add the butter. Bring up to the boil, then simmer until the water has evaporated, leaving the butter to colour the onions. Keep them just undercooked. Remove from the pan and cool a little, then cut each in half vertically.

pistachio oil
Place the pistachios and oil in a blender and pulse to break down. Don't make the nuts too fine as you want a little texture. Set aside.

pea purée
Set a medium saucepan on the heat, add the peas, water and half the butter, and bring to the boil. Cook for 2 minutes, stirring the peas. Place in a blender and blend to a smooth purée, adding the pistachios and remaining butter halfway through. Push through a fine sieve into a clean pan and season.

wilted lettuce
Remove any outer leaves from the lettuces that look old and limp. Then, picking the greenest from the remaining leaves, cut in

half lengthways through the stem. (Don't do this too far in advance of serving or the cut will start to brown.) Put the butter and water in a frying pan and bring to the boil to create an emulsion. Add the lettuce and turn around a little until the leaves are wilted. Season, remove from the pan and drain. Keep warm.

peas
Bring a saucepan of salted water to the boil. Add the peas and cook for 2–3 minutes. Refresh in cold water and drain. Pop them out of their skins. Return to the empty pan and add the butter and water. Set aside.

finishing the lobster
Heat the oil and butter in a large cast-iron frying pan. When hot, add the lobster tails and cook for about 3 minutes on each side; keep turning the tails over to make sure they do not burn. Season with lemon juice, salt and pepper. Remove from the pan and put to one side to rest. Add the claw and knuckle meat and heat through; do not overcook. Season with lemon juice, salt and pepper. Remove from the pan and keep warm with the tails and the pan juices until needed.

finishing the onions
Place a frying pan on the heat and oil the pan with a cloth dipped in olive oil. When it is very hot, place the onions, cut side down, in the pan and cook until they are lightly charred. Remove from the pan and season. Keep warm.

serving
Reheat the pea purée and the peas. Make 2 swipes of pea purée on each plate. Cut the lobster tails lengthways in half and place one half in the middle of each plate. Add the knuckle and claw meat. Arrange the peas, wilted lettuce and charred onions around and drizzle over the pistachio oil.

crab and peach salad, emulsion of brown meat, red pepper dulse, fresh almonds

Crab has such a lovely flavour and it brings back great memories for me of the British seaside and family holidays when I was young. I try to use crab whenever I can – its flavour complements both savoury and sweet. Peaches are one of my favourite fruits and they make a particularly successful pairing with crab. Here the brown crabmeat has been turned into its own mayonnaise, with some fresh almonds to give a textural crunch and a little seaweed for a briny flourish.

Serves 6

for the crab and peach salad
350g white crabmeat
100g mayonnaise
1 small ripe peach, peeled, stoned and finely diced
15g shelled fresh almonds, skinned and grated
juice of 1/2 lemon

for the crab legs
10g lemon juice
40g grapeseed oil
10 leaves of lemon verbena, finely chopped
18 pieces of crabmeat from the legs (taken in the piece)

for the brown crabmeat emulsion
80g brown crabmeat
10g fresh white breadcrumbs
3g English mustard
1 egg yolk
120g grapeseed oil
juice of 1/2 lemon

for the red pepper dulse
120g very young red pepper dulse fronds (preferably fresh)
20g soft brown sugar
25g red wine vinegar
50g red wine
125g olive oil

to serve
5 ripe peaches
borage leaves and flowers
24 fresh almonds, shelled and skinned

crab and peach salad
Mix the white crabmeat with the mayonnaise, peach and grated almonds. Mix in enough lemon juice to help the flavour but not overpower it. Season, then cover and keep in the fridge until needed.

crab legs
Mix together the lemon juice, oil and lemon verbena. Season. Set this dressing aside until needed.

brown crabmeat emulsion
Put the brown crabmeat in a blender with the breadcrumbs and mustard and blend until smooth. Add the egg yolk and blend in. With the machine running, gradually add the grapeseed oil until an emulsion is formed. Pass through a fine sieve, adding a little lemon juice to heighten the crab flavour. If the emulsion is too thick add a little water. Season. Keep in a cool place until needed.

red pepper dulse
Soak the dulse in fresh water for 10 minutes to get rid of a little of the saltiness; drain. Put the dulse in a medium pan, just cover with water and bring to the boil, then simmer very gently for 1 hour.

Meanwhile, make the dressing. Combine the sugar and vinegar in a small saucepan and bring to the boil, then add the red wine and cook for 12 minutes. Remove from the heat and leave to cool, then whisk in the olive oil.

Remove the dulse from the water and drain in a sieve. While still hot, pour the dressing over. Cover and leave to cool, then season.

serving
Slice 3 of the peaches into discs 2mm thick; you will need 12. Put to one side. Cut the other 2 peaches in half and remove the stone, then trim where the stone was and cut into half slices 3mm thick. Arrange on the plates. Put the white crab and peach salad between pairs of peach discs.
Pick a few of the smaller borage leaves and flowers and arrange on top, then set at the head of each plate. Dress the crab leg meat with the dressing. Remove the dulse from its dressing and drain. Add 3 little piles of dulse to each plate, then 4–5 blobs of brown crabmeat emulsion and the leg meat at different angles. Finally, dress with the borage leaves and flowers and almonds.

roasted hake, parsley root purée and rémoulade, chicken juices

Hake is a member of the cod family with a closer and finer flesh than that of its cousin. The Spanish love this fish and it is on many of their menus. I've served it here with a purée of parsley root – which looks like a parsnip, but with its own unique flavour – that is bound with a mustard mayonnaise. The chicken juices complement the roasted hake and match its meatiness, and the apple biscuit provides a sweet/sour crunch.

Serves 6

for the roasted hake
1 fillet of hake, skin on and scaled, about
   500g
50g olive oil
30g unsalted butter
juice of 1/4 lemon

for the chicken juices
50g olive oil
200g chicken wings, finely chopped
2 large shallots, finely sliced
100g button mushrooms, finely sliced
15g cider vinegar
75g Madeira
a sprig of thyme
125g white wine
600g chicken stock (see page 19)
30g unsalted butter

for the parsley root purée
200g parsley root
150g milk
125g double cream
75g unsalted butter

for the parsley root rémoulade
1 large parsley root, 200–250g
2 egg yolks
5g white wine vinegar
30g wholegrain mustard
300g groundnut oil
30g capers, finely chopped
30g gherkins, finely chopped
2 anchovy fillets, finely chopped

1 teaspoon chopped chervil
1 teaspoon chopped tarragon
1 teaspoon chopped parsley
1 Granny Smith apple, peeled, cored and
   finely diced

for the apple biscuit
100g unsalted butter, softened
100g caster sugar
110g plain flour
7g salt
1g freshly ground black pepper
75g apple juice
2g cider vinegar

for the parsley crumbs
100g flat-leaf parsley, chopped
75g fine breadcrumbs

to serve
1 apple, cut into 12 discs 4cm across and
   2mm thick
18 pieces of buck's horn plantain
tops from 12 cleavers

hake
Lay out some cling film on the work surface. Place the hake fillet on the cling film and wrap tightly, forming a perfect roll. Leave in the freezer for 2 hours, not to freeze but just to set the shape. Then remove from the freezer and cut the fillet into 6 even pieces. Keep in the fridge until needed.

chicken juices
Heat the oil in a saucepan and, when hot, add the chicken wings. Cook until well coloured, stirring occasionally. Remove the wings from the pan, then add the shallots and cook for 2 minutes. Add the button mushrooms and cook for another 2 minutes. Pour in the vinegar and reduce until completely evaporated. Add the Madeira followed by the thyme and white wine and reduce until the wine has evaporated. Add the stock and bring to the boil, then skim and simmer for 50 minutes.

Strain through a fine sieve and leave to cool. Remove any fat that has come to the surface, then pour into a saucepan and reduce to 200g. Set aside.

parsley root purée
Peel and slice the parsley root. Combine with the milk and cream in a saucepan and simmer on a low heat until tender. Transfer to a blender and blend to a smooth, velvety purée, adding the butter towards the end. Season, then leave to cool.

parsley root rémoulade
Peel the parsley root and remove the root top. Whisk the egg yolks, vinegar and mustard together, then slowly add the oil in a steady drizzle, whisking continuously. When all the oil has been incorporated, add the capers, gherkins, anchovies, chervil, tarragon and parsley. Mix well.

Cut the parsley root into long, thin slices on a mandolin, then cut the slices into julienne. Combine with the rémoulade sauce, mixing well. Add the apple and season. Cover and keep in the fridge until 30 minutes before serving.

apple biscuit
Put the butter and caster sugar in a mixing bowl and cream together until smooth. Beat in the flour, salt and black pepper. Finally, beat in the apple juice and vinegar until smooth. Chill in the fridge for at least 4 hours to set up.

Place a Silpat mat on a baking sheet. Spread out the mixture 2mm thick on the mat. Bake in an oven preheated to 160°C/Gas Mark 3 for 5 minutes until just turning golden. Remove from the oven and, while still warm, cut into rectangles about 7 x 3cm. Place the rectangles back in the oven to finish cooking until deep golden and crisp. Transfer to a wire rack to cool, then store in an airtight container.

parsley crumbs

Put the parsley and breadcrumbs in a food processor with a little seasoning. Pulse until the breadcrumbs have mixed with the parsley and taken on a green colour. Scatter onto a tray and leave to dry at warm room temperature for 4–5 hours.

roasting the hake

Heat the oil in a large frying pan. Season the hake and add to the pan. Cook for 2–3 minutes, then flip the fish over, add the butter to the pan and cook for a further 2 minutes, basting the top with the butter. Check to see if the fish is done (insert a fine skewer, then withdraw and touch it to your lips: if the skewer is warm the fish is cooked). If not, cook for another 1–2 minutes. Season, then squeeze a little lemon juice over. Remove from the pan and keep warm.

serving

Reheat the parsley root purée. Reheat the chicken juices, then whisk in the butter and season if needed. Keep warm. Place a little parsley root purée at one side of each bowl, then make a small mound of rémoulade on the other side. Top the rémoulade with an apple biscuit and stand an apple disc on each side of the mound. Dip one side of the hake in the parsley crumbs and place on the purée. Arrange the buck's horn plantain and cleavers around the dish. Finally, add a little of the chicken juices.

olive oil-poached pollock, salted pollock mousse, saffron potatoes

Pollock lends itself very well to the making of brandade-like dishes. Here it is simply poached, to retain its juiciness, and served with a salted pollock mousse to complement it. The pollock can, of course, be replaced with cod or hake, although the cooking will need to be watched. A salty anchovy and olive paste gives this dish a Mediterranean feel, and the potatoes poached in saffron add a little more substance.

Serves 6

for the salted pollock (for the mousse)
30g Maldon salt
5g caster sugar
grated zest of $1/2$ lemon
grated zest of $1/2$ orange
a sprig of thyme, chopped
2 juniper berries, ground
1 bay leaf
1 piece of skinned pollock fillet (middle section would be best), about 400g, pin-boned

for the salted pollock mousse
50g unsalted butter
50g olive oil
50g finely chopped onions
100g white of leek, finely chopped
100g sliced potatoes
450g double cream
11g bronze gelatine leaves

for the olive oil-poached pollock
3 pieces of skinned pollock fillet (middle section would be best), 300g each, pin-boned
2 juniper berries, crushed
grated zest of 1 lemon
leaves from 2 sprigs of thyme
30g Maldon salt
250g olive oil
juice of $1/2$ lemon

for the tapenade
250g stoned Nyons black olives, or good deeply coloured black olives
25g anchovy fillets, rinsed
50g baby capers
1 garlic clove, peeled
leaves from a sprig of savory or thyme
50g olive oil
a few drops of fresh lemon juice

for the saffron potatoes
6 small Aura potatoes, 3cm diameter, scrubbed
300g olive oil
100g finely chopped shallots
1 garlic clove, finely chopped
a good pinch of saffron strands
30g white wine vinegar
10g jasmine honey
100g white wine

sheep's sorrel and fine plantain leaves, to garnish

salted pollock

Mix the salt, sugar and all the aromatics together. Place the pollock fillet on a tray and sprinkle with half of the salt mixture, then turn it over and sprinkle with the remaining salt mixture. Cover with cling film and refrigerate overnight. Remove from the fridge and quickly rinse the salt off under cold running water, then dry well.

salted pollock mousse

Melt the butter with the olive oil in a pan, add the onions and leek, and sweat without colouring for 5 minutes. Add the potatoes and cook until translucent. Lay the salted pollock on top and cover with 250g of the cream. Poach gently for 10–15 minutes, until the pollock is cooked.

Soak the gelatine in some cold water for about 5 minutes. Meanwhile, transfer the pollock mixture to a blender and blend until smooth. Squeeze excess water from the gelatine and add to the blender. Blitz again, then pour into a bowl and leave to cool.

Whip the remaining cream to the ribbon stage and fold into the pollock mixture. Taste and season. Place in a lidded container and leave in the fridge overnight to set. When needed, spoon into a piping bag fitted with a plain nozzle.

olive oil-poached pollock

Sprinkle the pollock fillets with the juniper, lemon zest, thyme and salt. Wrap tightly in cling film and refrigerate for 2 hours. Remove the cling film and scrape the excess salt off the fillets. Warm the olive oil in a pan until it reaches 56°C, then slide in the fillets. Maintain the temperature at 56°C for 6–7 minutes, until the fish is just cooked (the exact timing will correspond to the thickness of the fillets). Remove from the oil and carefully flake the fish, getting as many nice big flakes as you can. Gently place in a bowl and cool, then add a couple of spoons of the cooking oil and the lemon juice. Cover and put to one side.

tapenade

Place all the ingredients, apart from the olive oil and lemon juice, in a food processor. Pulse to obtain a medium purée. Add the olive oil in a steady drizzle. Taste, then season with lemon juice and black pepper. Keep in a lidded container until needed.

saffron potatoes

Put the potatoes in a large saucepan, just cover with water and add some salt. Bring up to the boil, then simmer for 10 minutes; they will be undercooked.

Meanwhile, heat 30g of the olive oil in a small saucepan and sweat the shallots and garlic without colouring. Add the saffron and stir. Add the vinegar and honey and cook for 2 minutes, then add the white wine and reduce by half. Finally, add the remaining olive oil and warm through.

Drain the potatoes. Carefully remove the skins while still hot. Finely trim the end off each potato, then slice into 4. Place the potato slices in a lipped tray and pour over the hot saffron dressing. Immediately cover with cling film and leave at room temperature to finish cooking the potatoes. Turn them over every 30 minutes so they will take on the flavour and colour of the dressing. Keep in the dressing until needed.

serving

Place 4 potato slices on each plate, then add 4 pieces of poached pollock. Pipe on some blobs of the salted pollock mousse, then add some tapenade and garnish with the sheep's sorrel and plantain leaves.

red mullet, salt-baked kohlrabi, oyster and horseradish cream, ox-eye daisy

This is one of the simplest recipes in the book, and one of the tastiest. Red mullet, which appears quite a lot on our menu, has the ability to carry powerful flavours. Here it is cooked for the briefest of times to ensure it remains moist and then is partnered with salt-baked kohlrabi. Salt-baking intensifies the flavours of whatever is being cooked. Beetroot, sweet potato or celeriac could replace the kohlrabi, although I think the cabbage flavours of this vegetable complement the mullet very well. The horseradish and oyster cream give the dish silkiness. Ox-eye daisy, with its flavour of raw earthy beetroot, adds another dimension to the whole.

Serves 6

for the salt-baked kohlrabi
1kg plain flour
600g sel gris (grey sea salt)
5g thyme leaves, chopped
50g dried burdock root
5g burdock powder
550g water
2 medium kohlrabi, about 600g each

for the red mullet
50g olive oil
3 red mullets, about 400g each, scaled,
   filleted and pin-boned
50g unsalted butter
1/2 lemon

for the oyster and horseradish cream
3 large Whitstable oysters
3g finely grated fresh horseradish
20g creamed horseradish
1 egg yolk
150g rapeseed oil
1/2 lemon

to garnish
6 chives, finely snipped
30 small ox-eye daisy leaves

salt-baked kohlrabi
Put all the dry ingredients into a bowl. Pour in the cold water and mix well until a dough is formed. Remove all the long stems from the kohlrabi, then prick the heads all over lightly with a roasting fork. Roll out the salt dough to 7mm thickness and use to completely enrobe the kohlrabi. It is very important that there aren't any cracks in the dough crust. Place the 2 parcels on a baking sheet and bake in an oven preheated to 200°C/Gas Mark 6 for 2 hours. Remove from the oven and allow to cool.

Crack open the parcels and remove the kohlrabi, then peel and slice as thinly as possible (we use a meat slicing machine). Place in a bowl and keep covered until needed.

red mullet
Heat the olive oil in a large non-stick pan. Season the red mullet fillets. When the olive oil is hot, place the fillets in the pan, skin side down, and cook for 1–1 1/2 minutes, until the skin is golden. Flip the fillets over and add the butter, then remove from the heat and allow the fish to carry on cooking for 1 1/2–2 minutes in the residual heat from the pan. Season with the lemon juice and remove from the pan. Keep warm.

oyster and horseradish cream
Carefully open the oysters and remove the meat, making sure you keep the juices. Check the oysters for any bits of shell, then place them in a blender with the fresh horseradish and creamed horseradish. Blend until smooth. Add the egg yolk. Strain in the juice from 2 of the oysters through a fine sieve. Blend again. With the machine running, slowly add the rapeseed oil until an emulsion is formed. Pass through the fine sieve into a container and add a little lemon juice to heighten the oyster flavour. If the emulsion is too thick add a little water, then season.

serving
Add the chives and a little of the oyster and horseradish cream to the bowl with the kohlrabi, and mix well to coat. Place a line of kohlrabi along the right side of each plate, scrunching the slices slightly to form a pleasing shape. Arrange the ox-eye daisy leaves on top. Place the red mullet on the left side of the plate and drizzle a little more of the oyster and horseradish cream around.

witch with leek, salted wild garlic buds, pear and hairy bittercress

Witch, also called Torbay sole, is a member of the flatfish family. It has flaky flesh that is quite delicate, rather like lemon sole in texture. I have served it here with some salted wild garlic buds, which appear after the wild garlic has flowered. Once salted or pickled, they will last through the cold months. The pear adds a sweetness that goes well with the fieriness of the hairy bittercress.

Serves 6

for the leeks
12 small, thin baby leeks
50g olive oil
30g walnut oil
6 walnut halves

for the pears
2 Williams pears
30g walnut oil

for the hairy bittercress purée
400g fish stock (see page 19), reduced to
   150g
5g agar agar
100g watercress leaves
50g hairy bittercress
50g flat-leaf parsley leaves

for the witch
6 skinned and trimmed fillets of witch,
   about 140g each
50g olive oil
30g unsalted butter
a dash of lemon juice

to serve
25g Salted Garlic Buds (see page 14)
24 small stems of hairy bittercress
walnut oil

leeks
Remove any damaged outer leaves, then trim the bottoms of the leeks leaving 1cm of the root intact. Wash well and dry. Heat a large frying pan with the olive oil and add the leeks. When they are catching slightly, turn them. Repeat this until the leeks are sufficiently tender and charred all over.

Remove to a tray. Drizzle over the walnut oil and season. Grate the walnuts over using a fine grater (a microplane is best). Keep warm.

pears
Cut the 'lobes' off the opposite sides of each pear, then cut off the 2 'half-lobes' you have created. Place each piece, peel side up, on a chopping board and slice 2mm thick – just thick enough for them to stand up. Place in a bowl and sprinkle with the walnut oil and seasoning. Cover and put to one side.

hairy bittercress purée
Put the fish stock in a saucepan and whisk in the agar agar. Set aside for 5 minutes. Then set the pan on the heat and bring to the boil, whisking. Cook for 2–3 minutes. Pour into a blender and add the watercress, hairy bittercress and parsley. Blend until smooth. Season, then pass through a fine sieve into a container. Immediately place in the fridge and leave for 4 hours to set.

Tip the set mixture into the blender and blend again until smooth. Check the seasoning. Place in a squeezy bottle and keep at room temperature until needed.

witch
Lay the witch fillets out flat and season them. Heat the oil in a large frying pan and, when hot, add the butter. When it is foaming, place the fillets in the pan, skinned side up, and cook for 1 minute. Flip over and remove from the heat; the fish will finish cooking in the residual heat of the pan – when ready, they should have a little resistance to the finger. Squeeze a few drops of lemon juice over. Remove from the pan and keep warm. Pour the juices into a bowl and keep warm.

serving
Place a witch fillet on the left side of each plate. Neatly arrange the leeks to the right, then stand up the pear slices between the longer of the leek leaves. Scatter the garlic buds over the fish and leeks. Dot the bittercress purée over the fish and in between the leeks. Arrange the hairy bittercress stems on the fish and spoon a little of the cooking juices over and around. Finish with a drizzle of walnut oil.

fillet of cornish sea bass, wild mushroom tea, good king henry

The Cornish line-caught sea bass that my fishmonger Johnny gets me is the best I have ever seen – always firm and sparklingly fresh. Here I've served it with a mushroom tea, which is a very rich and concentrated mushroom stock mixed with a Japanese dashi to increase its savoury flavour. It is served with young Good King Henry leaves, wilted sea aster leaves and some tapioca poached in the mushroom tea. In the restaurant we serve the tea separately in little glass teapots with a few more dried wild mushrooms, a little lovage stalk and lemon verbena leaves. You could do this too, if you like.

Serves 8

for the sea bass
8 pieces of sea bass fillet (middle section, if possible), 100–120g each
grapeseed oil, for brushing
a little lemon juice

for the mushroom tea
50g olive oil
500g onions, finely sliced
50g dried ceps (porcini)
1.5kg brown chicken stock (see page 19)
500g Dashi (see page 20)

for the parsley oil
75g rapeseed oil
30g flat-leaf parsley leaves
juice of 1/4 lemon

for the tapioca
250g mushroom tea (see above)
40g tapioca

for the wilted sea aster
50g unsalted butter
50g water
200g sea aster leaves

to serve
Maldon salt
Good King Henry leaves

sea bass
Lay a sheet of cling film on the work surface and cut out a piece just large enough to wrap a portion of sea bass. Brush oil and lemon juice over a square in the centre of the piece of cling film and season. Place the sea bass portion on this, skin side down, and wrap the fish tightly. Repeat to wrap the remaining pieces of fish. Keep in the fridge until needed. Remove about 30 minutes before steaming.

mushroom tea
Heat the olive oil in a large saucepan, add the onions and stir well, then cover with a lid. Cook, stirring occasionally, for about 5 minutes, until the onions have collapsed and become translucent. Remove the lid and cook until the onions are a lovely deep golden-brown colour, stirring well. Add the ceps followed by the stock. Bring to the boil, then simmer for 50 minutes, skimming as necessary. Carefully strain through muslin into another pan.

Add the dashi, bring to the boil and simmer gently for 5–10 minutes so the flavours can develop. Remove from the heat. The tea should be extremely well flavoured by now; if it is a bit watery, place back on the heat and slowly reduce, without boiling. If it is too reduced add a little water. Leave to cool, then set aside.

parsley oil
Place all the ingredients in a blender and pulse to blend: the oil should have flecks of parsley, but not become a purée. Season and set aside.

tapioca
Pour 250g of the mushroom tea into a small saucepan and bring to the boil, then rain in the tapioca, stirring. Simmer gently until the tapioca is cooked, about 30 minutes. All the liquid should have been soaked up by the tapioca; if not, drain off

the excess. Season and keep warm.

steaming the sea bass
Place a steamer on the stove to heat up. Put the fish parcels in the steamer and steam for 5–6 minutes: timing depends on the thickness of the fish – you want it just cooked (check by inserting a fine skewer, withdrawing it and touching it to your lips; it should feel warm). Remove from the steamer, place on a tray and keep warm. When needed, carefully remove from the cling film.

wilted sea aster
Place a large sauteuse on the heat, add the butter and water, and bring to the boil. Add the sea aster leaves and cook for 1 minute, until just wilted. Season. Drain and keep warm.

serving
Reheat the mushroom tea without boiling. Place a little tapioca in the centre of each bowl. Arrange the wilted sea aster on top in a little pile and set the fish on this. Spoon a little of the parsley oil over the fish and sprinkle with Maldon salt. Arrange the Good King Henry leaves on top. Ladle over the tea or serve it in a little teapot, as described in the introduction.

roasted quail, lamb's sweetbreads, field mushroom purée

To my mind it takes a lot to beat the flavour and texture of sweetbreads. If they are on a menu, I have to admit that I generally order them as one of my courses. I use large quails here, but not jumbo ones, so they are the right size with the sweetbreads. Caramelised chicory is a perfect accompaniment to both the quail and the sweetbreads, giving a touch of sweetness, and the dandelion leaves balance that sweetness with bitterness.

Serves 4

for the chicory
300g red wine
a sprig of thyme
1 orange
50g caster sugar
10g salt
2 long, small heads of chicory
50g unsalted butter
25g olive oil
45g chestnut honey

for the dressing
200g rapeseed oil
1 shallot, finely chopped
leaves from a sprig of thyme
10g red wine vinegar
200g brown chicken stock (see page 19)

for the roasted quail
2 large quails
1 garlic clove, cut in half
a sprig of thyme
2 juniper berries
50g olive oil

for the sweetbreads
8 lamb's sweetbreads
50g olive oil
30g unsalted butter

for the field mushroom purée
30g unsalted butter
2 shallots, finely sliced
450g large field mushrooms, finely sliced

a sprig of thyme
100g chicken stock (see page 19)
200g double cream

a bunch of dandelion leaves, separated into individual leaves

chicory
Place the red wine and thyme in a saucepan large enough to take the chicory. Thinly peel the orange (without taking any of the pith) and add half of the peel to the red wine. Juice the orange and add the juice to the pan with the sugar and salt. Bring to the boil. Place the chicory in the boiling liquid and poach for 5 minutes, then remove from the heat and leave to cool in the liquid. Keep the chicory in the liquid for 2 hours to take on a little of the colour.

dressing
Heat 10g of the oil in a small saucepan, add the shallot and thyme leaves, and sweat for 2 minutes without colouring. Add the red wine vinegar and bring to the boil. Add the chicken stock and bring back to the boil, then reduce by half. Remove from the heat and leave to cool. Whisk in the remaining rapeseed oil and season.

roasted quail
Season the quail. Place half a garlic clove, half a sprig of thyme and a juniper berry in each of the quail. Heat the olive oil in a heavy ovenproof frying pan. When hot, add the quails, laying them on one side. Cook for 2 minutes until golden. Turn onto the other side and cook for another 2 minutes, then turn breast up and place in an oven preheated to 180°C/Gas Mark 4. Roast for 6–8 minutes, until cooked. Remove from the oven and leave to rest for 5 minutes, then joint each quail into 2 legs and 2 breasts. Keep warm.

sweetbreads
Place the sweetbreads in a bowl of cold salted water to cover and leave to soak for

2 hours. This will help pull the blood out of them. Drain and dry well with a cloth. Heat the oil in a large, heavy-based frying pan. Season the sweetbreads and place in the pan, then cook for 4–5 minutes, turning often, until golden. Add the butter and turn a few more times while the butter foams. Season again and drain. Keep warm.

field mushroom purée
Melt the butter in a large cast-iron frying pan and sweat the shallots until soft. Add the mushrooms with the thyme and cook until they are limp and have released all their juices. Add the stock and reduce by half, then add the cream and cook on a slow simmer for 10 minutes. Pour into a blender and blend until very smooth. Season. Pass through a fine chinois into a clean saucepan and keep warm.

finishing the chicory
Remove the chicory from the pan and squeeze out the excess liquid. Cut each chicory in half lengthways. Heat the butter and oil in a frying pan and, when hot, add the chicory, cut side down. Cook until starting to colour. Add the honey and cook for about 2 minutes longer, then turn the chicory over and cook until coloured on the other side. Remove from the pan, drain and season. Keep warm.

serving
Make a line of mushroom purée in the middle of each plate and use a small palette knife to flatten it and pull it along the plate. Pull the leaves of the chicory halves a little to fan them out, and place across this. Set a quail breast in the middle of the plate with a sweetbread at the head and the base. Cut each quail leg into drumstick and thigh and place on either side of the breast. Place a little of the dressing in a bowl; coat each dandelion leaf in the dressing, then arrange attractively down the middle of the plate top to bottom. Whisk the remaining dressing and drizzle around and over the quail.

pressed terrine of pork cheeks, smoked ham hock and leek

This is one of my favourite starters: a terrine of pig's cheeks, cooked slowly in duck fat, and poached smoked ham hock, served with home-cured pork jowl – yum! The terrine has just a little jus to help it set when pressed and to keep it moist. This porcine lover's delight is served with a pear purée, which helps cut the richness of the terrine, raw pear for texture and honeyed mustards seeds for a touch of heat. It is worth the wait for the home-cured jowl (which makes great bacon), although you could get it from a Spanish deli.

Serves 12–14

for the pork jowl
1 pork jowl, trimmed
20 black peppercorns
4 juniper berries
110g Maldon salt
50g granulated sugar
50g soft brown sugar
4 sprigs of thyme
3 bay leaves

for the pickled pears
600g demerara sugar
600g red wine vinegar
600g red wine
8g mustard seeds
strips of peel from 1 lemon
3 each allspice berries and cloves
4cm piece cinnamon stick
20g peeled fresh ginger
10 coriander seeds
6 Williams pears

for the ham hock
350g smoked ham hock
200g roughly chopped carrots
100g each roughly chopped onion, leek and celery
2 garlic cloves, crushed
2 bay leaves
a sprig of thyme
10 white peppercorns

for the terrine
1 medium celeriac, about 700–800g
100g unsalted butter
24 pig's cheeks, trimmed
salt and aromatics as for Confit of Duck Leg (see page 22)
750g duck fat
25 thin baby leeks
400g brown chicken stock (see page 19), reduced to 100g

for the pear purée
6 Williams pears (or another similar variety)
juice of 1/2 lemon
50g unsalted butter
30g caster sugar
75g water

for the banyuls syrup
2 bottles of Banyuls
1 bottle of red wine
30g golden raisins
25g demerara sugar

for the garnish
4 Williams pears
Honeyed Mustard Seeds (see page 16)
60–70 orpine leaves
48–56 small sea purslane leaves
30g olive oil
Maldon salt and crushed black peppercorns

pork jowl
Check the jowl to see if there is any hair on the skin. If there is, use a blowtorch to singe the hairs, then remove with a dry cloth. Turn the jowl over and remove any glands that may be there.

Crush the peppercorns using a pestle and mortar. Add the juniper berries and crush, then add the remaining ingredients and mix well. Rub this mixture over the jowl and massage it in for 3 minutes on each side. Place the jowl in a vacuum bag or a zip freezer bag and seal. Leave in the fridge for 6–8 days, until the flesh is firm to the touch. Remove from the bag and dry well. Using a trussing needle, thread a little string through the meat, form a tied loop and hang in a cool, dry place (7–10°C) for 2–3 weeks. The jowl will become duller in colour and get harder as the time progresses and it dries out. When ready, wrap the jowl in baking parchment, place it in a container and keep in the fridge until needed.

pickled pears
Put all the ingredients, except the pears, in a saucepan and bring to the boil. Cook for 20 minutes. Meanwhile, peel the pears and cut each one lengthways in half, then remove the cores with a small parisienne scoop or a teaspoon. Add the pears to the pickling juices and bring back to the boil, then lower the heat to a simmer and poach gently for 8–12 minutes, until the pears are tender but still holding their shape.

Remove the pears from the pickling juices and leave to cool. Reduce the pickling juices by half, then remove from the heat and cool. Pack the pears in a sterilised Kilner jar and pour the pickling juices over. Keep in the fridge for at least 3 days to allow the pears to gain a deep red colour.

ham hock
Soak the smoked ham hock overnight in cold water to remove excess salt. The next day, place it in a large saucepan with the vegetables and aromatics. Cover with water and bring to the boil, then skim and simmer for 3 1/2–4 hours, until the meat is coming easily away from the bone. Lift out the hock (strain the stock and keep for a soup or broth). Remove the meat from the bones, discarding the skin and picking off any bits of gristle and fat. Place in a container.

(continued on page 63)

(continued from page 61)

celeriac

Peel the celeriac and slice as finely as possible. Line a baking tray, about 52 x 32cm, with baking parchment. Melt the butter in a small saucepan, then brush the baking parchment with a little of it. Season, then cover with overlapping slices of celeriac to form a rectangular sheet about 25 x 36cm in size. Brush with more butter and season. Place in an oven preheated to 180°C/Gas Mark 4 and cook for 5 minutes. Turn the celeriac sheet over (this manoeuvre will need another baking tray lined with buttered parchment) and cook for a further 5 minutes.

Remove from the oven and place a sheet of baking parchment on top of the celeriac. Set a baking tray of the same size on top and add a heavy weight. Cool, then place in the fridge to chill. When cold, remove from the trays and remove the paper. Cut into two equal rectangles, about 36 x 12cm, for the top and bottom of the terrine.

pig's cheeks

Salt the pig's cheeks as for Confit of Duck Leg (see page 22) but for 6 hours only. Remove the salt and herbs by quickly rinsing under cold water and dry well. In a heavy-based ovenproof pot or a high-sided baking tray large enough to fit the cheeks, melt the duck fat over a low heat. Add the cheeks, which should be completely covered with fat. Cover with foil, then place in an oven preheated to 150°C/ Gas Mark 2 and simmer gently for 2–2$\frac{1}{2}$ hours, until tender. To check, prick with a fork: there should be no resistance. Keep warm in the fat until needed.

leeks

Remove any damaged outer leaves from the leeks and trim the green end, then carefully trim the bottom, leaving the smallest amount of root intact. Bring a large pan of salted water to the boil, add the leeks and cook for 3–4 minutes, until tender. Place on a tray and squeeze the excess water out of them. Keep warm.

building the terrine

The ham hock, pig's cheeks and reduced stock should be warm, so reheat if necessary. Place a frame, about 36 x 12 x 4cm, on a tray and line with 2 layers of cling film, overlapping the sides of the frame. Carefully place one of the celeriac rectangles on the bottom of the frame and drizzle over a little of the reduced chicken stock. Neatly arrange the pigs' cheeks next to each other, 3 across and 8 along, in a layer on the celeriac. Press down well with a board that fits inside the frame. Season and drizzle with chicken stock, then add the leeks, arranged top to tail along the length of the terrine. Press down well again. Drizzle with chicken stock and season.

Evenly place a layer of smoked ham hock all over the leeks. Drizzle with the last bit of stock and season. Carefully lay the other rectangle of celeriac on top and press down well with the board. Bring the cling film up and over the terrine, and seal. Prick lightly with a fork and place the board on top. Place 2 heavy weights on the board and leave in the fridge overnight to set. About 40 minutes before serving, take the terrine from the fridge, to take the chill off it, and remove it from the frame, leaving the cling film on.

pear purée

Peel, core and finely slice the pears, then toss in a little lemon juice. Melt the butter in a medium saucepan, add the pears and sweat for 3 minutes without colouring. Add the sugar, water and a squeeze of lemon juice and stir. Simmer for about 5 minutes, until the pear slices collapse and most of the moisture has evaporated.

Tip the pears and remaining juices into a blender and blend until smooth. Pass through a fine sieve and season. Allow to cool, then cover and keep in the fridge until needed. Remove from the fridge 30–40 minutes before serving.

banyuls syrup

Place all the ingredients in a heavy-based saucepan and reduce on a slow simmer to 275g. Strain through a fine sieve and cool. Keep in a small squeezy bottle.

finishing the components of the dish

Cut the terrine into 12–14 slices through the cling film (it will help keep the terrine intact). Remove the cling film and place the terrine on a tray. Slice the salted, dried jowl as finely as you wish on a meat slicer or with a very sharp knife, allowing 3–4 slices per person.

Remove the pickled pears from their syrup and cut into 6mm dice. Peel the pears for the garnish and cut into 1mm slices, then cut out discs using a 2cm cutter.

serving

Make 2 lines of pear purée 4cm apart on the left side of each plate. Place the terrine at an angle and arrange the slices of cured jowl in between the purée lines. Add the pear discs and pickled pear dice to the plates. Dot with little piles of honeyed mustard seeds and garnish with the orpine and sea purslane leaves. Drizzle a little olive oil on the terrine and sprinkle with Maldon salt and crushed black peppercorns.

tartare of dexter beef, home-made corned beef, wasabi mayonnaise

This dish has become a bit of a favourite of our customers and I must admit it covers all the bases as a good starter, in flavour, texture and presentation. We always have it on our tasting menu, which means the portions are small, but you can serve larger portions to your requirements. Sea radish is another idea for garnishing the plate. Horseradish could replace the wasabi, but to me the wasabi just delivers that extra bit of zing that the dish needs.

Serves 12

for the brine
1kg water
50g salt
a strip of orange peel
5 juniper berries, crushed
2 cloves
1 bay leaf
10 black peppercorns

for the corned beef
1kg beef brisket
500g pork back fat
250g pork belly
15g chopped parsley
50g baby capers
120g wholegrain mustard

for the pickled onions
450g lager
50g honey
a sprig of thyme
50g white wine vinegar
2 juniper berries, crushed
a strip of orange peel
1kg small button onions, peeled and soaked
  in salted water for 24 hours, then drained

for the poaching liquid
1kg water
100g white wine
1 onion, chopped
2 celery sticks, chopped
1 carrot, chopped

2 garlic cloves, crushed
1 teaspoon coriander seeds
1 teaspoon black peppercorns
a sprig of thyme
1 bay leaf

for the wasabi mayonnaise
2 egg yolks
15g white wine vinegar
100g olive oil
100g grapeseed oil
60g double cream
100g spinach
1g xanthan gum
3g ultratex
30–40g wasabi paste (to taste)

for the maury syrup
2 bottles Maury
1 bottle red wine
100g verjus
30g golden raisins
4 dried figs, chopped
25g demerara sugar

for the bread crisps
2 bread rolls or a 15cm piece of baguette

for the beef tartare
400g boneless blade of beef (preferably
  Dexter), trimmed
10g wholegrain mustard
40g baby capers
15g chopped parsley
60g olive oil
40g finely chopped shallots

to serve
96 small Pickled Shimeji (see page 17)
48–60 small pieces of stonecrop

brine
Combine the ingredients in a large saucepan and bring up to the boil. Simmer for 2 minutes. Remove from the heat and leave to cool. Add all of the meat to the brine and leave in the fridge for 1 week. Drain.

pickled onions
Combine all the ingredients, apart from the onions, in a medium saucepan and bring to the boil. Remove from the heat and leave to cool slightly. Cut the onions in half and pack into a sterilised Kilner jar, then pour the pickling juices over them. Seal the jar and leave to cool. Keep in a cool place for a week. When needed, remove 24 onions and cut into quarters.

poaching liquid
Put all the stock ingredients in a large saucepan and bring to the boil. Simmer for 10 minutes, then add the brined meats and cook gently for 4 hours. Remove from the heat and leave to cool a little in the stock. Remove the meats from the warm stock and drain. Strain the stock and keep 150g.

corned beef
Mince the cooked meat, preferably using a medium mincer although a food processor could be used. Beat in the reserved stock. Add the parsley, capers and wholegrain mustard. Season well.

Place a frame 36 x 12 x 4cm on a tray and line with 2 layers of cling film, letting the film hang over the edges of the frame. Spoon the corned beef mixture into the frame and push out into the corners. Wrap the film around the frame. Place a board that will fit inside the frame on top of the corned beef, then set a weight on the board. Leave to press in the fridge overnight. When needed, slice into 3cm pieces and trim the sides.

wasabi mayonnaise
Place the egg yolks and vinegar in a mixing bowl and whisk together to combine.
Mix the two oils together. Slowly drizzle in the oils, whisking constantly. When all the oil has been incorporated you will have a lovely thick mayonnaise. Keep in the fridge until needed.

Put the double cream in a small saucepan and bring to the boil, then add the spinach. Remove from the heat and pour into a blender. Blend until smooth; halfway through add the xanthan gum and ultratex to the vortex in the middle. Add 30g wasabi paste and blend again. Pass through a fine sieve into a bowl. Cool, then place in the fridge to chill for 2 hours.

When cold, whisk the mayonnaise bit by bit into the wasabi mixture. Taste and season, adding a little more wasabi paste if needed, or a squeeze of lemon juice. Transfer to a large squeezy bottle and keep in the fridge until needed.

maury syrup

Place all the ingredients in a heavy-based saucepan and reduce on a slow simmer to 300g. Strain through a fine sieve and leave to cool. Keep in a small squeezy bottle.

bread crisps

Leave the bread rolls or baguette in the freezer overnight. Slice wafer thin (2mm) on a slicing machine or with a sharp knife. Spread on a tray and leave to dry out overnight.

The next day, bake in an oven preheated to 160°C/Gas Mark 3 until crisp and slightly golden. Remove from the oven and leave to cool and become crisp. Store in an airtight container until needed. When needed, break up into small shards.

beef tartare

Trim off any last traces of fat and sinew from the blade. Wrap in cling film and firm up in the freezer for 4–5 hours. Remove the cling film, then slice finely, 2mm thick. Place the slices on top of each other and cut into 2mm strips, then turn and cut those into 2mm dice. Place the diced beef in a bowl and allow to come to room temperature.

Add all the other ingredients, mixing well, then season. Place 12 ring moulds, about 4cm across and 4cm deep, on a tray lined with baking parchment or brushed with a little olive oil. Fill the rings with the tartare. Cover and place to one side while you dress the plates.

serving

Make a smear of wasabi mayonnaise in the centre of each plate. Add a piece of corned beef. Put some blobs of wasabi mayonnaise on the corned beef, then add a few pickled onion segments, shimeji and stonecrop stems, placing them at an angle on the plate. Set the beef tartare on the plate and remove the ring, then place a shimeji, a stonecrop stem and a segment of pickled onion on top. Dress the rest of the plate with the remaining onions, shimejis and stonecrop stems. Scatter bread crisps around, then place a few drops of Maury syrup on the plate.

slow-cooked duck egg, white asparagus with maple syrup, hazelnut bon bons, duck crumble

There is something luxurious about eating this dish, with the richness of the yolk concentrated because of the slow cooking and the egg flavour complementing the asparagus so well. The sweetness of the maple seems to heighten the richness and duck crumble adds texture. I serve this with little hazelnut purée 'bon bons', which have been set with a Japanese root starch called kuzu, something fairly new to me that is becoming a very useful part of our larder. When cooking eggs in this way, the key to perfection is to use only the freshest of eggs.

Serves 6

6 fresh duck eggs

for the duck crumble
500g duck skins
150g water

for the craquant
400g glucose syrup
400g caster sugar
100g water
200g hazelnuts, toasted and skinned

for the hazelnut bon bons
200g milk
150g water
100g hazelnuts, roasted and skinned
25g kuzu, ground to a powder in a spice mill
200g toasted hazelnuts, finely ground
50g unsalted butter

for the caramelised white asparagus
12 white asparagus spears
50g unsalted butter
50g maple syrup

for the white asparagus velouté
100g unsalted butter
100g chopped onions
50g white of leek, chopped

250g white asparagus stalks (from above)
150g potatoes, peeled and sliced
500g milk
500g vegetable stock (see page 19)

for the hazelnut purée
200g hazelnuts, toasted and skinned
250g milk
100g double cream
40g water
3.5g bicarbonate of soda
12g hazelnut oil

to serve
12 hazelnuts, toasted, skinned and broken
  into medium pieces
3 fat white asparagus spears, sliced wafer
  thin and kept in cold salted water
6 sprigs of hedge bedstraw

duck crumble

Lay the duck skins out on a board and burn off any stubble with a blowtorch, being careful not to scorch the skin. Roll up individual skins like a Swiss roll. Leave in the freezer overnight.

Mince the frozen duck skins through a fine-medium mincing plate. Place in a saucepan and add the water. Bring up to the boil and cook slowly, stirring from time to time, until the water has evaporated, leaving some rendered duck fat in which to cook the rest of the duck skin 'bits'. Cook until the duck skin solids are golden and crisp. Drain well on kitchen paper. Season and keep warm.

duck eggs

Fill a water bath or large saucepan with water and heat to 64°C. Add the eggs and keep the temperature at a constant 64°C for 2½ hours. Drain and keep warm.

craquant

Place the glucose syrup, caster sugar and water in a heavy-based saucepan and dissolve on a gentle heat, then bring up to the boil and cook until caramelised to a golden amber colour. Fold in the hazelnuts, then immediately pour on to an oiled lipped baking tray. Put to one side until cold and very crisp. Then break up the caramel, place in a food processor and pulse to a coarse powder. Store in an airtight container until needed.

hazelnut bon bons

Place the milk, 100g water and the skinned hazelnuts in a saucepan and bring up to the boil. Pour into a blender and blend until smooth. Season, then leave to cool. When cool, pour the hazelnut mixture back into the saucepan and whisk in the kuzu. Place on the heat and beat until the mixture starts to thicken and then becomes very thick. Remove from the heat and spoon into a piping bag fitted with a 1cm nozzle.

Scatter the ground hazelnuts in a tray and pipe on 18 blobs of the thick hazelnut mixture; each blob or 'dumpling' should be about 6mm high (this will make more mixture than you need, so freeze the rest for a later date). Place in the fridge to set.

caramelised white asparagus

Carefully bend the asparagus spears; they will snap just at the right point above the tough bottoms. Keep the bottom parts for the velouté. Peel the top parts to within 2cm of the tips. Keep the peelings for the velouté. Bring a large pot of water to the boil, add the trimmed asparagus and blanch for 3 minutes, then refresh and drain. Place on a towel to dry.

white asparagus velouté

Melt the butter in a medium heavy-based saucepan. Add the onions, leek and asparagus stalks and peelings and cook for 5 minutes without colouring. Add the potatoes, milk and stock and bring to the boil, then simmer for 20 minutes. Pour into a blender and blend to a smooth, fine purée. Push through a fine sieve and season. Keep warm until needed.

hazelnut purée

Combine all the ingredients, apart from the hazelnut oil, in a medium heavy-based saucepan. Bring to the boil, then turn the heat down and simmer very gently for 10 minutes. Pour into a blender and blend until smooth, drizzling in the hazelnut oil at the end. Season. Keep warm.

finishing the caramelised asparagus

Melt the butter in a cast-iron frying pan, add the blanched asparagus and cook until golden. Add the maple syrup and cook until caramelised. Season and keep warm.

finishing the bon bons

Heat the remaining 50g water and the unsalted butter in a saucepan and bring to the boil, then season. Add the 18 little 'dumplings', then remove the pan from the heat and leave to warm through in the residual heat for 2 minutes. Scatter 100g of the craquant on a tray and roll the 'dumplings' around in this until coated. This needs to be done at the last minute to make sure you retain the texture from the craquant.

serving

Make a swipe of the hazelnut purée on each plate, then place 2 asparagus spears coated in a little of the duck crumble and craquant. Crack an egg and carefully remove the cooked egg from the shell, then place it on the plate. Top with crumble and add the bon bons and cracked toasted hazelnuts, then lay 3 pieces of sliced raw asparagus on the plate and garnish with hedge bedstraw. Finally, place the velouté in a jug and serve with the egg at the table.

gayette of pig's trotter and whelks

The idea for this dish came to me when Johnny, my fishmonger, gave us some whelks to play with one day. They arrived in the same delivery as some stonkingly fresh mackerel. From this the seeds for the dish were sown. It has taken a little while for it to come together, but now I am extremely happy with it. It is a real chef's dish with its contrasting flavours, textures and temperatures.

Serves 8

for the gayette of trotter and whelks
300g poached and shelled whelks
125g belly pork
70g lean pork
20g pork back fat
50g white breadcrumbs
1 egg
125g meat from poached pig's trotter, finely diced (poach trotter as for ham hock in Pressed Terrine of Pork Cheeks, Smoked Ham Hock and Leek on page 61)
65g finely chopped onions
juice of ¹/₂ lemon
60g olive oil
a sheet of caul, about 150g
50g unsalted butter

for the mackerel
75g salt
50g light brown muscovado sugar
20g grated lemon zest
20g grated orange zest
10g coriander seeds, crushed
2g mustard seeds, crushed
6 black peppercorns, crushed
20 leaves of lemon verbena, shredded
3 mackerel, about 350g each, trimmed and filleted
50g olive oil

for the cardamom yoghurt
250g milk
8g dried skimmed milk
3 cardamom pods, slightly crushed
50g natural cultured yoghurt

for the pickled mooli
1 medium mooli
300g orange juice
200g caster sugar
100g white wine vinegar

grated zest and juice of 1 orange

for the gozmasio
50g peanuts, toasted and peeled
50g sesame seeds, toasted
13g salt

radish shoots, to garnish

gayette of trotter and whelks
Mince the whelks, belly pork, lean pork and back fat through a fine/medium mincing plate. Place in a mixing bowl. Add the breadcrumbs and beat in the egg, then add the diced trotter, onions, lemon juice and seasoning and mix well. To check the seasoning, take a small spoonful of the mixture and shape into a flat burger, then cook in 10g of the oil in a small frying pan for 1 minute on each side. Remove from the pan and taste. Add more seasoning if required.

Divide the mixture into 55g balls. (You only need 8, but it is difficult to make a smaller quantity of mixture; you could shape all the gayettes and serve the rest on the side.) Lay the sheet of caul on the work surface. Wrap each ball in caul, cutting it as necessary. Flatten the balls to resemble burgers and trim. Place on a tray and keep in the fridge until needed.

mackerel
Put all the ingredients, except the mackerel and olive oil, in a food processor and blitz to break down the aromatics a little. Place the mackerel fillets skin side down on the work surface and sprinkle the flesh with the aromatic mixture. Place one mackerel fillet on top of another, flesh sides in, and tightly wrap the pairs in cling film. Place on a lipped tray and leave in the fridge for 2 hours. After this curing time, rinse quickly under cold running water and pat dry with a cloth. Keep in the fridge until needed.

cardamom yoghurt
Place the milk in a saucepan and whisk in the skimmed milk powder, then add the cardamom and bring to the boil. Remove from the heat and cool down to 35°C. Strain through a fine sieve. Mix in the

cultured yoghurt and place in a yoghurt-maker. Leave for 8–10 hours. Keep the yoghurt in the fridge until needed.

pickled mooli
Peel the mooli, then use a mandolin to cut it into long, thin strips. If you don't have a mandolin, then grate the mooli. Place in a bowl of salted water and leave for 1 hour. Meanwhile, bring all the remaining ingredients up to the boil in a small saucepan. Cook for 1 minute, then remove from the heat and leave to cool. Pour the pickling solution into a bowl. Drain the mooli well and add it to the pickling solution. Leave to marinate for about 1 hour. When needed, drain.

gozmasio
Put all the ingredients in a food processor and process to a coarse powder (it can be finer if you wish; I quite like a coarse texture).

finishing the gayettes
Heat the remaining oil in a large pan. Place the gayettes seam side up in the pan and cook for 3 minutes, until golden. Flip them over, add the butter and continue cooking for 2 minutes. Remove from the pan to a tray and keep warm.

finishing the mackerel
Heat the olive oil in a large frying pan. Place the mackerel fillets, skin side down, in the pan and cook for 1 minute. Flip them over, then remove the pan from the heat and let the mackerel finish cooking in the residual heat of the pan for a further 1 minute. Remove from the pan and place on a tray. Keep warm.

serving
Split each mackerel fillet lengthways, then cut the pieces across in half. Make 2 swipes of cardamom yoghurt on each plate, then place a cross of mackerel on it. Put a gayette at the opposite side of the plate and add a small mound of the gozmasio. Place a third piece of mackerel on top of the gayette and garnish the plate with a small mound of the drained mooli and the radish shoots.

summer truffle risotto

Working in the restaurant trade, we occasionally have customers or suppliers walking in off the street and asking if we would be interested in buying their wares, anything from damsons to ceps. Sometimes someone really special appears with something amazing. Alfredo came into the restaurant with a big poly-box and asked if we were interested in summer truffles. Normally I would steer clear but he was so genuine that I had a look. Boy, am I glad I did. The truffles were the best I had ever seen. They were from Umbria, and perfect – a good size, with an intoxicating and heady aroma. So I bought a couple of kilos there and then. Ever since, for the last 6–7 years in the season, he gets a phone call or two from me to order a supply. The risotto rice that we use for this dish is a carnaroli called Acquerello. It has been aged in vats for at least a year, so when cooking it absorbs more liquid than traditional carnaroli and it does take longer to cook, but the result is perfection.

Serves 4–6

2 summer truffles, 50g each
1kg good chicken stock (see page 19)
75g unsalted butter
4 large shallots, finely chopped
225g Acquerello risotto rice
125g white wine
3g truffle oil
40g Parmesan cheese, finely grated
30g unsalted butter, finely diced and chilled
30g mascarpone

Finely peel the truffles and place the peelings in the stock. Heat the stock in a medium saucepan. Heat the butter in a medium sauteuse, add the shallots and cook for 3 minutes, until translucent without colouring. Add the rice and stir well to coat the grains with butter, then cook for 3–4 minutes, until the rice becomes translucent, being careful it doesn't catch on the bottom of the pan. Add the white wine, bring to the boil and stir until the wine has evaporated.

Add 200g of the hot stock, pouring it in through a sieve to remove the truffle peelings, and bring to the boil, stirring continuously. Once this stock has been absorbed, add more of the strained stock, 100g at a time, continuing to stir, until the rice is just cooked. You may not need all the stock – you want the rice to have a little bite to the teeth, although it mustn't be chalky.

Add the truffle oil. Working quickly, finely grate in half of one of the truffles. Add the Parmesan and butter, beating well to emulsify, then add the mascarpone and bring the risotto back to the boil. If it is too thick, add a little more stock.

Spoon into serving bowls as soon as possible. Finely shave the remaining truffles over the surface of the risotto and serve.

risotto of oat groats, snails and nettles, braised pig's cheek

Oat groats have a tough texture, so need to be soaked and then cooked for quite a long time, but they have good flavour and are very nutritious. Spelt could be used instead, as could whole wheat berries. Snails and nettles are a good combination and the ever-so-slightly chewy texture of the snail works well with the risotto as does the braised pig's cheek, meltingly unctuous and sticky. We serve this topped with a crisp pig's ear wafer for a little added texture, but it is a wonderful dish without.

Serves 6

for the braised pig's cheeks
6 plump pig's cheeks
50g olive oil
1 celery stick, chopped
1 onion, chopped
1 carrot, chopped
10g tomato paste
400g red wine
4 garlic cloves, crushed
a sprig of thyme
1 bay leaf
600g brown chicken stock (see page 19)

for the snails
100g unsalted butter
1 onion, chopped
2 garlic cloves, chopped
45 prepared snails
2g dried burdock root
2 bay leaves
2 sprigs of thyme
100g port
150g red wine
500g brown chicken stock (see page 19)

for the oat groat risotto
1kg brown chicken stock (see page 19)
50g olive oil
4 shallots, finely chopped
2 garlic cloves, finely chopped
150g oat groats
150g white wine
leaves from 2 sprigs of thyme

30g unsalted butter
200g young nettles, blanched and finely chopped
50g mascarpone
30g Parmesan cheese, finely grated

for finishing the snails
50g unsalted butter
1 garlic clove, finely chopped
5g chopped parsley

roughly chopped flat-leaf parsley, to garnish

braised pig's cheeks
Trim any bits of sinew or fat from the cheeks. Heat half the oil in a large frying pan. When hot, fry the cheeks on both sides until well coloured. Remove from the pan to a flameproof casserole.

Place the frying pan back on the heat, add the remaining oil and then add the celery, onion and carrot and cook until golden, then add the tomato paste and cook for 2 minutes, stirring. Add to the casserole. Pour the red wine into the frying pan, add the garlic and herbs, and scrape the sediment from the bottom of the pan. Reduce by two-thirds, then add to the casserole.

Pour in the stock and bring to the boil, then cover the casserole and place in an oven preheated to 160°C/Gas Mark 3. Braise for 3–3½ hours, until the meat is extremely tender. Remove the cheeks. Strain the stock into a clean pan and reduce to a sticky glaze. (This can be done up to a day in advance.) Add the cheeks and set aside until needed.

snails
Melt the butter in a medium saucepan, add the onion and garlic and cook for 3–4 minutes, until soft and translucent without colouring. Add the snails, burdock, bay leaves and thyme and cook for a further 5 minutes, again without colouring. Pour in the port and red wine and reduce slowly by half. Finally,

add the chicken stock and bring to the boil, then simmer for 1–1½ hours, until the snails are tender. Drain the snails and chop 15 for the risotto. Reserve these with the remaining whole snails. Strain the stock and reserve.

oat groat risotto
Bring the stock to the boil in a medium saucepan. Heat the olive oil in another medium saucepan, add the shallots and garlic, and cook for about 4 minutes, until translucent without colouring. Add the oat groats and cook for a further 3 minutes, stirring. Add the white wine and bring to the boil, then reduce until the wine has evaporated. Add the thyme leaves and a third of the hot stock and simmer, stirring all the time, until the stock has almost all been absorbed. Repeat two more times.

Add the chopped snails and 50g of their stock. Bring to a low simmer and cook until the oat groats are tender with just a little bite. When cooked, raise the heat and cook quickly to evaporate any remaining liquid. Season and add the butter.

To finish the risotto, add the chopped nettles and mix in well. Bring to the boil. Add the mascarpone and stir well, then add the Parmesan. Check the seasoning. If the risotto is too stiff add a little stock; if too sloppy, cook a little more. Keep warm.

finishing the snails
Melt the butter in a pan, add the garlic and cook for 1 minute. Add the whole snails and cook for 2 minutes, then season and add the chopped parsley. Keep warm.

serving
Reheat the cheeks in their glaze: they should be shiny and sticky. Divide the risotto among 6 bowls, place a cheek in the middle and surround with the whole snails. Drizzle some of the sticky glaze around plus a little of the snails' butter, then sprinkle with a little chopped parsley.

kid cannelloni, land cress purée, goat's curds

This starter is a regular on our menus. The rich and tender braised meat forms a sticky, unctuous filling for the cannelloni, working so well alongside the land cress purée with its touch of bite and natural acidity. The dish is served with some creamy goat's curds that are mellow with a little acidity too.

Serves 6

for the kid
150g olive oil
2 kid shoulders, 600g each
1 onion, coarsely chopped
1 celery stick, coarsely chopped
1 carrot, coarsely chopped
3 garlic cloves, peeled
1 pig's trotter, split in half (ask your
    butcher to do this)
100g red wine
1kg brown chicken stock (see page 19)
1 bay leaf
2 sprigs of mugwort
50g unsalted butter
200g hogweed, chopped
100g double cream

for the mooli cannelloni
1 medium-thick mooli
20g unsalted butter, for greasing the baking
    tray

for the land cress purée
100g land cress
75g watercress leaves
25g double cream
50g water
50g unsalted butter

for the goat's curds
1kg goat's milk
1g salt
3g rennet
5g lemon juice

for the asparagus
18 Evesham asparagus spears
50g unsalted butter
50g water

land cress, to garnish

kid
Heat the olive oil in a large frying pan and, when hot, add the shoulders and fry until golden brown on all sides. Transfer the shoulders to a flameproof casserole big enough to hold them. Add the vegetables and garlic to the frying pan and cook until golden, then transfer to the casserole. Add the trotter and red wine to the casserole and place on the heat, then bring to the boil. Add the chicken stock, bay leaf and mugwort. Bring back to the boil. Cover and place in an oven preheated to 160°C/Gas Mark 3. Braise for 3^1/$_2$–4 hours, until the veal is very tender.

Remove the shoulders and trotter. Strain the braising juices into a saucepan and reduce by half. Set aside until needed. Take the meat from the shoulders and trotter and pull apart into long shreds, discarding any fat, skin and bone. Chop the trotter meat and add to the shreds of shoulder meat. Put to one side.

Heat the butter in a large saucepan, add the hogweed and wilt down. Add the meat and the cream and bring to the boil, then add 200g of the reduced braising juices (keep the rest for serving). Cook over a medium high heat for 5–10 minutes, until the mixture is cohesive and not too sloppy, stirring so it doesn't catch. Season, then put to one side.

mooli cannelloni
Bring a large pan of salted water to the boil. Using a Japanese turner slicing machine, create a long sheet of mooli 2mm thick. Place the sheet in the boiling water and cook for 30 seconds. Remove and drain. Cut into 12 rectangles, each about 9 x 7cm. Lay them on a tray. Place a spoonful of the kid mixture in the centre of each mooli slice and roll up, to form 12 small cannelloni. Trim the ends and keep on a buttered baking tray until needed.

land cress purée
Bring a large pan of salted water to the boil. Blanch the land cress and watercress, then refresh in cold water. Drain and squeeze out excess moisture, then chop finely. Bring the cream, water and butter to the boil in a saucepan. Place the chopped cresses in a blender, add the boiling liquid and blend to a fine purée; it should be very smooth. Cool quickly. Season and reheat when needed.

goat's curds
Place the milk and salt in a medium saucepan and heat the milk to 30°C. Stir in the rennet and lemon juice, then remove from the heat, cover the pan and leave to set for 10 minutes. Cut a criss-cross pattern into the curds with a knife, then leave to settle for 30 minutes.

Line a colander with muslin and set it over a large bowl. Strain the milk mixture through the muslin: the curds will be in the cloth and the whey in the bowl (the whey can be used for poaching fish or poultry). Gather up the curds in the muslin and tip them into a container. Season. Cover and keep in the fridge until needed.

asparagus
Carefully bend the asparagus stalks; they will snap at the right point above the tough bottom part. Discard this. Peel the spears to within 2cm of the tip and trim the bottom to a point as if sharpening a pencil. Put the butter and water in a sauteuse and bring to the boil. Add the asparagus and cook for 2 minutes, until tender. Drain and season. Keep warm.

serving
Reheat the cannelloni, covered, in an oven preheated to 180°C/Gas Mark 4 for 3–4 minutes, until hot. Place the goat's curd on another baking tray and warm through in the oven for 1 minute. Reheat the remaining reduced braising juices from the kid.

Make a swipe of land cress purée in the middle of each plate. Place 2 cannelloni on each plate at different angles. Dot some goat's curds around the plate, then add the asparagus and garnish with the land cress. Drizzle with the braising juices and serve.

witchill potatoes, caramelised onion purée, buffalo milk, turkey prosciutto

This is one of the newer dishes in the restaurant, created as a course for our tasting menu. All elements for the dish work perfectly together – the sweet caramelised onion purée with the creamy buffalo milk jelly, these with the smokiness of the leek ash, then the salted garlic buds and the pickled green elderberries, and finally the saltiness of the cured turkey breast. Perfect! We use Witchill potatoes, a small variety that we get from our 'potato lady', Lucy, from Carroll's Heritage Potatoes.

Serves 6

for the brine and the turkey prosciutto
1kg red wine
1kg water
225g salt
1 head garlic, cut across in half
150g roughly chopped carrots
200g roughly chopped onions
2 sprigs of thyme
2 bay leaves
1 sprig of rosemary
20 black peppercorns
400g piece of skinless turkey breast, sinew-
*   free*

for the turkey coating
6g black peppercorns
8g coriander seeds
8g mustard seeds
2g cumin seeds
5g fennel seeds
8g Maldon salt

for the buffalo milk jelly
450g buffalo milk (available at
*   supermarkets)*
80g double cream
50g dried buffalo milk
1.8g agar agar

for the witchill potatoes
6 Witchill potatoes, about 40g each,
*   scrubbed*
50g unsalted butter
4g Leek Ash (see page 16)

for the caramelised onion purée
50g duck fat
600g onions, finely sliced
30g unsalted butter

for the spring onions
12 pencil-thin spring onions, trimmed
5g olive oil

to serve and garnish
10g Pickled Green Elderberries (see page 14)
10g Salted Garlic Buds (see page 14)
chickweed

brine
Combine all the ingredients, except the turkey, in a large saucepan and bring to the boil. Cook for 5 minutes to start the aromatics off. Remove from the heat and leave to cool. Place the turkey in the brine, cover and leave in the brine in the fridge for 4–5 days.

turkey coating
Toast all the ingredients, apart from the sea salt, in a dry pan until the seeds start popping and the mixture smells aromatic. Remove from the heat and leave to cool, then grind in a blender, or in a spice mill or clean coffee grinder. Mix with the salt and keep in a sealed jar until needed.

turkey prosciutto
Drain the turkey, rinse briefly and dry with a cloth. Roll the turkey in the spiced coating mixture, then roll it in a piece of muslin. Tie both ends with string, making a loop at one end. Hang up and leave to air-dry for 1–2 weeks in a cool, airy place. When needed, remove the cloth and slice as finely as possible. You will need 4–5 slices per portion.

buffalo milk jelly
Place all the ingredients in a medium saucepan and whisk together, then leave to sit for 5 minutes. Heat up the mixture, whisking occasionally, and boil for 2 minutes. Season. Strain through a fine chinois into a stainless-steel tray, about 150 x 30 x 4mm. Leave to cool, then cover and leave in the fridge for about 4 hours, until set. Remove from the fridge 30 minutes before needed.

witchill potatoes
Put the potatoes in a large saucepan, just cover with water and add some salt. Bring up to the boil, then simmer for 10–15 minutes, until tender. Drain and leave to cool. When needed, cut each potato into 4 even slices. Warm the butter in a medium pan, add the potatoes and turn around in the butter, then add the leek ash. Turn the potatoes in the ash and butter until coated. Season and keep warm until needed.

caramelised onion purée
Heat the duck fat in a large saucepan, add the onions and stir well, then cover with a lid. Cook for about 5 minutes, stirring occasionally, until the onions have collapsed and become translucent. Remove the lid and cook until the onions are a lovely deep golden-brown colour, stirring well to prevent them from catching. Transfer the onions to a blender and blend until smooth. Add the butter and blend again. Remove from the blender to a small saucepan and season. Keep warm until needed.

spring onions
Heat a large frying pan. While it is getting hot, toss the spring onions in the oil and seasoning. Place them in the pan and keep turning until wilted, golden and cooked.

serving
Make a smear of onion purée down the centre of each plate. Sprinkle with green elderberries and garlic buds. Using a teaspoon, place 4 scoops of buffalo milk jelly on each plate, then add the spring onions. Now, add the potatoes, 4 slices per plate. Arrange 4–5 slices of turkey prosciutto on each plate, bending them a little. Finally, add the chickweed and dust a band of leek ash over the centre of the plate.

main courses

fillet of brill, wilted sea beet, girolle purée

Brill is a member of the turbot family. The flesh is a little finer and softer than that of turbot, but to my mind it eats just as well. We have served it in the past with red wine and liquorice jus, so know that it can stand up to the bold flavours of our kitchen. Here it is poached with flavoursome fish stock and served with some wilted sea beet, a sort of sea spinach with slightly denser leaves (it has that lovely briny taste that so many sea vegetables and plants that grow near the sea have). Girolles always seem to evade me when we go mushrooming, so I have only ever brought a handful back with me, but it's easy enough to get them from Scotland, which has the best girolles in the world.

Serves 6

for the brill
600g fish stock (see page 19), reduced to 200g
50g white wine
a sprig of thyme
1/2 slice of lemon
6 skinless portions of brill fillet from a large fish, 200g each

for the girolle purée
25g unsalted butter
500g large girolles, trimmed, cleaned and finely sliced
100g double cream

for the girolle and hazelnut juices
30g unsalted butter
50g sliced shallots
150g white wine
500g fish stock (see page 19)
50g double cream
30g hazelnut oil

for the girolles
30g olive oil
250g medium girolles, cleaned
30g unsalted butter

for the sea beet
50g unsalted butter
40g water
200g sea beet

brill
Place the reduced stock, white wine, thyme and lemon slice in a large sauteuse. Bring to the boil. Add the brill and bring back to the boil, then immediately turn down the heat to barely simmering. Cook for 3 minutes. Remove from the heat and leave the fish to finish cooking in the residual heat of the pan for 2–3 minutes, depending on the thickness of the fish. It is cooked if it feels firm when you prod it with your finger. Remove from the stock and keep warm under buttered paper. The stock can be strained through a fine chinois, cooled and frozen for another day.

girolle purée
Heat the butter in a large, heavy-based pan. Add the girolles and cook for 5 minutes, tossing them occasionally so they don't catch. You are looking for a little colour but not much. Add the cream and cook for 1 minute, then transfer to a blender and blend until smooth. Season and keep warm.

girolle and hazelnut juices
Melt the butter in a saucepan, add the sliced shallots and sweat for 3 minutes without colouring. Add the white wine and reduce to a glaze. Add the fish stock and reduce by half. Add the cream and 50g of the girolle purée and bring to the boil. Remove from the heat. Drizzle in the hazelnut oil while blending with a stick blender. Pass through a fine chinois and season. Keep warm.

girolles
Heat the olive oil in a frying pan. When hot, add the girolles and sauté for 1 minute. Add the butter and sauté for a further 2–3 minutes, until cooked. Drain and season. Keep warm.

sea beet
Heat the butter and water in a frying pan, then add the sea beet and cook until wilted. Drain, season and keep warm.

serving
Make a swipe of girolle purée on each plate, then add a loose mound of wilted sea beet. Place the brill on next and scatter the girolles around. Finally, froth the juices with a stick blender and spoon on to the plate.

butter-fried ray, peas, wilted hogweed and pink purslane

One of the great things about having a good fishmonger (as we do with Johnny) is that he can advise you on what is sustainable and what is not. Skate is one of those fish that are not sustainable and Johnny suggested that blond ray could be used instead. This fish has the same lovely meaty taste and gelatinous texture so praised by skate-lovers. Here, it is served quite simply because it tastes so good just as it is. Pink purslane is a fleshy-leaved plant with a beautiful pink flower and a very succulent stem that tastes of raw beetroot, and is lovely to eat.

Serves 4

for the butter-fried ray
4 blond ray wings, 500g each, filleted and
   trimmed
125g unsalted butter
juice of 1/2 lemon
20g chopped parsley

for the buttered hogweed
250g young hogweed shoots
100g unsalted butter

for the peas
100g podded fresh peas
25g unsalted butter
2 teaspoons water

200g pink purslane leaves, to garnish
Maldon salt, to serve

butter-fried ray
Remove any whitish skin on the ray wings, then place a top wing and a bottom wing together, skin side inwards. Wrap in cling film and leave in the fridge for a couple of hours. Remove from the fridge 30 minutes before cooking.

buttered hogweed
Peel the bottom 3cm of the hogweed shoots. Bring a large pan of salted water to the boil, add the hogweed and cook for 2 minutes, until tender. Refresh in cold water – the hogweed should be vibrant green. Drain. When needed, heat the butter in a pan and, when hot, add the hogweed shoots. Season and keep turning over until hot. Keep warm.

peas
Bring a saucepan of salted water to the boil. Cook the peas for 2–3 minutes, then refresh in cold water and drain. Pop them out of their skins. When needed, reheat the peas in the butter and water, then drain and season.

cooking the ray
Heat the butter in a large frying pan that will take the wings (or cook in 2 batches). When the butter starts foaming, add the wings and season. Cook for 3 minutes, then turn and cook for another 3 minutes. Remove from the heat and leave to finish cooking in the residual heat of the pan for a further minute, then remove from the pan to a tray and keep warm.

Place the pan with the juices back on the stove and, when hot, squeeze in the lemon juice. Pass through a fine sieve and add the parsley. Season, then keep warm.

serving
Place the ray wings on one side (the front) of the plate and the buttered hogweed on the opposite side. Scatter the peas over the wings and then some pink purslane shoots. Drizzle the parsley sauce over the fish and around. Sprinkle with Maldon salt. Serve with boiled buttered heritage potatoes or a loose buttered mash.

spiced monkfish poached in brown butter, split pea and cumin, cardamom yoghurt

Monkfish is one of the meatiest fish in the sea and has a wonderful firm texture. It is also easy to fillet – just a central bone to remove and no pin bones to catch you out. I love cooking it in brown butter – it's almost caramelised because the butter gives a nutty taste. It goes so well with the rest of the dish: my take on a dahl, confit of garlic and a coriander, rocket and coconut salad.

Serves 6

for the garlic confit
24 garlic cloves, peeled
200g olive oil or duck fat
20g unsalted butter

for the cardamom yoghurt
1kg milk
10 cardamom pods, slightly crushed
200g natural cultured yoghurt

for the spiced monkfish
5g cumin seeds
5g fennel seeds
5g coriander seeds
2g cardamom pods, crushed
2g mustard seeds
6 monkfish fillets, 220g each, trimmed and membrane removed
50g olive oil
300g unsalted butter
juice of ¹/₂ lemon

for the split peas
200g yellow split peas
3 garlic cloves, 1 crushed and 2 finely sliced
3g ground turmeric
800g water
50g sunflower oil
3g cumin seeds
2g mustard seeds
20 coriander leaves, chopped

for the coriander, coconut and rocket salad
30g coconut milk
¹/₂ garlic clove, finely sliced

30g palm sugar
juice of 1 lime
30g olive oil
100g coriander leaves
30g water
3g cumin seeds
200g fresh coconut, grated
50g desiccated coconut
1 green chilli, deseeded and finely diced
125g rocket leaves

garlic confit
Put the garlic cloves in a small saucepan, add the olive oil and cook on a slow simmer for 20 minutes. Remove from the heat and leave to cool in the oil. The garlic can be kept in a jar, covered with the oil, in the fridge for 2–3 weeks.

cardamom yoghurt
Place the milk and cardamom in a saucepan and bring to the boil. Remove from the heat and cool down to 35°C. Pass through a fine sieve into a jug. Mix in the yoghurt and place in a yoghurt maker. Leave for 8–10 hours. Keep the yoghurt in the fridge until needed.

spiced monkfish
Heat a large frying pan. When hot, add all the spices and dry-roast until the fragrance is released and the seeds start 'popping'. Remove from the heat and leave to cool, then grind the spices in a spice grinder to a fine powder. Pass through a sieve to remove any larger bits. Lightly coat the monkfish with the spices (any not used can be stored in a jar for another day). Wrap the fish in cling film and leave in the fridge for 2 hours. Remove from the fridge 30 minutes before cooking.

split peas
Place the split peas, crushed garlic, turmeric and water in a pan, stir well and bring to the boil. Skim, then cover the pan and simmer, stirring regularly, for 40–50 minutes, until the split peas are very tender. If they get

too dry, add a little more water. When cooked, beat with a spoon just to break them down a little more.

Heat the oil in a cast-iron frying pan on a moderate heat. Add the cumin seeds and mustard seeds and fry for 20–30 seconds, until fragrant and 'popping'. Add the sliced garlic and fry until golden brown (any more than this and the garlic will taste bitter). Immediately pour the contents of the pan into the split peas. Stir and season. Keep warm. Add the chopped coriander just before serving.

cooking the monkfish
Heat the oil in a large frying pan. Add the monkfish fillets, 2 at a time, and quickly sear on all sides. Remove from the pan and put to one side. Clean the pan, then melt the butter in it and cook until it is just starting to turn a light brown colour. Remove from the heat and immediately pass through a sieve. Cool down to 60–62°C.

Arrange the monkfish fillets, in one layer, in a wide flameproof casserole or roasting tin with high sides. Pour the browned butter over them. Place on the heat and raise the temperature of the butter to 60–62°C again. Keep at this temperature and poach for 20–25 minutes, turning the monkfish around every 5 minutes. Remove and keep warm.

coriander, coconut and rocket salad
Put the coconut milk, garlic, palm sugar, lime juice, oil and 50g of the coriander leaves in a blender with the water. Blend until smooth. Place to one side. Dry-roast the cumin seeds until fragrant. Just before serving, mix the fresh and desiccated coconut with the remaining coriander leaves, the roasted cumin seeds and chilli. Add the blended mixture and

(continued on page 82)

(continued from page 81)

toss together using 2 spoons. Add the rocket and season. Mix well.

finishing the garlic confit

Heat a little of the garlic oil, add the garlic and the butter, and cook until golden. Drain, season and keep warm.

serving

Place a monkfish fillet on the left side of each plate, sitting on a little mound of split peas. Season the fish with the lemon juice. Arrange the salad to the right. Place the garlic confit around the monkfish and drizzle the yoghurt around. Serve the remaining split peas in a bowl.

Note: Instead of making your own yoghurt, you could buy some natural yoghurt, add crushed cardamom pods and leave to infuse overnight. Strain out the cardamom before using.

chicken-glazed cod, surf clams, sea lettuce jelly, clam jus

Cod is without doubt Britain's favourite fish. Its lovely big flakes, moist meatiness and glistening white flesh are beautiful, and there is nothing like its taste when freshly cooked. Here I have given it an added savoury element with a reduced chicken glaze, and served it with a sea lettuce jelly and some wonderful little surf clams, which add to the dish's taste of the sea. If you can't find clams, then cockles will do. The seaweed jelly could be made with parsley, spinach or orache instead.

Serves 6

for the surf clams
750g live surf clams
50g olive oil
2 large shallots, finely sliced
a sprig of thyme
200g white wine
150g fish stock (see page 19)

for the sea lettuce jelly
200g fish stock (see page 19)
50g fresh sea lettuce
2.5g agar agar

for the cod
6 skinless portions of cod fillet from a 4kg
    fish, 200g each
50g olive oil
30g unsalted butter
juice of 1/2 lemon
400g brown chicken stock (see page 19),
    reduced to 125g

for the clam sauce
25g unsalted butter
50g finely sliced shallots
3g lemon verbena
50g vermouth
125g double cream
3g lecithin powder

for the sea lettuce
60g fresh sea lettuce
juice of 1/4 lemon

for the choy sum
50g unsalted butter
12 stems choy sum

surf clams
Wash the clams under cold running water to remove grit. Heat a large saucepan, add the olive oil, shallots and thyme, and cook for 30 seconds. Add the surf clams, pour in the white wine and stock, and immediately place the lid on the pan. Cook for 1 minute, shaking the pan frequently from side to side. The clams should now have opened. Remove them from the stock as quickly as possible and leave to cool a little, then remove the meat from the shells. Pass the stock through damp muslin (to catch any grit) into a container. Add the clams and set aside. When needed, drain the clams, reserving the clam stock for the jelly and clam sauce. Set the clams and stock aside.

sea lettuce jelly
Place the fish stock and 50g of the clam stock in a saucepan and bring to the boil. Rinse the sea lettuce 2 or 3 times to get rid of any grit, then squeeze out the moisture. Add the lettuce to the pan and poach on a low simmer for 5 minutes. Remove from the heat and cool down a little, then add the agar agar and stir. Leave to one side for 3 minutes. Bring back to the boil. Transfer to a blender and blend until smooth. Pass through a fine sieve and season. Pour on to a stainless steel tray to a depth of 2mm; tilt the tray slightly to help move the liquid. Set on a level surface to cool, then place in the refrigerator to set.

Cut the set jelly into 5cm discs using a round cutter; you will need 18 discs. Place on a greased tray (this will make it easier to pick up the discs with a small palette knife). Keep in the fridge until needed. Remove from the fridge 30 minutes before serving.

cod
Lightly season the fish and set aside for 15 minutes. Place a cast-iron frying pan on the heat and add the oil. When hot, add the cod and cook for 3 minutes, then flip over, add the butter and cook the other side for 2 minutes. Add the lemon juice. Pour in the chicken stock and bring to the boil. Spoon the stock over the fish, then transfer to an oven preheated to 200°C/Gas Mark 6 and

cook for 4 minutes; spoon the stock over the fish again halfway through. The cod should be very shiny and just cooked. Remove from the oven and leave to rest, in the pan, in a warm place, basting with the stock every now and again.

clam sauce
Melt the butter in a medium saucepan, add the shallots and cook for 3 minutes. Add the lemon verbena and vermouth and reduce to a glaze, then add 300g of the clam stock. Cook for 3–4 minutes. Add the cream and bring to the boil. Using a stick blender, blend in the lecithin. Pass through a fine chinois into another pan, season and keep warm.

sea lettuce
Bring a pan of salted water to the boil. Add the sea lettuce and cook for 6–8 minutes, until tender. Remove from the pan and drain, then season and add a little lemon juice. Keep warm.

choy sum
Put the butter and a little water in a medium sauté pan. Heat until the water boils and forms an emulsion, then add the choy sum. Cook quickly until tender. Season and drain. Keep warm.

serving
Warm the clams in the clam sauce until hot, but do not boil. Place 3 discs of jelly on each plate, then flash under a preheated grill to warm through. Set the cod in the middle of the plate, then place the choy sum on each side. Add a little of the sea lettuce to each plate and then the surf clams. Finally, froth the clam sauce with a hand blender and drizzle around the plate.

fillet of plaice, alexander purée, scarlet elf caps

Plaice has a lovely softness to its flesh and is quite delicate. When buying it from your fishmonger, always check that its spots are bright orange, eyes are bright and protruding, and gills are very red, not brown at all. The fish works well with scarlet elf caps, which are gorgeous, brightly coloured mushrooms that look like – well, as the name suggests – upturned little red hats. They are about at the same time as wild garlic and from my experience grow in the same proximity. The mushrooms will retain their colour when cooked, but only if cooked quickly. An alexander purée provides a pleasing contrast. Alexanders taste like strong celery so if you can't get them you can substitute lovage or celery tops or even angelica.

Serves 6

for the banyuls and white balsamic vinegar reduction
25g wild garlic
750g Banyuls
250g white balsamic vinegar
50g olive oil

for the alexander purée
200g peeled Desiree potatoes, each cut into 6
100g milk
30g unsalted butter
120g alexander leaves

for the plaice
30g unsalted butter, softened
4 plaice fillets, 200g each, skinned
50g olive oil

for the scarlet elf caps
36 scarlet elf caps
30g olive oil

for the alexander shoots
50g unsalted butter
40g water
18 young alexander shoots

banyuls and white balsamic vinegar reduction
Chop the wild garlic and place in a saucepan with the Banyuls and vinegar. Bring to the boil and simmer until reduced to 100g. Remove from the heat and pass through a fine sieve. Leave to cool, then add the olive oil. Keep in a squeezy bottle.

alexander purée
Cook the potatoes in a saucepan of boiling salted water until tender. Drain well and leave to dry out with their natural heat, then place in a blender. Bring the milk and butter to the boil in a small saucepan. Add the alexander leaves to the blender and pour on the boiling milk mixture. Blend immediately until smooth. Season. If the purée is a little too thick, add more hot milk. Pass through a sieve. Keep warm.

plaice
Line a baking sheet with baking parchment and butter it with the soft butter, then season. Lay the plaice fillets on the buttered paper, tucking the tail end under. Drizzle over the olive oil and season. Place in a preheated 180°C/Gas Mark 4 oven and cook for 4 minutes, until just done: the thickness of the fillet will determine the cooking time. Plaice can be easily overcooked, so take care; it is done when it is firm to the touch and not mushy. Remove from the oven, cover and keep warm.

scarlet elf caps
Make sure the elf caps are free from grit, and trim the bases. Heat the olive oil in a large frying pan, add the elf caps and sauté very quickly, for just 30 seconds, then season and drain. Keep warm.

alexander shoots
Place a large sauteuse on the heat, add the butter and water, and bring to the boil. Add the alexander shoots and cook until wilted. Drain and season. Keep warm.

serving
Make a swipe of alexander purée in the middle of each plate and set the plaice on top. Arrange the alexander shoots over the plaice, then scatter the scarlet elf caps over. Finally, shake the squeezy bottle and dot the Banyuls reduction on the plates.

85 beyond *essence*   main courses

poached flounder, trotter and crayfish, broad bean and lovage mousseline

Flounder is a flat fish that is best cooked very quickly, otherwise it will dry out due to its low oil content. The fish has a mild to medium flavour and can stand a little lifting from more powerful ingredients. So here it is served with a pig's trotter compote and crayfish. Broad bean and lovage mousseline complements the entire dish. The lovage can be replaced with celery leaves, and the broad beans with peas or fresh soya beans.

Serves 6

for the trotter compote
3 pig's trotters
80g olive oil
2 large onions, 1 roughly chopped and 1 finely chopped
2 carrots, roughly chopped
1 celery stick, roughly chopped
3 garlic cloves, chopped
1 bay leaf
a sprig of thyme
2kg brown chicken stock (see page 19)

for the crayfish
2kg water
1 celery stick, chopped
1 small onion, sliced
1 leek, finely sliced
juice of 1 lemon
a sprig of thyme
2 bay leaves
10 black peppercorns
24 raw crayfish

for the flounder
12 flounder fillets (skin on), about 100g each, trimmed
about 30g unsalted butter
200g fish stock (see page 19)

for the broad bean and lovage mousseline
100g peeled potatoes, diced
50g unsalted butter
300g podded broad beans, skinned by blanching
25g lovage

for the baby broad beans
50g water
5 small lovage leaves
40g unsalted butter
120g podded baby broad beans, skinned by blanching

trotter compote
Remove any dirt or nails from the trotters. Singe any hairs with a blowtorch, then rinse under cold water. Heat 50g of the olive oil in a large flameproof casserole, add the roughly chopped onion, the carrots and celery and cook until golden. Add the garlic, bay leaf and thyme, then add the brown chicken stock and trotters. Bring to the boil. Place a lid on the casserole and transfer to an oven preheated to 150°C/Gas Mark 2. Cook for 3–4 hours, until the trotter meat is tender.

Remove from the oven and leave to cool. When cool, lift out the trotters, remove the skin and meat from the bones, and cut into 5mm dice. Put to one side. Strain the cooking stock and skim off the fat. Measure 250g of the stock into a pan and reduce by two-thirds. Meanwhile, heat the remaining olive oil in a sauteuse, add the finely chopped onion and cook until soft and translucent. Add the reduced stock, then stir in the trotter dice and season. Put to one side.

crayfish
Put all the ingredients, except the crayfish, in a large saucepan, bring to the boil and boil for 10 minutes. Add the crayfish and cook for 2–3 minutes, depending on their size. Remove the crayfish and refresh in cold water; when cold, drain. Detach the heads, then shell the crayfish, trim and devein. Keep the crayfish in a covered bowl in the fridge until needed. Freeze the shells and heads for another use, such as for a soup or a stock.

flounder
Lay the flounder fillets on the work surface and season. Sandwich pairs of fillets together, skin sides in, both in the same direction. Butter a baking tray with sides that is large enough to take all the paired fillets in one layer. Place the paired fillets in the tray. Bring the stock to the boil and pour over the fillets, then cover with buttered paper or foil. Place in an oven preheated to 180°C/Gas Mark 4 and cook for 4–6 minutes, starting to check the fish after 3 minutes – carefully pierce with the point of a knife: when the fish is cooked, there will be very little resistance. When the fish is ready, remove from the oven and keep warm.

broad bean and lovage mousseline
Place the potatoes in a small saucepan, add the butter and just cover with water. Bring to the boil, then lower the heat to a simmer and cook until the potatoes are tender. Add the broad beans and cook for a further 2 minutes. Transfer the contents of the pan to a blender and blend until smooth, adding the lovage halfway through. Pass through a sieve and season. Keep warm.

baby broad beans
Heat the water, lovage and butter in a sauté pan. Add the beans and cook for 1–2 minutes, to heat through. Drain and season, then keep warm.

serving
Reheat the crayfish in the trotter compote, then form a line of compote down the right side of each plate. On the left, make a swipe of mousseline. Place the flounder on the mousseline. Put the crayfish on the trotter compote in a line and scatter on the baby broad beans. Heat up the flounder juices and season, then whisk in a knob of butter and drizzle over the fish. Finally, dot a little more mousseline about the plate.

roasted huss glazed with cider vinegar, pappardelle of celeriac, pork mince and apple

I remember that, as a child, whenever I used to visit my grandmother she always got us rock and chips – a lovely treat. That 'rock', or rock salmon, is in fact huss, also known as dog fish, which isn't found on restaurant menus very often. Whatever you call it, it's a fish with a firmish texture that can be creamy, and I like to cook it very quickly in a similar way to monkfish. When buying huss, make sure it is fresh as it goes off very quickly: check that the blood looks very red and fresh; if it is dull and brown, choose something else. Get your fishmonger to trim, skin and portion it for you. Because of its meaty taste, I have paired the huss with some pork mince and, to cut that, some apple and celeriac. If you want to make an all-fish dish, the huss would be great with pumpkin and maybe a lobster mince.

Serves 6

for the roasted huss
6 skinless portions of huss fillet, 200g each, membrane removed
50g olive oil
25g unsalted butter
10g demerara sugar
45g cider vinegar

for the celeriac pappardelle
1 large celeriac, peeled
50g unsalted butter
50g water
salt

for the pork mince
30g olive oil
175g good-quality lean pork mince
1 garlic clove, finely chopped
15g roughly chopped flat-leaf parsley
2 Granny Smith apples, peeled, cored and cut into fine julienne
200g brown chicken stock (see page 19)

Maldon salt, for sprinkling

roasted huss
Season the huss well. Heat the olive oil in a large, heavy-based frying pan. When hot, add the huss and cook until golden brown on one side. Flip over and add the butter, then cook until golden on the other side. The total browning time will be 2–3 minutes, depending on the thickness of the fish. Add the sugar and vinegar and swirl in the pan so the huss is glazed. Continue cooking until the liquid has evaporated. The fish is cooked if it gives a little and feels springy when you prod it. Remove from the pan. Season again and leave to rest in a warm place.

celeriac pappardelle
We have a special Japanese turning slicer, which allows us to create sheets of vegetables. If you have one of these slicers, create long sheets of celeriac. Then stack them on top of each other and cut into long strips 2cm wide. If you don't have a slicing machine, then cut the celeriac horizontally into quarters through the centre. You will have 4 discs. Using a peeler in a steady motion, peel around each celeriac disc, trying to get as long a strip as possible, then cut the strip in half down the length.

Put the butter, water and a good pinch of salt in a large saucepan and bring to the boil to create an emulsion. Add the celeriac pappardelle and cook for about 1 minute. Drain quickly and scatter on to a tray. Put to one side to cool down.

pork mince
Heat the olive oil in a large frying pan and, when very hot, add the pork mince. Cook for 4–5 minutes, until golden brown. Just before it is all browned, add the garlic and stir. Add the parsley to the mince and then the celeriac pappardelle. Stir gently, turning the celeriac until coated with the mince mixture, then add the apple julienne and stir to mix. Tip out on to a warm tray. Pour the stock into the pan and stir to release any sediment, then bring to the boil. Strain this sauce and keep warm.

serving
Place the roasted huss on the left side of each deep soup plate, then carefully arrange the celeriac pappardelle on the right side. Top with the mince, then spoon the sauce over the fish and a little on the celeriac. Sprinkle a little Maldon salt on the huss.

megrim sole with winkles, pickled green elderberries and marrow

Megrim sole, also called whiff and lately Cornish sole, has a flavour that is somewhat sweeter and cleaner than lemon sole, with a texture that is a little more coarse. Salted and pickled green elderberries, which are rather like a more solid baby caper, provide a nice acidity for the megrim sole and complement the winkles and the buttered and peppered marrow. The black cardamom used in this recipe has a more smoky taste than green cardamom and is more powerful, so don't be tempted to add more!

Serves 6

for the winkles
1 carrot, sliced
1 onion, sliced
1 celery stick, sliced
a sprig of thyme
1/2 bay leaf
2 slices of lemon
15g white wine vinegar
60 winkles
50g unsalted butter
1 garlic clove, crushed

for the lemon and cardamom butter
juice of 1 lemon
10g pickling juices from the green elderberries (see below)
1 black cardamom pod, crushed
50g dessert wine, such as a Monbazillac
200g fish stock (see page 19)
100g unsalted butter, chilled and diced

for the marrow
1 medium vegetable marrow
50g unsalted butter
50g water
1 black cardamom pod, crushed
a sprig of thyme

for the megrim sole
75g olive oil
6 megrim sole fillets, 140g each, skinned and trimmed
30g unsalted butter
5g pickling juices from the green elderberries (see below)

to serve
24 young fat hen shoots, washed and dried
Pickled Green Elderberries (see page 14)

winkles
Place the vegetables, thyme, bay leaf, lemon slices and vinegar in a medium saucepan. Cover with a little water. Bring to the boil and cook for 30 minutes. Add a little salt and then the winkles and cook for 2–3 minutes. Remove from the heat and leave for 5 minutes, then drain the winkles. Hook the winkles out of their shells. Remove the black part at the end (the intestine), then place the winkles to one side to cool.

lemon and cardamom butter
Place the lemon juice, pickling juices and cardamom in a small saucepan and bring to the boil. Reduce to a glaze, then add the dessert wine and reduce by half. Repeat with the stock, then whisk in the butter, bit by bit – if you add the butter too quickly the mixture might split. Pass through a fine sieve, season and keep warm.

marrow
Peel the marrow lightly just to remove the outer tougher skin. Then using a sharp peeler, peel 6 long, thin strips from the length of the marrow. Trim the strips and cut each lengthways into 3. Place to one side. Using a sharp knife, cut the outside of the marrow (without seeds) into 4mm thick slices, so you get the nice light green marrow flesh. Cut these slices into batons, about 6cm long and 6mm wide; you need 34 batons.

Place the butter, water, cardamom pod and thyme in a sauteuse and bring to the boil. Add the marrow batons and cook for 3–4 minutes, until tender. Use a slotted spoon to remove them from the pan and season. Cut 10 of the batons into small dice. Add the marrow strips to the emulsion and cook for 1 minute. Drain and season. Put with the batons and dice and keep warm.

megrim sole
Heat the olive oil in a large frying pan and, when hot, add the sole fillets, presentation side down. Cook for 1 minute, then add the butter. When it froths, turn the fish over. Remove from the heat and drizzle over the elderberry pickling juices. Leave for about 1 minute to finish cooking in the residual heat of the pan. Remove the fish from the pan and keep warm.

finishing the winkles
Heat the butter in a frying pan and, when foaming, add the garlic and cook for 10 seconds. Add the winkles and just heat them through. Keep warm.

serving
Place the sole on the plates. Scatter over the diced marrow, winkles and pickled green elderberries. Curl the marrow strips and lay about the plate. Arrange the marrow batons and the fat hen shoots on and around the fish, then drizzle over the sauce.

ballotine of sea trout, lobster blancmange and dressing

This dish is for one of those rare occasions in this country when we get a few uninterrupted hot days. It is a room-temperature main course that is a pleasure to eat when the weather is hot. The sea trout I use is called sewin in Wales and it comes from Welsh waters – the fish has a particularly good flavour and texture. I've served it with a lobster blancmange made from a very rich lobster stock and lobster dressing. Crab or langoustine could be used instead of lobster. The fish is served with wilted and raw beetroot stems and red amaranth.

Serves 6

for the ballotine
1 sea trout, 2.5–3kg, filleted and skinned
100g parsley leaves
30g chervil
30g salad burnet leaves
30g borage leaves
30g dill
olive oil, for brushing

for the lobster jus
shells from a lobster
100g olive oil
1 onion, chopped
1/2 carrot, chopped
1 celery stick, chopped
100g chopped fennel
2 garlic cloves, crushed
6 tarragon leaves
50g tomato paste or 200g chopped ripe
  tomatoes
50g Cognac
200g white wine
2kg brown chicken stock (see page 19)

for the lobster blancmange
100g double cream
1g carrageen powder
2g agar agar
a few squeezes of lemon juice

for the lobster dressing
70g olive oil
juice of 1/4 lemon

for the beetroot stems and spring onions
24 beetroot stems
12 spring onions
olive oil, for dressing

to serve
a large handful of red amaranth
Maldon salt and crushed black peppercorns

ballotine
Season the 2 sea trout fillets all over and set aside for 5 minutes. Meanwhile, chop all the herbs very finely; put to one side in a covered bowl. Cut each fillet lengthways down the middle. Lay out a sheet of cling film that is longer than the fillets by 5cm at each end. Place another sheet on top. Brush with a little olive oil and season, then scatter over a quarter of the chopped herbs, only to the length of the fillets. Place the fatter piece from one fillet, skin side down, on the herbs and cover with the thinner piece from the same fillet, skin side up, arranging the pieces head to tail. Sprinkle another quarter of the herbs over the fish, then roll up in the cling film as tightly as possible. Twist the ends of the roll and tie with string. Roll this parcel in a J-cloth and tie. Repeat with the other sea trout fillet.

Heat a large pan of water and bring the temperature to 62°C, then remove from the heat. Lower the fish parcels into the water and leave to poach for 10–20 minutes, depending on the size of the roll. When the internal temperature reaches 58–60°C (it must not go above this), remove the parcels from the pan and place in an ice bath. Leave for 2–3 minutes to stop the cooking, then remove and cool. Keep in the fridge overnight to set. Remove from the fridge 30 minutes before serving.

lobster jus
Using the end of a rolling pin, smash the lobster shells in a deep pan until well crushed. Heat the olive oil in a large saucepan until very hot, then add the shells and cook until golden. Remove from the pan. Add the vegetables, garlic and tarragon to the pan and cook until golden. Return the lobster shells to the pan and stir in the tomato paste. Cook for 2 minutes, stirring. Deglaze with the Cognac and cook to evaporate the liquid, then add the white wine and reduce by half. Add the stock, bring back to the boil and simmer gently for about 2 hours. Strain the stock through a sieve into a clean pan – do not push it through. Place back on the heat and reduce to about 600g. Cool.

lobster blancmange
Place 400g of the lobster jus and the cream in a pan and whisk in the carrageen and agar agar powders. Leave to rehydrate for 3–4 minutes, then place on the heat and bring up to the boil. Cook for 2 minutes, whisking occasionally. Remove from the heat and season with the lemon juice and salt and pepper to taste. Pour into a tray, about 17 x 13 x 4cm, and leave to cool. Cover and place in the fridge to finish setting.

lobster dressing
Place 200g of the lobster jus in a saucepan and reduce to 125g. Remove from the heat and slowly drizzle in the oil while blitzing with a stick blender. Season with the lemon juice and salt and pepper to taste, then pass through a fine sieve. Leave to cool. Place in a squeezy bottle and keep in the fridge until needed.

beetroot stems and spring onions
For the beetroot stems, bring a large pan of salted water to the boil, add the beetroot stems and cook for 20 seconds. Remove and refresh, then drain well. Place on a large tray lined with a J-cloth.

For the spring onions, bring a large pan of salted water to the boil, add the spring onions and cook for 1–2 minutes, until limp. Remove and refresh, then drain well. Place on the tray alongside the beetroot stems.

Dice 8 of the beetroot stems and toss with a little oil and seasoning. Season the remaining beetroot stems and the spring onions and dress with a little oil.

serving
Unwrap the 2 ballotines and cut each into 6 slices. Place 2 ballotine slices on each plate. Remove the blancmange from the fridge and, using a wet teaspoon, place 2 scoops on each plate. Arrange the spring onions and beetroot stems, sprinkle with the diced stems and scatter the red amaranth over the plate. Drizzle the lobster dressing over and place a little Maldon salt and freshly crushed black peppercorns on the ballotine.

roasted turbot with salsify, sheep's sorrel and herbed crumbs

Quite rightly known as the king of fish, turbot has a wonderful texture that lends itself to roasting just as well as poaching. Here, it is cooked on the bone, which helps the fish to retain a little moisture and improves the flavour. I've served it with salsify in different guises and added some fried herb breadcrumbs, which add a pleasing texture to the dish. You could replace the salsify with Jerusalem artichokes or turnips.

Serves 6

for the herbed breadcrumbs
100g fresh white breadcrumbs
25g chopped parsley
4g chopped thyme
4g chopped rosemary
25g unsalted butter
75g olive oil
2 garlic cloves, finely chopped

for the red wine juices
30g olive oil
3 shallots, finely sliced
1/2 bay leaf
a sprig of thyme
200g fish stock (see page 19)
200g port
300g red wine
30g unsalted butter

for the roasted turbot
50g olive oil
6 turbot tronçons, 300g each, cut across the bone to resemble an 'A'
50g unsalted butter
juice of 1/2 lemon

for the salsify purée
250g peeled salsify, sliced
125g milk
100g double cream
50g unsalted butter

for the salsify
6 thin salsify sticks
juice of 1 lemon
2 very thick salsify sticks
50g olive oil
100g unsalted butter
45g maple syrup

100 sheep's sorrel, to serve

herbed breadcrumbs
Place the breadcrumbs and herbs in a food processor and blitz until the breadcrumbs take on a green colour; take care not to process too long as you still want crumbs and not a lump of dough. Heat the butter and oil in a frying pan over a medium heat. Add the garlic and fry for 1 minute. Add the herbed breadcrumbs and fry for a further 3 minutes, until crisp. Season, then drain on kitchen paper to soak up any excess fat; do this 2 or 3 times. Leave to cool. Store in an airtight container until needed.

red wine juices
Heat the olive oil in a medium saucepan and, when hot, add the shallots, bay leaf and thyme. Cook for 2 minutes without colouring. Deglaze with the fish stock and reduce to 2 tablespoons. Add the port and reduce by half, then add the red wine and reduce by a third. Pass through a fine chinois into a clean pan, pressing on the shallots to get as much of the juice out as possible. Place on the heat and whisk in the butter. Bring back to the boil and season. Keep warm until needed.

roasted turbot
Heat a large cast-iron frying pan until hot. Add the oil and then the turbot, dark skin side down, and brown quickly. Turn and brown the other side. Season with salt and white pepper, then transfer to an oven preheated to 200°C/Gas Mark 6. Roast for 6–7 minutes, turning the fish over halfway through and adding the butter. When done, the fish should only just spring back when touched. The cooking time will depend on the thickness of the steaks, so give them a light prod every now and again. Remove from the oven, squeeze over the lemon juice and season. Keep warm until needed.

salsify purée
Put the salsify, milk and double cream in a medium saucepan and cook on a low simmer until tender. Transfer to a blender and blend to a smooth, velvety purée, adding the butter towards the end. Season. If the purée is slightly thick, add a little warm milk. Keep warm.

salsify
Peel the thin salsify sticks, trim the ends and cut lengthways in half to make batons. As you prepare each baton, place in a bowl of cold water mixed with half of the lemon juice. Bring a medium pan of salted water up to the boil, add the salsify batons and cook for 3 minutes, until just tender but still with a little bite. Refresh in cold water and drain, then dry thoroughly.

Peel the thick sticks of salsify, then cut into long, thin strips with a mandolin (failing this, use a peeler to create the long strips). Keep in cold water with the remaining lemon juice added.

Heat the oil in a medium frying pan, add the salsify batons and cook to a golden colour. Add half of the butter and the maple syrup and toss until well coated and caramelised. Season and drain. Keep warm. Heat the remaining butter with a little water in a medium saucepan, add the salsify strips and cook for 30 seconds just to warm them through but still be crunchy. Season and drain, then keep warm.

serving
Make a swipe of salsify purée on the right side of each plate. Cut the caramelised salsify batons in half at an angle and place along the purée. Carefully fold some of the salsify strips and place between the caramelised salsify. Sprinkle some breadcrumbs over the salsify, then scatter on the sheep's sorrel. Place the roasted turbot to the left and drizzle the red wine juices over.

seared ling, duxelle of saffron milk cap, chestnut velouté

The perfect season for ling is just when chestnuts and saffron milk caps are around. We find the wonderful-tasting milk caps when walking in the forest. They have a unique appearance, with flecks of orange and green. As they are hard to source, blue limbs (also called wood blewits) could be used instead. We pick chestnuts at the same time as the mushrooms. The chestnut velouté has a natural sweetness that complements the seared flesh of the ling. To make the dish a little more luxurious, you could drizzle over some white truffle oil – not too much though as you don't want to overpower the fish.

Serves 6

for the saffron milk cap duxelle
250g saffron milk caps
30g olive oil
50g finely chopped shallots
1 garlic clove, finely chopped
15g finely chopped parsley

for the chestnut velouté
530g duck fat
30g smoked bacon, chopped
75g chopped onions
50g chopped white of leek
a sprig of thyme
225g peeled chestnuts
15g sherry vinegar
15g Cognac
200g white port
200g white wine
750g good fish stock or chicken stock
  (see page 19)
300g milk
125g double cream
50g unsalted butter

for the seared ling
6 portions of ling fillet (skin on), 225g
  each, pin-boned
10g Maldon salt
10g cep powder
50g olive oil
25g unsalted butter

for the sea beet and sea purslane
50g unsalted butter
30g water
200g sea beet
30g sea purslane leaves

for the chestnuts
3 raw chestnuts, peeled

olive oil, for drizzling

saffron milk cap duxelle
Remove the bottom third of the mushroom stems and put to one side for the velouté. Wipe the mushrooms with a damp cloth to remove any grit. Chop finely, then place in a bowl to one side. Heat the olive oil in a large frying pan, add the shallots and cook for 1 minute without colouring. Add the garlic and cook for a further minute, then add the chopped mushrooms and cook on a moderately high heat, stirring occasionally, until all the liquid that has been produced by the mushrooms has evaporated. Stir in the parsley and cook for a minute longer. Season and remove from the heat.

chestnut velouté
Melt the duck fat in a heavy-based saucepan. When it is good and hot, add the smoked bacon and render the fat a little without colouring. Add the onions and leek, cover and cook until translucent without colouring. Add the thyme, chestnuts and mushroom trimmings and cook for a further 3 minutes, then deglaze with the vinegar and cook until it has evaporated. Add the Cognac and cook for 1 minute, then add the white port and cook until evaporated. Add the white wine and reduce by half. Stir in the stock and milk and cook for 50 minutes on a slow simmer.

Pour into a blender and blend until smooth, then pass through a fine chinois into another saucepan. Add the cream and bring to the boil. Whisk in the butter and season, then remove from the heat and set aside.

seared ling
Sprinkle the ling fillets with the Maldon salt and put to one side for 30 minutes. Then rinse under cold running water to remove the salt and dry thoroughly. Season the ling with a little pepper and the cep powder. Heat the olive oil in a large, heavy-based frying pan. When hot, add the ling fillets, skin side down, and cook for 2 minutes, until the skin starts to colour. Flip over and add the butter, then cook for 1 minute. Turn back on to the skin side and cook for a further 2 minutes. Remove the pan from the heat. The fish should be just cooked: when you prod it, it should give a little and feel springy. Remove from the pan. Season again and leave to rest in a warm place.

sea beet and sea purslane
Place the butter and water in a pan and bring to the boil. Add the sea beet and turn around in the emulsion until wilted and nearly cooked, then add the sea purslane and cook for a further minute. Season and drain. Keep warm.

chestnuts
Finely slice the chestnuts with a truffle slicer, or carefully use a peeler.

serving
Heat the chestnut velouté and the duxelle. Spoon the duxelle into the bottom of the shallow soup plates. Carefully place the sea beet on top with a little of the sea purslane, keeping the rest to scatter around at the end. Ladle a little of the chestnut velouté around the sea beet and place the seared ling on top. Drizzle over a little olive oil. Drizzle the sliced chestnuts with olive oil and season. Scatter them over and around the fish. Finally, scatter the remaining sea purslane around and season.

dover sole, *mussel and carrot purée, mussel juices, wild cabbage*

This country has the best Dover sole in the world so it is a shame not to use it. It is the most sought-after member of the sole family and the meatiest. I think it is best cooked simply and served with other things around or under it. Here I've put together mussels and carrots, which have a natural affinity for each other, and made them into a purée. The Dover sole then has the mussel juices to finish. It is also served with some wild cabbage that Yun, one of my fantastic suppliers, gets for us from the coast. Only use wild cabbage from a reliable forager who will pick where there is an abundance and have proper respect for the area.

Serves 4

for the dover sole
80g sunflower oil
2 Dover sole, 600g each, filleted and
  skinned (8 fillets)
a squeeze of lemon juice
50g unsalted butter

for the mussel juices
50 fresh, live mussels in shell
30g olive oil
2 shallots, chopped
1 garlic clove, crushed
5 parsley stalks
200g white wine
200g fish stock (see page 19)
100g double cream
a little lemon juice, if needed

for the mussel and carrot purée
100g unsalted butter
500g carrots, finely sliced
100g double cream
100g milk

for the wild cabbage
240g wild cabbage
50g unsalted butter
50g water

dover sole

Heat half of the sunflower oil in a large, heavy-based saucepan. Add 4 of the Dover sole fillets, presentation side down, and cook for 3 minutes, then flip over, season and cook for a further minute. Sprinkle with the lemon juice, then remove from the pan and pair the fillets up, setting them one on top of the other, skin side inwards. Place on a buttered baking tray. Repeat with the other 4 fillets. You will now have 4 double fillets of sole on the tray. Set aside in a cool place.

mussel juices

Scrub the mussels well under cold running water, discarding any that do not close when tapped, and removing any 'beards'. Warm the olive oil in a large pan over a medium heat. Add the shallots, garlic and parsley and sweat for 2 minutes. Turn the heat up and add the mussels and white wine. Cover and cook for about 4 minutes, shaking the pan halfway through, until the mussels have opened. Remove the mussels from the pan. Strain the mussel stock through dampened muslin into a clean saucepan; reserve. Remove the mussel flesh from the shells and put to one side.

mussel and carrot purée

Heat 50g of the butter in a saucepan, add the carrots and cook for 5 minutes without colouring. Add the cream and milk and cook for a further 15 minutes, until very tender. Transfer to a blender and add 30 of the cooked mussels and 30g of the reserved mussel stock. Blend to a smooth purée, adding the remaining butter while still hot. Pass through a fine chinois, season and keep warm.

finishing the mussel juices

Add the fish stock and cream to the remaining mussel stock and bring to the boil. Cook for 2–3 minutes. Season, then add a little lemon juice, if needed. Keep warm.

wild cabbage

Remove the central core from the cabbage. Separate the leaves from the stems and peel the stems. Bring a pan of salted water to the boil, add the stems and cook for 3–4 minutes, until tender. Refresh in cold water and drain. Add the leaves to the boiling water and cook for 2–3 minutes, until tender. Refresh in cold water and drain. Place a large sauteuse on a moderate heat, add the butter and water, and bring to the boil. Add the leaves and stems and turn over in the butter emulsion until hot. Season, then drain. Keep warm.

serving

Warm the paired Dover sole fillets in an oven preheated to 180°C/Gas Mark 4 for 2 minutes while you dress the plates. Make a good swipe of mussel and carrot purée on the left side of each plate. Tear the cabbage leaves and place on the right, then arrange the mussels and cabbage stems over the leaves. Remove the Dover sole from the oven and set on the carrot and mussel purée. Froth the mussel juices with a stick blender, then spoon over the fish and around.

wild sea bass with coconut and turnip 'gnocchi', coconut broth, razor clams and salad burnet

There is nothing like a nice thick piece of line-caught Cornish sea bass, and my fishmonger Johnny Godden supplies me with the best I have seen. Here I've paired it with a coconut and turnip 'gnocchi', which isn't gnocchi in the traditional form. To make it, I set a purée with a Japanese root starch called kuzu, which I learnt about from Mugaritz restaurant in Spain. This gives a lovely light texture and enables you to make gnocchi from any purée. The dish includes razor clams, with their juices giving the coconut broth a fantastic taste, and it is finished with salad burnet, with its haunting cucumber flavour.

Serves 6

for the coconut and turnip gnocchi
300g peeled turnips, finely sliced
225g coconut milk
37g kuzu
olive oil, for drizzling

for the razor clams
50g olive oil
2 shallots, finely chopped
15g salad burnet
8 large live razor clams
200g white wine

for the turnips
2 medium turnips
a little unsalted butter

for the coconut broth
30g unsalted butter
1/2 stem of lemongrass
50g peeled turnips, finely sliced
400g coconut milk
100g salad burnet

for the sea bass
6 pieces of sea bass fillet, 140g each, scaled
*   and pin-boned*
30g olive oil
6 sprigs of salad burnet
juice of 1/2 lemon

18 sprigs of salad burnet, to garnish

coconut and turnip gnocchi

Put the turnips in a saucepan with the coconut milk. Bring to the boil, then reduce the heat and simmer until tender. Transfer the contents of the pan to a blender and blend until smooth. Pass through a fine chinois and season. Measure out 450g of the purée into a clean pan and leave to cool.

Place the kuzu in a spice mill and grind to a fine powder, then add to the turnip purée in the pan and stir well. Set on the heat and cook, stirring all the time, until the mixture is very thick. Spoon into 30 small semi-sphere moulds (you will need 24 gnocchi, plus 6 extra just in case) – we use a silicone sheet of deep hemisphere moulds 30mm diameter and 20mm deep. Leave to cool, then place in the fridge to set.

razor clams

Heat a large saucepan with a tight-fitting lid. When hot, add the olive oil, shallots and salad burnet. Cook for 30 seconds, then add the razor clams and pour in the white wine. Immediately put on the lid. Shaking the pan from side to side, cook for 1 minute. This should have opened the clams. Remove them from the stock as quickly as possible and leave to cool a little. Strain the stock through a piece of damp muslin to catch any grit; put to one side. Remove the long white muscle of the clams; discard the rest. Slice the clams on a diagonal and put to one side.

turnips

Peel and finely slice the turnips. Using a cutter, cut perfect discs from 18 of the slices. (Keep the trimmings for the coconut broth.) Blanch the discs in salted boiling water, then refresh and drain; set aside. When needed, reheat in a little butter without colouring, and season.

coconut broth

Melt the butter in a medium saucepan, then add the lemongrass, turnips and turnip trimmings. Sweat for 4 minutes without colouring. Add the coconut milk, 200g of the razor clam stock and the salad burnet, and simmer for 10 minutes. Strain through a fine chinois into a clean saucepan and keep warm.

sea bass

Heat a steamer to boiling. Brush the sea bass fillets with olive oil and season, then add a salad burnet sprig to each fillet. Sprinkle with a little lemon juice. Carefully wrap each fillet in cling film (make tidy parcels so that none of the juices can escape). Place the wrapped sea bass in the steamer and cook for 5 minutes. Remove from the steamer and allow to rest for 2 minutes before unwrapping them.

finishing the gnocchi

Heat a non-stick frying pan and drizzle in a little olive oil. Push the gnocchi out of the moulds, place in the frying pan and gently colour on each side. Season, then remove from the pan and place on a buttered tray. Keep warm.

serving

Bring the coconut broth to the boil, then remove from the heat and add the clams to warm through. Place a sea bass fillet in each shallow soup plate with 4 gnocchi, then place 3 turnip discs and some razor clams in each. Froth up the broth with a stick blender and spoon over and around. Garnish with salad burnet sprigs.

john dory with a sauté of baby squid, asparagus and samphire, nero sauce

John Dory is quite a firm-fleshed, meaty fish, and I often pair it with meat like oxtail or a little stew of pig's trotter. Here, I have put it with one of my favourite seafoods, baby squid. These lovely little squid require very little cooking to become tender – any longer and they would be rubbery. Asparagus and samphire are perfect bedfellows, the asparagus adding a touch of bitterness and the samphire a natural saltiness.

Serves 4

for the baby squid
12 baby squid
50g olive oil
50g unsalted butter

for the nero sauce
100g vermouth
250g white wine
300g fish or chicken stock (see page 19)
200g double cream
40g fresh squid ink or 5 sachets of squid ink
juice of 1/2 lemon

for the asparagus
12 Evesham asparagus spears
50g unsalted butter
40g water

for the samphire
125g samphire
30g unsalted butter
40g water

for the john dory
4 john dory fillets (skin on), 150–170g each
30g olive oil
30g unsalted butter
a squeeze of lemon juice

baby squid
With one hand on the body of a squid and the other holding the tentacles, pull gently so the tentacles and body separate from each other. Trim the head away from the tentacles by cutting just below the eyes; discard the head. Remove the 'beak' from the middle of the tentacles if it's there. There is a transparent quill in the squid's body; pull this out and discard. Remove anything else in the body, then rinse under cold running water. I like to leave on the pink skin when the squid are small. Repeat with the remaining squid, so you have 12 cleaned small bodies and 12 small piles of tentacles. Put all of these on a tray lined with a damp cloth. Cover and keep in the fridge until needed. Remove 5 minutes before cooking.

nero sauce
Heat the vermouth in a medium saucepan and reduce until syrupy. Add the white wine and reduce until almost evaporated, then add the fish stock and reduce by two-thirds. Add the cream and reduce by half. Whisk in the squid ink. Heat gently but do not boil. Season, then add a few drops of lemon juice. Pass through a fine sieve and keep warm until needed.

asparagus
Carefully bend the asparagus stalks: they will snap just at the right point above the tough bottoms. Peel the stalks to within 4cm of the top. Place the butter and water in a sauteuse and bring to the boil, then add the asparagus spears and cook until tender – check by piercing with a knife through the thickest part of a spear. Season and drain. Keep warm.

samphire
Pick through the samphire, removing any dead bits. Bring the butter and water to the boil in a sauteuse, then add the samphire and cook for about 1 minute – I like it to keep a bit of texture. Season with pepper and a little salt, remembering that samphire can be quite salty, then drain and keep warm.

john dory
Season the John Dory fillets on both sides. Heat the olive oil in a thick-based pan until very hot. Add the John Dory, skin side down. Cook on a medium/high heat for 2–3 minutes, until golden. Flip the fish over carefully, then add the butter and cook for a further 1–2 minutes. Squeeze over the lemon juice. The fish should be golden but only just cooked. Remove from the pan and keep warm.

cooking the baby squid
Heat a large, heavy-based frying pan. When you can feel the heat coming off it, add half of the olive oil and then the squid bodies. Season. Cook for 30 seconds, then add half of the butter. Cook for a further 30–60 seconds. Remove to a warm plate. Wipe the pan and repeat with the tentacles and remaining oil and butter – the tentacles are nicer if a little more crisp than the bodies. Keep warm.

serving
Arrange the John Dory on the plates with the squid bodies and tentacles and drizzle over the sauce, then add the asparagus and samphire.

fillet of cornish pollock, tapioca and cep compote, malt garganelli

Pollock holds a special place in my heart because it was the first sea fish I caught when I was a little boy, on a family holiday in Looe. I was actually trying to catch bass, but you can't have everything. Pollock has a firmer texture than cod and is able to handle more powerful flavours, so here I've paired it with a cep compote – sort of like a rough duxelle – to which I have added some tapioca to give another texture. The pasta came about when I was playing with some malt flour we had just had delivered. It is a good match for the mushrooms.

Serves 6

for the malt garganelli
300g Malt Pasta Dough, made with 1 egg
   and 2 egg yolks (see page 21)
semolina, for sprinkling
olive oil, for coating
50g unsalted butter
50g water

for the herb oil
50g olive oil
10g tarragon leaves
5g parsley leaves

for the tapioca and cep compote
225g fish stock (see page 19)
40g tapioca
200g ceps, wiped clean and trimmed
30g olive oil
30g finely chopped shallots
1 garlic clove, finely chopped

for the pollock
5g fennel seeds
6 portions of pollock fillet (skin on), 200g
   each
50g olive oil
30g unsalted butter

for the ceps
50g olive oil
6 nice medium-sized ceps, wiped clean,
   trimmed and each sliced into 4

25g unsalted butter

malt garganelli
Roll out the pasta dough in a pasta machine to the last (thinnest) setting. Lay the sheet of dough flat on a floured work surface and cut into 4cm squares. Now, to shape the garganelli you need a piece of dowelling 6–7mm in diameter. Place the dowelling across a corner of one square and roll up the pasta around the dowelling to make a pointed tube. Roll this in turn over a gnocchi board to make lines in the pasta, then carefully slide off on to a semolina-dusted tray. (If you don't have a gnocchi board you can use a clean comb to make the lines.) Repeat until the pasta has been used up. When all the garganelli have been shaped, leave to dry a little before cooking.

Bring a large pan of salted water up to the boil, then add half of the pasta and cook until al dente. Remove from the pan with a slotted spoon and refresh, then drain and coat with a little olive oil. Repeat with the other half of the pasta. Set aside.

herb oil
Place all the ingredients in a blender and pulse to break the herbs down. They just need to be fine but not a purée – you want to see specks of herbs. Keep in a jar until needed.

tapioca and cep compote
Put the fish stock in a small saucepan and bring to the boil, then rain in the tapioca, stirring. Simmer gently for about 30 minutes, until the tapioca is cooked. Ideally, all the liquid should have been soaked up by the tapioca, but if not drain off the excess.

Finely dice the ceps. Heat the olive oil in a large frying pan and, when hot, add the shallots and sweat for 3 minutes without colouring. Add the garlic and ceps and cook until all the moisture that comes out of the ceps has disappeared. Remove from

the heat and stir in the tapioca, then season. Transfer to a bowl and keep warm.

pollock
Heat a large frying pan. When hot, add the fennel seeds and dry roast until fragrant. Remove from the pan and leave to cool, then place them in a spice grinder and grind to a fine powder. Season the pollock with salt, then sprinkle both sides lightly with the fennel powder. Heat the olive oil in the frying pan and, when hot, add the butter. Place the pollock, skin side down, in the pan. Cook for 3–4 minutes, until golden, then turn the heat down and flip the fish over. Cook for a further minute. The pollock should be just cooked: it should give a little when prodded and feel springy. Remove from the pan and keep warm.

finishing the garganelli
Heat the butter and water in a medium sauteuse to make an emulsion, then add the pasta and warm through. Season well (there is nothing worse than bland pasta). Remove from the heat and keep warm.

ceps
Heat the olive oil in a large frying pan. When hot, add the ceps and sauté until nearly cooked, then add the butter and finish cooking until golden. Season. Keep warm.

serving
Drizzle a little of the herb oil on the drained pasta. Place the pasta on the right side of each shallow soup plate, then make a line of tapioca and cep compote to the left and sit the pollock on this. Scatter the ceps over the pasta, and drizzle herb oil over the fish and around the plate.
The moisture from the tapioca and cep compote, teamed with the herb oil, makes enough of a sauce for the dish, but a little cep sauce could also be made if preferred.

loin of rabbit with beech nuts and dried cranberries, mead butter

The rabbits used for this are not wild rabbits, and because of that their loin meat is so much more plump and juicy than that of their wild brothers or sisters. I've used a topping made with beech nuts, which I am sure wild rabbits invariably have their fill of. Beech nuts can be picked from windfall in the autumn. They can be slightly tannic but generally have a lovely nutty flavour, and combined with dried cranberries make a good flavouring with texture. I have also added a mead butter. Mead was once a popular drink all over the world. Because of the honey used to make it, it has a lovely rounded sweetness that complements the sweet-sour of the cranberries.

Serves 4

for the saddle of rabbit
50g duck fat
50g chopped shallots
1 garlic clove, chopped
100g spinach, blanched and chopped
50g trompette noire mushrooms, trimmed, washed and dried
50g shelled beech nuts, toasted and chopped
50g dried cranberries, chopped
the offal from the rabbit (livers, kidneys and hearts – see below)
unsalted butter, for greasing
2 boned saddles of rabbit (ask your butcher to bone them for you, keeping each in one piece)

for the mead butter
120g unsalted butter
50g finely chopped shallots
300g mead
200g chicken stock (see page 19)
15g dried cranberries
30g double cream
juice of 1/2 lemon (if needed)

for the savoy cabbage
1 small savoy cabbage, cored and cut into rough 2cm squares
50g unsalted butter
250g baby spinach
50g shelled beech nuts, toasted

for the button onions
20 small button onions, peeled
30g dried cranberries
50g unsalted butter

saddle of rabbit
Heat the duck fat in a frying pan until hot, then add the shallots and garlic and cook for 5 minutes without colouring. Add the spinach and then the trompette noire mushrooms and cook until the moisture evaporates. Stir in the beech nuts and cranberries. Remove from the pan and leave to cool. Mince all the offal and mix with the spinach mixture. Season.

Place a large sheet of foil on the work surface and fold it double, then grease it with a little butter and season. Lay a saddle of rabbit, skin side down, on the foil and open out. Place half of the spinach stuffing mixture in the middle. Roll up the saddle to a cylinder, then roll the foil tightly around it several time to form a long sausage and twist the ends to seal. Repeat to stuff and wrap the second saddle. Place in an oven preheated to 200°C/Gas Mark 6 and cook for 10–12 minutes. Remove from the oven and leave to rest in a warm place for 10 minutes or until needed.

mead butter
Place a medium saucepan on the stove, add 20g of the butter and melt it. Add the shallots and sweat for 4 minutes without colouring. Add the mead and reduce until it is a glaze, then add the chicken stock and cranberries and reduce by half. Add the cream and bring to the boil. Whisk in the remaining butter, a little at a time, making sure it has been incorporated before adding the next bit. Bring to the boil, then remove from the heat and pass through a fine chinois into a clean pan. Season. If the butter sauce tastes a bit too sweet, add a little lemon juice. Keep warm, but not hot.

savoy cabbage
Bring a large saucepan of salted water to the boil. Add the cabbage and cook for 3 minutes, then refresh quickly in a bowl of cold water. Remove from the water and gently squeeze any excess water out of the cabbage. Put to one side. When needed, heat the butter in a large pan and, when hot, add the cabbage. Season, then add the spinach. When it has wilted, add the toasted beech nuts. Drain off any excess liquid and keep warm.

button onions
Place the onions in a medium frying pan with the cranberries and add enough water to half cover the onions. Add the butter. Bring up to the boil, then simmer the onions until tender, reducing the water at the same time. You want all the water to evaporate, leaving the butter to colour the onions. When ready, season and keep warm.

serving
Cut the ends off the foil packages. Carefully unwrap the rabbit saddles and cut each into 4 nice pieces. Place 2 slices overlapping on the left side of each plate and arrange a little mound of the cabbage and spinach to the right, making sure you get beech nuts in every portion. Scatter the button onions and cranberries around, then drizzle the mead butter/sauce over the rabbit and around the plate. This would be good served with a little wholegrain mustard mash.

roasted partridge, blood purée, baby parsnips with woodruff

For this dish we use grey-legged partridge, which I much prefer. We have a person who shoots for us, so have no problem in game season getting the birds we require. I have teamed the partridge with poached baby wild figs, blood purée – a rich, dark and masculine flavour – and some baby parsnips cooked with woodruff and glazed in maple syrup. Woodruff has a light taste of marzipan, and is used to flavour anything from beer and wine to sausages. It also makes a great ice cream to go with apples or pears. We add a touch of bitterness to this dish with some local cavolo nero, but you could use another brassica like kale.

Serves 4

for the partridges
4 juniper or sloe berries
4 sprigs of thyme
4 grey-legged partridges
50g olive oil
25g unsalted butter

for the partridge juices
25g Madeira
250g brown chicken stock (see page 19)
10g hazelnut oil

for the blood purée
30g duck fat
100g good-quality black pudding, finely sliced
175g milk
75g double cream

for the baby parsnips
12 sprigs of fresh woodruff
250g unsalted butter
12 baby parsnips, peeled
50g olive oil
30g maple syrup

for the parsnip cream
200g peeled parsnips, sliced
150g milk
125g double cream
75g unsalted butter

for the wild baby figs
25g demerara sugar
20g red wine vinegar
125g red wine
125g port
2cm piece cinnamon stick
1/2 star anise
8 dried baby wild figs

for the cavolo nero
12 small cavolo nero leaves, stalks trimmed
30g unsalted butter
30g water

partridges
Place a sloe or juniper berry and a sprig of thyme in each bird's cavity. Season the birds. Heat the oil and butter in a cast-iron or other ovenproof frying pan. When sizzling, add the partridges, placing them on one of the leg sides first. Cook for 1 minute until golden, then turn on to the other leg and cook for another minute, until golden. Finally, turn breast down and cook for 1 minute, until golden. Turn the birds breast up and transfer to an oven preheated to 220°C/Gas Mark 7. Cook for 7–8 minutes for a nice pink bird. Remove from the oven and leave to rest in a warm place for about 5 minutes. Remove the breasts and keep warm.

partridge juices
Deglaze the frying pan with the Madeira and cook until almost all evaporated. Add the chicken stock, together with the juices that escape from the birds during resting, and bring to the boil. Simmer for 3–4 minutes, then add the hazelnut oil and season. Strain through a fine sieve. Keep warm.

blood purée
Heat the duck fat in a medium saucepan and, when hot, add the black pudding. Cook for 2 minutes, turning often. Add the milk and cream and bring to the boil. Cook for 3–4 minutes. Pour the contents of the pan into a blender and blend until smooth. Pass through a fine chinois, then season. If the purée is too thick, add a little water; if too thin, reduce a little. Place in a squeezy bottle and keep warm.

baby parsnips
Strip the woodruff leaves from the stalks and set aside; keep the stalks. Melt the butter in a wide-based pan, add the parsnips and woodruff stalks, and poach gently until the parsnips are just cooked. Meanwhile, chop the woodruff leaves finely. Remove the parsnips from the butter and reserve. Pour the butter from the pan into a bowl and reserve. Put a little oil in the pan and heat, then add the parsnips and cook until golden. Add the maple syrup and turn the parsnips around to glaze. Add a little of the cooking butter and sprinkle with the chopped woodruff leaves. Turn the parsnips over in the maple syrup and woodruff. Season and keep warm until needed.

parsnip cream
Combine the parsnips, milk and cream in a pan and cook on a low simmer until tender. Transfer to a blender and blend to a smooth, velvety purée, adding the butter towards the end. Season and keep warm.

wild baby figs
Place the sugar and vinegar in a small saucepan and cook to a light caramel. Add the red wine, port and spices (take care as it will splutter). Bring to the boil, then add the figs and slowly poach until tender. Remove the figs from the pan and keep warm while you reduce the juices to a syrup; keep this warm.

cavolo nero

Blanch the cavolo nero in some salted boiling water; refresh and drain. Put the butter in a pan with the water and bring to the boil. Add the cavolo nero and turn around in the emulsion until hot. Season and drain.

serving

Make a slash of parsnip cream on each plate. Put 2 partridge breasts on top of each other and place across the purée. Dress the plate with the figs and baby parsnips. Add blood purée in blobs on the plate and drizzle a little fig syrup around. Lay the cavolo nero on the plate and drizzle over the partridge juices.

pork belly, pressed ham hock croquettes, confit shallots, pickled apple

The idea for this recipe was created by Mark Stinchcombe, a talented young chef who is a welcome member of our brigade. I first met Mark when judging the Young Chef of the Year competition, a title which he then went on to achieve. There are many layers to this dish: the crisp pork and the lovely little smoked ham hock croquettes, offset with the acid from the pickled apple and the sweetness from the confit shallots. It takes a little while to prepare, but it is well worth it.

Serves 8

for the pork belly
1 large leek, sliced
2 sprigs of thyme
1 piece of boned belly pork, about 1.5kg (keep the rib bones for the sauce)
1 head of garlic, cut across in half
750g chicken stock (see page 19)
50g olive oil

for the ham hock
1 medium ham hock, soaked overnight in cold water
1 pig's trotter, slit down the centre
500g cider
2kg water
100g roughly chopped carrots
100g roughly chopped onions
100g roughly chopped celery
2 garlic cloves, peeled
1 bay leaf
10 black peppercorns
a few sprigs of thyme

for the pressed croquettes
30g wholegrain mustard
5g vinegar
50g plain flour
3 eggs, whisked to mix
200g fresh breadcrumbs
oil for deep-frying

for the pickled apple purée
400g demerara sugar
400g red wine vinegar
400g red wine
5g mustard seeds
2 allspice berries
2 cloves
3cm piece cinnamon stick
15g peeled fresh ginger
8 coriander seeds
5 Granny Smith apples

for the pork sauce
50g olive oil
200g rib bones from the pork (see above), chopped into small pieces
1 red onion, finely sliced
1 celery stick, finely sliced
1 garlic clove, finely sliced
2 sprigs of thyme
100g port
200g red wine
1kg brown chicken stock (see page 19)
30g unsalted butter

for the confit shallots
30g olive oil
10 medium shallots, finely sliced
a sprig of thyme
250g red wine

for the trompette noires and baby leeks
16 large trompette noire mushrooms, washed and dried
30g olive oil
16 baby leeks, trimmed
50g unsalted butter

pork belly
Spread the leek slices and thyme sprigs in a baking tray just large enough to take the pork. Place the pork belly in the tray and put the garlic halves in two of the corners. Pour in the stock. Cover tightly with foil and bring to the boil, then place in an oven preheated to 160°C/Gas Mark 3. Cook for 3½–4 hours, until very tender.

Carefully remove the pork belly from the stock and place on a tray lined with cling film. Cover with more cling film and set another tray on top. Put a couple of heavy weights on this to press the pork and leave in the fridge overnight. The next day, trim the pork to a neat rectangle, then cut it into 8 even pieces. Set aside in a cool place.

ham hock
Rinse the ham hock and pig's trotter in cold running water. Put them in a large saucepan with all the other ingredients. Bring to the boil, then simmer gently for 2–2½ hours, skimming well occasionally. The meat should now be very tender and coming off the bone: you should be able to remove the small bone from the hock. If there is any resistance, cook for a little longer. When cooked, lift the ham hock and trotter from the stock. Remove the fat and bones from the hock and flake the meat. Remove the bones from the trotter and cut the meat into fine dice.

pressed croquettes
Mix together the meat from the ham hock and trotter and season with a little pepper plus salt if needed. Add the wholegrain mustard and vinegar and mix well. Spoon into a cling film-lined frame, about 18 x 12 x 4cm, and spread evenly into the corners. Place a board that fits inside the frame on top and set a weight on this to press the meat. Leave in the fridge overnight.

Remove from the fridge and remove the cling film. Cut the pressed meat into 8 even pieces, each 6 x 2.5cm. Put the flour in a bowl, the whisked eggs in another bowl and the breadcrumbs in a third. Coat the meat pieces with flour, shaking off the excess, then place in the egg and coat evenly. Lift out, shaking off excess, and roll in the breadcrumbs, coating evenly. Place in the fridge to set a little, then dip again in the egg and then the breadcrumbs.

The pieces must be totally covered or they will leak when fried, so check all over carefully. Keep in the fridge until needed.

pickled apple purée

Bring all the ingredients, except the apples, to the boil in a saucepan and cook for 20 minutes. Peel the apples, cut in half and remove the cores. Add the apples to the pickling juices and poach gently for 5–10 minutes, until tender but still holding their shape. Remove the apples from the pickling juices with a slotted spoon and leave to cool down. Reduce the pickling juices by half, then leave to cool. Place the apples in a container and pour the pickling juices over. Keep in the fridge.

When needed, warm the apples in a little of the pickling juices, then transfer to a blender. Blend until smooth. Pass through a fine chinois and season. Keep warm.

pork sauce

Heat the olive oil in a large saucepan, add the rib bones and cook until deep brown. Remove the bones and a little of the resultant fat. Add the vegetables, garlic and thyme to the pan and cook for 2–3 minutes. Add the port and stir to loosen the sediment on the bottom of the pan, then cook until completely evaporated. Add the red wine and reduce by half. Finally, add the chicken stock. Bring to the boil and skim. Return the rib bones to the pan and then simmer for 1–1$\frac{1}{2}$ hours; remove any fat that comes to the surface. Pass through a fine chinois into a clean pan and reduce to 400g, then whisk in the butter and season. Keep warm.

confit shallots

Heat the oil in a medium saucepan, add the shallots and sweat without colouring for 2 minutes. Add the thyme and red wine. Bring to the boil, then cook until the shallots are tender and the wine has reduced to a glaze. Season. Keep warm.

trompette noires and baby leeks

Rip the trompette noires into halves. Sauté in the olive oil for 30 seconds, until limp. Season and drain. Keep warm.

For the baby leeks, place a large sauteuse on the heat and add the butter, baby leeks and enough water to half cover. Bring to the boil and cook for about 5 minutes, turning over, until tender. Drain and season. Keep warm.

finishing the pork belly

Heat a large cast-iron frying pan and add the olive oil. When very hot, place the pork, skin side down, in the pan and turn the heat down to moderate. Cook until crisp, then turn over and cook for a further 3–4 minutes, until the pork is hot.

finishing the croquettes

Heat oil for deep-frying in a deep-fat fryer or a large, deep saucepan to 165°C. Carefully place the croquettes in the oil and cook until golden on all sides. Remove from the oil and drain on kitchen paper. Season and keep warm.

serving

Make a teardrop swipe of pickled apple purée along the middle of each oval plate. Place the crisp pork belly, skin side up, to the right at an angle. Arrange a loose line of the confit shallots across the plate, left to right. Put the ham hock croquettes on top of the shallots and dress with the trompette noires and the baby leeks. Drizzle over the sauce.

roasted wood pigeon, beetroot purée, rosehip jelly

Wood pigeon is my favourite of all the game birds. This may have something to do with the fact that it is available all year round, although it is at its best when crops are being gathered and the birds have plenty to eat, getting nice and plump. Here it is served with another of my favourite things, beetroot – as a purée, pickled and roasted. I have also used some of the young beetroot tops or greens. Rosehip jelly gives the whole dish a light sweetness. This could be replaced with crab apple and rowan jelly or a haw and apple jelly.

Serves 6

for the rosehip jelly
1.25kg dog rose hips
400g crab apples, roughly chopped (peel left on)
1kg water
450g caster sugar for every 500g of juice
3g agar agar

for the pickled beetroot slices
2 large golden beetroot, peeled
100g apple juice
75g caster sugar
50g cider vinegar
grated zest of 1/2 orange

for the roasted wood pigeon
6 good wood pigeons
50g olive oil
30g unsalted butter

for the pigeon sauce
50g olive oil
50g chopped onions
1 celery stick, chopped
2 garlic cloves, chopped
50g red wine vinegar
100g port
200g red wine
100g beetroot juice (made with a juicer)
1kg brown chicken stock (see page 19)
500g water

4 juniper berries, crushed
a sprig of thyme

for the roasted beetroot
24 baby beetroots
50g olive oil
25g unsalted butter

for the beetroot purée
500g small peeled beetroots
150g beetroot juice (made with a juicer)
125g double cream
5g grated fresh horseradish
75g unsalted butter

for the garnish
50g unsalted butter
12 tops from the baby beetroots (see above)
12 choy sum stems

rosehip jelly

Remove the stalk and the bottom bit from the rosehips. Place them in a food processor with the crab apples and blitz. Put the water in a large saucepan, bring to the boil and add the blitzed rosehip and apple mixture. Return to the boil, then reduce the heat to a rolling simmer and cook for 45–60 minutes. Pour into a jelly bag, or gathered piece of muslin, and hang it over a large bowl to catch the juices. Leave to drain overnight.

In the morning, measure out the juice and calculate the correct amount of sugar. Combine the juice and sugar in a large saucepan and bring to the boil, stirring. Skim. Put the agar agar in a little water to swell, then add to the boiling mixture. (The agar agar gives the jelly a slightly firmer set so it will hold on a warm plate without melting too quickly.) Cook to 105°C. Remove from the heat and strain into sterilised jars while still warm. Leave to cool, then store in the fridge (the jelly will keep for 2–3 weeks).

pickled beetroot

Slice the beetroot as thinly as possible and place in a stainless steel bowl. Put all the other ingredients into a small saucepan and bring to the boil. Remove from the heat and leave to cool, then pour over the beetroot slices. Set aside in a cool place for 12 hours, then keep in the fridge until needed.

wood pigeon

Check the pigeons for quills and stray bits of feather. Remove the legs and the bottom part of the backbone from each pigeon; retain these for the sauce. Remove the skin from the breasts, leaving a nice crown of pigeon. Keep in a cool place until needed.

pigeon sauce

Heat the oil in a large saucepan and fry the pigeon legs and bones until golden all over. Remove and put to one side. Add the onions, celery and garlic and colour. Put the pigeon legs and bones back in the pan. Pour in the vinegar and cook until evaporated, then add the port and cook until it has evaporated. Add the red wine and beetroot juice and cook until reduced by half. Add the chicken stock, water, juniper and thyme and bring to the boil, then reduce the heat to a simmer and cook for 1 hour. Strain into a clean pan. Remove any grease and reduce by two-thirds. You should now have a wonderful rich sauce for 6 portions. Check the seasoning. If the sauce is too thick, add a little water; if too thin, reduce a little more. Set aside.

roasted beetroot

Wash the beetroot and trim the tops, leaving 2–3cm of stalks (keep the trimmed-off leafy tops). Toss the beetroot in the olive oil and season, then wrap in foil to form a sealed bag. Place on a baking sheet and roast in an oven preheated to 180°C/Gas Mark 4 for 15–20 minutes,

(continued on page 108)

(continued from page 107)

until tender (timing depends on the size of the beetroots). Remove from the oven and leave to cool until warm, then peel the beetroot. Cut each into quarter wedges. Heat the butter and colour the beetroot. Season and keep warm.

roasting the wood pigeons

Heat the oil in a heavy roasting tray and colour the pigeons for about 30 seconds on each side. Add the butter and season, then transfer to an oven preheated to 220°C/ Gas Mark 7 and cook for 5–8 minutes. Check to see if the birds are cooked by pressing the breast meat with your fingers: it should give a little when pinched, then spring back. Remove from the pan and leave to rest in a warm place for 10 minutes.

beetroot purée

Slice the beetroot and place in a saucepan with the beetroot juice and cream. Bring to the boil, then reduce the heat and simmer gently until tender. Add the grated horseradish and cook for 1 minute. Transfer to a blender and blend to a smooth, velvety purée, adding the butter towards the end. Season and keep warm.

garnish

Divide the butter between 2 pans, add a little water to each and bring to the boil. Place the beetroot tops in one and the choy sum in the other. Cook just long enough to wilt. Season and drain. Keep warm.

serving

Reheat the pickled beetroot in a little of its marinade. Reheat the pigeon sauce. Remove the pigeon breasts from the carcass and season the inside of each breast a little. Make a streak of beetroot purée on each plate and place 2 pigeon breasts to the left. Scoop a little of the rosehip jelly on to the plate, then arrange the roasted beetroot, pickled beetroot, beetroot greens and choy sum around. Finally, spoon over the pigeon sauce.

wild rabbit with hazelnut gnocchi, apple and kohlrabi

The crisp tartness of Granny Smith apples pairs very well with the slight cabbagey/turnip flavours of kohlrabi. Gnocchi, made with a potato base, provides the starch element and, with the hazelnuts, add a roundness to the dish that complements the distinctively gamey flavour of the wild rabbit. You could replace the hazelnuts with walnuts, the apple with pear.

Serves 6

for the wild rabbit
3 wild rabbits, with their offal (kidneys,
   livers, hearts)
75g olive oil
35g unsalted butter

for the wild rabbit jus
rabbit bones (from above)
50g olive oil

3 shallots, chopped
1 garlic clove, crushed
100g button mushrooms, sliced
50g cider vinegar
100g Madeira
200g red wine
1kg brown chicken stock (see page 19)
30g hazelnut oil

for the hazelnut gnocchi
1kg Desiree potatoes
2 egg yolks
30g hazelnut oil
125g type '00' pasta flour
ground nutmeg, to taste
50g toasted hazelnuts, chopped
olive oil, for sprinkling and frying
50g unsalted butter
12 sprigs of watercress, leaves removed and
   chopped (stems kept for the garnish)

for the kohlrabi
2 medium kohlrabi, peeled
30g olive oil
30g cider vinegar
100g apple juice
200g cider
50g unsalted butter

for the garnish
2 Granny Smith apples
50g unsalted butter
50g water
50g toasted hazelnuts, crushed

wild rabbit

Remove the rabbit meat from either side of the backbone (keep the bones for the jus). Trim off any silver skin. You should now have 6 nice rabbit fillets. Remove the skin from the kidneys, and trim the livers and hearts. Keep in the fridge until needed, removing 5 minutes before cooking.

wild rabbit jus

Chop up the rabbit bones into small pieces. Heat the olive oil in a large saucepan, add the bones and cook until golden. Add the shallots, garlic and mushrooms and cook for 2–3 minutes. Deglaze with the vinegar and cook until it has evaporated. Add the Madeira and cook to a glaze, then add the red wine and reduce by half. Add the stock and bring to the boil, then simmer for 40 minutes. Strain through a fine sieve into a clean pan and reduce to 250g. Set aside.

hazelnut gnocchi

Bake the potatoes in an oven preheated to 200°C/Gas Mark 6 until cooked. Scoop out the flesh and push through a sieve or potato ricer into a bowl. While still warm, beat in the egg yolks, hazelnut oil and flour, incorporating these thoroughly, but trying not to work the mixture too much. Season with nutmeg, salt and pepper, then mix in the chopped hazelnuts. Roll the mixture into balls, each weighing about 12g. Press a fork on the back of each ball to make indentations.

Bring a large pan of salted water to the boil. Add the gnocchi and cook until they float to the surface. Scoop out and place in a bowl of cold water. Drain, then place in a container. Sprinkle with olive oil and turn the gnocchi over in the oil to coat. Keep in the fridge until needed.

kohlrabi

Cut each kohlrabi into 3 discs about 1cm thick, then use a cutter to make perfect rounds. Heat the oil in a sauteuse, add the kohlrabi and fry until golden on both sides. Remove from the pan. Deglaze the pan with the vinegar, then reduce by half. Add the apple juice and cider, then place the kohlrabi discs back in the pan. Add the butter and bring to the boil. Simmer until the liquid has evaporated and the kohlrabi is tender. Remove from the heat, season and keep warm.

cooking the rabbit

Heat 50g of the olive oil and 25g of the butter in a frying pan. When sizzling, add the rabbit fillets and season, then brown quickly on all sides. Lower the heat and cook for a further 3–4 minutes, until just cooked – test by pressing: the fillets should feel springy. Remove from the pan and keep warm.

Wipe out the pan, then heat the remaining oil and butter. Add the kidneys, livers and hearts and cook for 1 minute, turning halfway through. They should be golden but still pink inside. Remove from the pan and keep warm.

finishing the gnocchi

Heat a little olive oil in a large frying pan and, when hot, add the gnocchi. Toss until golden. Finish with the butter and chopped watercress. Drain to remove the excess oil and butter, then season. Keep warm.

garnish

Peel and core the apples, then cut into fine strips; set aside. Heat the butter and water in a sauteuse and, when boiling, add the reserved watercress stems. Drain and season.

serving

Quickly reheat the jus. Blitzing with a stick blender, drizzle in the hazelnut oil, then season. Cut the rabbit fillets in half at an angle and arrange with the offal on the left side of each plate. Place the kohlrabi in the centre right of the plate, then scatter the gnocchi over the kohlrabi. Arrange the watercress stems in a line across the gnocchi and sprinkle with the crushed hazelnuts and apple strips. Drizzle over the jus.

hare with cauliflower, cocoa nib jus

The first time I had cauliflower and chocolate together was at Heston's restaurant The Fat Duck, in the form of a risotto. Here, I've used the flavour combination with braised and roasted hare. A little chocolate works well in a sauce for game, and pungent cauliflower can stand up to strong game flavours, so it seemed natural to put the three elements together. Instead of making a normal cauliflower purée you could roast the cauliflower. Or replace the cauliflower with pumpkin, or with onions in various forms (puréed, pickled and roasted).

Serves 4

for the hare
100g olive oil
105g unsalted butter
1 hare, broken down into 2 saddle fillets,
    2 legs and 2 shoulders
1 onion, chopped
2 carrots, chopped
1 celery stick, chopped
2 garlic cloves, crushed
200g port
6g cocoa nibs (grue de cacao)
6 juniper berries, crushed
500g red wine
500g brown chicken stock (see page 19)

for the hare cannelloni
1/2 large celeriac, peeled
a little grated fresh horseradish or
    wholegrain mustard
100g spinach, blanched and chopped

for the cauliflower purée
1 medium cauliflower
125g unsalted butter
milk, if needed

for the garnish
25g olive oil
1/2 cauliflower, broken into small florets
75g unsalted butter
12 trompette noire mushrooms, washed
    and dried

30g water
6 choy sum stems, split lengthways
3 medium cauliflower florets, thinly sliced

braising the hare shoulders and legs
Heat 50g of the olive oil and 25g of the butter in a flameproof casserole large enough to take the legs and shoulders. First, colour the shoulders on both sides; remove from the casserole. Then add the legs and colour on both sides; remove. Add the chopped vegetables and garlic to the casserole and cook until golden. Add the port, half of the cocoa nibs and the juniper berries and reduce to a glaze, stirring in the sediment from the bottom of the casserole. Put the shoulders and legs back in the pot. Add the red wine and reduce by two-thirds. Add the stock and bring to the boil, then cover and place in an oven preheated to 150°C/Gas Mark 2. Braise for 2–2½ hours, until very tender.

Remove from the oven. Spoon out three-quarters of the cooking stock and strain through a fine sieve into a saucepan. Add the remaining 3g cocoa nibs and reduce to 200g, then whisk in 50g butter and season. Set this sauce aside.

Lift the shoulders and legs from the casserole. Trim the legs and shoulders to yield 4 little leg and shoulder joints (shanks). Put these in a little of the remaining cooking stock and set aside.

Flake the meat from the shoulders and thighs of the hare, discarding the bones, and chop roughly, then bind with a little of the remaining cooking stock. Reserve for the cannelloni filling.

hare cannelloni
Bring a medium pan of salted water to the boil. Slice the celeriac with a mandolin to get 4 good thin slices. Blanch them in the boiling water for about 1 minute, until translucent. Refresh in cold water, then drain and place on a cloth to dry a little. Add a few gratings of fresh horseradish or

a little wholegrain mustard to the chopped hare meat. Add the blanched spinach and season. Wrap in the blanched celeriac slices to create 4 cannelloni; trim the ends. Season and place on a buttered baking tray. (You can serve the rest of the hare meat in a little dish.)

cauliflower purée
Bring a large saucepan of water to the boil. Trim the cauliflower, removing all the green and the major part of the stalk; discard these. Break down the rest of the cauliflower into small florets and place in a cooking bag. Add the butter and seasoning and seal. Place the bag in the boiling water and cook for 30–40 minutes, until very soft. Remove the bag and empty the contents into a blender. Blend until fine and smooth. The purée needs to be thick enough to hold its shape, so if it is too thick add a little milk; if it is too thin, cook it a little. Check the seasoning and keep warm.

Alternatively, if you do not have a cooking bag, put the cauliflower in a saucepan with 250g milk and bring to the boil, then cover and simmer gently for 10–15 minutes, until very tender. Drain, keeping the milk. Place the cauliflower in a blender, add 50g unsalted butter and blend until smooth; add a little of the reserved milk if the purée is too thick. Keep warm.

roasting the hare fillet
Melt the remaining 30g butter with the remaining olive oil in a frying pan until hot. Add the hare saddle fillets and cook gently for 4–5 minutes, until golden on both sides. The cooking time depends on the size of the fillet; it should be very pink inside. Remove from the pan and leave to rest in a warm place. Season before serving.

garnish
For the caramelised cauliflower, heat half of the olive oil in a medium frying pan. Add the cauliflower florets and cook gently until tender and a light golden brown.

Add a little of the butter and cook until mid-brown, then season and drain. Keep warm.

For the trompette noire mushrooms, heat the remaining olive oil a frying pan, add the mushrooms and sauté very quickly until limp, then season and drain. Keep warm.

For the choy sum, put the remaining butter and the water in a medium sauté pan and heat until the water boils and forms an emulsion. Add the choy sum and cook quickly until tender. Season and drain. Keep warm.

serving
Reheat the sauce. Glaze the little hare shanks in the sauce until shiny. Quickly warm the cannelloni through in an oven preheated to 180°C/Gas Mark 4. Make a line of cauliflower purée in the centre of each plate. Slice each hare fillet in half and place on the plates, then add a shank and a cannelloni. Scatter on the caramelised cauliflower and neatly arrange the remaining garnishes. Finally, spoon the sauce over and around.

pavé of winchcombe roe deer, nasturtium millet, smoked almonds

Winchcombe is just down the road from us and we get most of our venison from around that area. It has a wonderful flavour, sort of like the best beef but a little gamier. Here, I have put it with millet and run a purée of nasturtium through this, which gives it a wonderful pepperiness. The nasturtiums that we use are grown for us by Justyna Juszczuk, our waitress. The venison is served with wonderful smoky almonds, a flavour that most game loves, and sautéed meaty eryngii mushrooms. The dish is finished off with a biting land cress and wild watercress pesto to add even more depth.

Serves 4

for the venison sauce
75g olive oil
300g venison bones, chopped small, plus
    any trimmings from the fillet (see below)
2 shallots, finely chopped
2 garlic cloves, crushed
6 juniper berries, crushed
3 sprigs of thyme
1 bay leaf
50g Madeira
200g red wine
600g brown chicken stock (see page 19)
50g unsalted butter

for the pesto
75g wild watercress leaves
1 garlic clove, peeled
50g land cress
50g toasted pine kernels
125g olive oil
40g Parmesan cheese, finely grated

for the nasturtium millet
50g watercress
50g spinach
75g nasturtium leaves
75g unsalted butter
50g finely chopped onions
150g millet
300g chicken stock (see page 19)

for the smoked almonds
50g unsalted butter
24 smoked almonds

for the venison
750g venison fillet, taken from the saddle
25g duck fat
25g unsalted butter

for the choy sum
50g unsalted butter
30g water
12 choy sum stems

for the sautéed eryngii
25g duck fat
12 medium eryngii mushrooms, halved
25g unsalted butter

16 nasturtium leaves, to garnish

venison sauce
Heat the olive oil in a large saucepan and, when hot, add the venison bones and trimmings and cook until golden brown. Add the shallots, garlic, juniper, thyme and bay leaf. Cook until the shallots are a deep golden brown and caramelised. Add the Madeira and cook until it has evaporated, then add the red wine and reduce by two-thirds. Add the brown chicken stock and simmer until reduced by two-thirds. Strain through a fine sieve into a clean pan. Whisk in the butter. The sauce should coat the back of a spoon. If it is too thin, reduce a little more; if too thick, add a little more stock. Set aside.

pesto
Bring a large pan of salted water to the boil. Add the wild watercress leaves, then immediately refresh. Place in a blender with the garlic, land cress and pine kernels. Pulse until broken down. Then, with the machine still running, drizzle in the olive oil. Finally, add the Parmesan and blend until smooth. Season. Place in a squeezy bottle and set aside until needed.

nasturtium millet
Bring a large pan of salted water to the boil and blanch the watercress, spinach and 50g of the nasturtiums for 30 seconds. Refresh in iced water, then drain. Place in a blender and blend until smooth. Put to one side.

Heat 50g of the butter in a wide-based saucepan, add the onions and cook without colouring for 3–4 minutes, until translucent and soft. Pour in the millet and stir until coated. Cook for 2 minutes. Add the chicken stock and bring to the boil, then simmer for 15 minutes, until the millet is tender. If a little undercooked, add some water and continue cooking. The millet should have absorbed all the liquid. Remove from the heat. Add the green purée, then mix in the remaining 25g butter and season. Chop the remaining nasturtium leaves and mix in. Keep to one side until needed.

smoked almonds
Place a small frying pan on the heat, add the butter and, when foaming, add the smoked almonds. Season and toss until golden. Drain on kitchen paper and keep warm.

venison
Cut the fillet into 4 equal portions. Season. Heat the duck fat in a heavy cast-iron or other ovenproof frying pan and, when hot, add the butter and then the venison. Sear quickly all over to brown, taking care not to burn. Transfer the pan to an oven preheated to 180°C/Gas Mark 4 and cook for 4–6 minutes, depending on the thickness of the fillet. When cooked, the venison will be springy to the touch. Leave to rest in a warm place for 3–4 minutes. Season again before serving.

choy sum
Place a medium sauté pan on the stove and add the butter and water. Heat until the water boils and forms an emulsion, then add the choy sum. Cook quickly until tender. Season and drain. Keep warm.

sautéed eryngii
Heat a cast-iron frying pan and, when hot, add the duck fat followed by the mushrooms, cut side down. Cook gently for 2 minutes, then flip the mushrooms over and add the butter. Season and cook until tender. Drain and keep warm.

serving
Quickly reheat the sauce and the nasturtium millet. Cut each piece of venison fillet in half. Place a spiral of pesto in the centre of each plate. Dress the millet to the left of the plate and place the venison on top. To the right, place the choy sum, then the sautéed mushrooms and smoked almonds. Carefully arrange the nasturtium leaves on top. Drizzle the sauce around.

mallard, celeriac cream, braised celery, pickled walnuts

I can't wait for the game season to arrive with its bounty of wonderful birds. Mallard is a favourite of mine, being leaner and with a more powerful and pronounced flavour than farmed ducks, and it stands up well to most accompaniments. If the mallards are truly wild, they can be a little tough, but there are a lot bred for the shoot and generally these are more tender with plumper breasts. I usually serve them with something acidic, to help cut through the richness of the meat – here this is in the form of pickled walnuts, but crab apple can be used or pickled pears. The mallard is also wonderful roasted on some dried lovage stalks, with lemon verbena.

Serves 4

for the mallard
2 large mallards, with giblets (for the sauce)
2 dried lovage stalks
4 juniper berries
2 sprigs of thyme
50g olive oil
25g unsalted butter

for the duck sauce
50g olive oil
250g duck bones
1 onion, sliced
2 garlic cloves, crushed
1 celery stick, sliced
100g Madeira
500g brown chicken stock (see page 19)
25g unsalted butter
giblets from the mallards (see above), chopped
30g walnut oil

for the braised celery
50g olive oil
1 head of celery, de-stringed and cut into 6cm lengths
400g chicken stock (see page 19)
25g unsalted butter

for the celeriac cream
2 medium celeriac, peeled and chopped
200g milk
200g double cream
100g unsalted butter

for the pickled walnuts
25g unsalted butter
6 Pickled Walnuts (see page 17), cut into quarters

4 shelled walnuts, to garnish

mallard
Remove the duck legs (keep them for another occasion), leaving 2 duck crowns. Season the crowns and place the lovage stalks, juniper berries and thyme sprigs in the cavity. Heat the oil and butter in a large frying pan and sear the birds on one side for about 1 minute, until golden. Flip over and sear the other side. Turn the crowns breast side down and sear until golden. Transfer to a roasting tray and place in an oven preheated to 200°C/Gas Mark 6. Roast for 20 minutes; the duck will be rare to medium-rare. Leave to rest under some loose foil in a warm place for at least 15 minutes; keep any juices that escape for the sauce. When needed, take the breasts off the carcass – if they are too rare, put back in the oven, skin side down, and cook for a further 2 minutes.

duck sauce
Heat the olive oil in a large saucepan, add the duck bones and brown all over. Pour off some of the fat. Add the onion, garlic and celery and cook until golden. Add the Madeira and reduce by half, then add the brown chicken stock and bring back to the boil. Skim, then reduce the heat to a simmer and cook for 30 minutes.

Melt the butter in a small frying pan. When foaming, add the chopped giblets and cook for 2–3 minutes. Add to the sauce and cook for a further 5 minutes. Remove the duck bones, then pass the sauce through a fine sieve into a clean pan. Blitzing with a stick blender, drizzle in the walnut oil to emulsify the sauce. Season and set to one side.

braised celery
Heat the oil in a small flameproof casserole, add the celery and cook until lightly caramelised. Add the chicken stock and butter and bring to the boil. Season. Cover with baking parchment, then place in an oven preheated to 200°C/Gas Mark 6 and cook for 40 minutes, basting every 10 minutes. Keep warm until needed.

celeriac cream
Put the celeriac, milk and cream in a medium saucepan, bring to the boil and simmer until the celeriac is tender. Place in a blender and blend to a fine, smooth purée. Add the butter, bit by bit. Season and keep warm.

pickled walnuts
Heat the butter in a large frying pan. Add 15g of the walnut pickling juice and then the pickled walnuts and gently warm through. Keep warm.

serving
Add any juices from the duck to the sauce and quickly reheat. Place a spoonful of the celeriac cream on one side of each plate and set a mallard breast on top. Arrange the pickled walnuts and braised celery on the other side. Spoon over the sauce. Finally, grate the shelled walnuts over the celery.

pheasant, pumpkin, honeyed mustard seeds

Pheasant has its place on our menu at the end of December and beginning of January. By this time, the birds have filled out a little and put on a little more fat. Pheasant has a wonderful gamey taste and, when served slightly pink, is the most succulent of birds. Here I've partnered it with roasted pumpkin, the sweetness of which complements the game flavour. Pheasant also takes to spices so I've added some honeyed mustard seeds, which are perfect with all game as well as with beef and terrines. Buttered kale makes a good accompaniment.

Serves 4

for the pheasant
2 plump pheasants, with neck and giblets
   (for the juices)
2 garlic cloves, crushed
4 juniper berries
2 sprigs of thyme
50g duck fat
50g unsalted butter

for the pheasant juices
50g olive oil
200g pheasant bones, chopped into small
   pieces
100g chopped celery
50g chopped shallots
a sprig of thyme
1 bay leaf
5 juniper berries, crushed
100g port
100g white wine
750g brown chicken stock (see page 19)
30g unsalted butter
30g walnut oil

for the pumpkin
1 smallish Crown Prince pumpkin
75g unsalted butter
25g white port
4 sprigs of thyme
2 juniper berries, crushed
200g chicken stock (see page 19), reduced
   to 100g

to serve
Maldon salt
buttered kale (optional)
Honeyed Mustard Seeds (see page 16)

pheasant
Remove any little feathers from the pheasants and quickly blowtorch all over, then wipe clean. Remove the neck and any giblets that may be inside the birds (reserve for the juices). Place a crushed garlic clove, 2 juniper berries and a sprig of thyme in the cavity of each bird. Set aside in a cool place.

pheasant juices
Heat the olive oil in a large saucepan, add the bones and the pheasant necks, and cook until golden brown all over. Add the vegetables, herbs and juniper berries and cook for a further 2 minutes. Deglaze with the port, scraping the pan for the sediment, and cook until completely evaporated. Add the white wine and reduce by half. Finally, add the chicken stock and bring to the boil. Skim, then leave to simmer for 45 minutes while you roast the pheasant.

roasting the pheasant
Heat a small roasting tray or a heavy cast-iron pan and, when hot, add the duck fat. Season the birds and place them, leg side down, in the pan. Cook for 1 minute just to brown lightly. Flip on to the other leg and brown. Finally, add the butter, turn the birds breast down and cook for 1 minute (this will give them a head start before putting them in the oven). Place the birds on their backs in the tray and transfer to an oven preheated to 180°C/Gas Mark 4. Roast for about 30 minutes, depending on the size of the birds. Remove from the oven and set aside to rest in a warm place for 10–15 minutes.

When needed, remove the legs and cut through the thigh and drumstick joint. If the meat is still pink, return to the oven to cook for a further 1–2 minutes. Remove the breasts carefully and season the undersides. Keep warm.

pumpkin
Peel the pumpkin and cut across into slices about 12mm thick (don't worry about the seeds; you can take them out later). Using a round 5cm cutter, cut out 8 discs of seedless pumpkin flesh from the slices. (You could use the pumpkin trimmings to make a little purée or a shot of soup to serve with the pheasant.) Heat the butter in a cast-iron or other heavy ovenproof frying pan that is just large enough to take the discs. Place them in the pan and cook for 2 minutes. Add the port, thyme and juniper, bring to the boil and cook for 1 minute. Add the stock, which should come no more than halfway up the pumpkin discs, and bring to the boil again.

Transfer the pan to an oven preheated to 200°C/Gas Mark 6 and cook for 15–20 minutes. The liquid should have been absorbed by the pumpkin, leaving the butter to give the discs a golden glaze. Check for tenderness with the point of a knife: it should go through very easily. Remove the discs carefully – they will be very fragile – and put on a parchment-lined tray. Keep warm.

finishing the juices
Finely chop the pheasant giblets and add to the sauce. Immediately remove the pan from the heat and stir the giblets around a little, then leave to sit for 5 minutes before passing the sauce through a muslin-lined sieve into a clean pan. Skim off any fat that rises to the surface, then use a stick blender to blend in the butter and walnut oil. Season and keep warm.

serving
Place 2 pumpkin discs on the left side of each plate and sprinkle a little Maldon salt on top. Set a pheasant breast on top of the pumpkin. Add some buttered kale, if using, in a little mound and place a pheasant thigh and drum-stick against it. Dot some of the honeyed mustard seeds over the breast and the plate, and drizzle the juices over and around.

cinderford lamb, bay boletus cream, sautéed ceps and walnuts

Here in Cheltenham we are very lucky to be so close to such wonderful produce: terrific cheeses, lamb and game as well as an abundance of wild mushrooms and other foraged foods. In this dish I am using some of these wonderful ingredients – lamb from nearby Cinderford, which we drive through to get to the Forest of Dean where we get the bay boletus for this dish.
You could, of course, use ceps instead as they are from the same family. The walnuts give the dish a slight bitterness and a crunchy texture. The sauce is finished with a little walnut oil to complement the addition of the walnuts.

Serves 4

for the lamb jus
100g Madeira
120g red wine
20g dried ceps (porcini)
1kg lamb stock (see page 20)
30g walnut oil
30g unsalted butter

for the cinderford lamb
50g olive oil
4 boned chumps of lamb, 225–250g each
30g unsalted butter

for the bay boletus cream
30g olive oil
350g bay boletus mushrooms (or ceps), sliced
125g double cream
20g walnut oil
30g unsalted butter

for the sautéed ceps
25g duck fat
8 small fresh ceps, cut in half

for the raw ceps
2 large fresh ceps with no blemishes
20g walnut oil

for the baby leeks
30g unsalted butter
30g water
8 baby leeks

16 walnut halves, to serve

lamb jus
In a medium saucepan, reduce the Madeira until it has almost all evaporated, then add the red wine and dried ceps and reduce by two-thirds. Add the lamb stock and bring to the boil. Cook for about 20 minutes to reduce to 250g. Whisk in the walnut oil and butter, then strain through a fine sieve and check the seasoning. Keep warm.

cinderford lamb
Heat the olive oil in a cast-iron or other heavy ovenproof frying pan. Season the lamb, then brown on the fatty side until golden. Flip over, add the butter and cook on the other side for 1 minute. Place back on the skin side, then transfer to an oven preheated to 220°C/Gas Mark 7 and cook for 10–12 minutes. Remove the meat from the pan and season again, then leave to rest in a warm place for 4–8 minutes.

bay boletus cream
Heat the olive oil in a large, heavy-based pan. Add the mushrooms and sauté until a light golden colour. Add the cream, bring to the boil and cook for 2 minutes. Pour into a blender and blend until smooth. With the machine running, slowly drizzle in the walnut oil and add the butter, bit by bit. Pass through a fine sieve and season. Keep warm.

sautéed ceps
Heat the duck fat in a frying pan and, when hot, add the ceps. Cook until golden, tossing occasionally, then season, drain and keep warm.

raw ceps
Slice the ceps finely; you need 14–16 slices. Carefully toss with the walnut oil, without breaking the slices, and season.

baby leeks
Heat a wide-based pan, then add the butter and water to create an emulsion. Add the baby leeks and poach in the emulsion until tender. Season and drain. Keep warm.

serving
Cut the lamb chumps in half. Make 2 slashes of bay boletus cream on each plate, then add the lamb. Dress with the sliced raw ceps, sautéed ceps and baby leeks. Toss the walnuts in the lamb jus and add to the plate, then drizzle the lamb jus over and around.

grouse with elderberry vinegar, compote of brambles, caramelised chicory

The 'Glorious 12th' of August, when the grouse season starts, is much anticipated. The birds are very expensive at the beginning so I prefer to wait a little while for the price to come down and for the birds to develop a little more. Their wonderful gaminess cries out for deep flavours to accompany. Because grouse is associated with heather, I've used that in the birds as well as flavouring the brambles with it. The elderberry vinegar balances the sweetness of the brambles and the caramelised chicory, which has been poached in a red wine and elderberry vinegar syrup. This is very good served with buttered cavolo nero or another brassica such as kale.

Serves 4

for the chicory
2 small heads of chicory
200g red wine
25g Elderberry Vinegar (see page 16)
25g muscovado sugar
25g unsalted butter
25g olive oil
25g maple or birch sap syrup
juice of 1/2 lemon

for the grouse jus
50g olive oil
1 small red onion, finely chopped
1 garlic clove, crushed
30g Elderberry Vinegar (see page 16)
100g port
200g red wine
3 juniper berries, crushed
3 sprigs of heather
500g brown chicken stock (see page 19)
30g unsalted butter

for the grouse
4 small heather twigs
4 grouse
25g olive oil
25g unsalted butter

for the compote of brambles
40g caster sugar
30g Elderberry Vinegar (see page 16)
2 sprigs of heather
75g red wine
100g brambles

chicory
Remove the central core from the chicory. Put the red wine and elderberry vinegar in a pan just large enough to take the chicory and bring to the boil. Add the sugar and a little salt and bring back to the boil. Place the chicory in the boiling liquid and poach for 5 minutes. Drain, reserving the cooking liquid. When cool enough to handle, squeeze the excess moisture out of the chicory and cut in half lengthways. Set aside.

grouse jus
Heat the olive oil in a large saucepan, add the red onion and garlic, and cook for 3 minutes to colour. Deglaze with the elderberry vinegar and cook until evaporated. Add the port and reduce by half. Add the red wine and reduce by half, then add the juniper, heather and brown chicken stock. Bring to the boil and simmer for 45 minutes. Meanwhile, roast the grouse.

grouse
Place a heather twig in the cavity of each bird. Heat the oil and butter in a large frying pan, add the grouse, leg side down, and sear for 15–20 seconds until golden. Turn over and repeat. Finally, turn on to the breasts and colour. Transfer the grouse to a baking tray. Place in an oven preheated to 200°C/Gas Mark 6 and roast for 15–20 minutes, depending on the size of the grouse.

Remove from the baking tray. Take the legs off the birds, chop them up and keep for the jus. Leave the crowns to rest for about 5 minutes under some loose foil. When needed, remove the breasts from the birds; add any juices that have come out to the jus.

finishing the jus
Skim the jus, then strain through a fine sieve into a clean pan. Add the grouse legs and reduce to 250g. Pass through a sieve into another pan. Using a stick blender, blend in the butter. Season and keep warm.

caramelising the chicory
Heat the butter and oil in a frying pan and, when hot, add the chicory, cut side down. Cook until starting to colour. Add the maple syrup and a little of the reserved cooking liquid and cook for about 2 minutes, until golden brown. Turn the chicory over and cook until golden brown on the other side. Remove from the pan, drain and season with lemon juice. Keep warm.

compote of brambles
Combine the sugar and elderberry vinegar in a small saucepan. Cook until a syrup is formed and is almost caramelised. Add the heather and red wine (take care as it may splutter) and bring to the boil, then add the brambles. Immediately remove from the heat so the brambles just warm through. Keep warm. When needed, remove the brambles with a slotted spoon.

serving
Arrange 2 grouse breasts on one side of each plate. Place a chicory half on the other side. Spoon a little of the grouse jus around the plate and then the bramble compote.

guinea fowl with buckwheat cream, roasted buckwheat and dandelions

A good guinea fowl has a lovely flavour – sort of like the best chicken with a little pheasant thrown in. Younger birds are best for roasting and sautéing. Here the guinea fowl is served with buckwheat, which isn't really a wheat – it is related to sorrel and rhubarb. You can get it green or already roasted. For this recipe, I've used the roasted variety, which has a light smoky flavour. For the dandelions, I recommend the white blanched leaves as they are less bitter; if you use wild green ones, select small young leaves.

Serves 6

for the guinea fowl
50g olive oil
3 guinea fowl crowns
50g unsalted butter, softened
3 sprigs of lemon thyme, leaves and stalks separated
2 garlic cloves, crushed

for the roasted buckwheat
25g unsalted butter
25g sunflower oil
1 large shallot, finely diced
1 garlic clove, finely chopped
150g roasted buckwheat
150g brown chicken stock (see page 19)
50g trompette noire mushrooms, chopped
50g chopped parsley

for the buckwheat cream
30g olive oil
45g roasted buckwheat
50g chopped white of leek
50g Madeira
500g brown chicken stock (see page 19)
100g double cream
25g hazelnut oil

for the trompette noire mushrooms
100g trompette noire mushrooms, washed and dried
25g duck fat

for the dandelions
75g smoked bacon lardons (fatty preferably)
200g blanched dandelion leaves, trimmed, washed and dried

guinea fowl

Heat the olive oil in a heavy baking tray just large enough to hold the 3 guinea fowl crowns. Quickly sear the crowns for 1 minute on each side, then turn them breast up. Cover with the butter, season and sprinkle with the lemon thyme leaves. Place the thyme stalks in the tray with the garlic. Transfer to an oven preheated to 190°C/Gas Mark 5 and cook for 20–25 minutes; baste the birds with the pan juices after 10 minutes. The breast meat should still be slightly pink; do not overcook. Transfer to another tray and leave in a warm place to rest under some foil.

When needed, add any juices that have escaped to the buckwheat cream. Carefully remove the breasts and season the flesh side.

roasted buckwheat

Heat the butter and oil in a heavy-based saucepan. Add the shallot and garlic and sweat without colouring until translucent. Stir in the buckwheat and cook for 1 minute. Add the stock and bring to the boil, then simmer until the liquid had been absorbed and the buckwheat is tender but still with a tiny bit of bite. Add the mushrooms and parsley, and season. Keep warm.

buckwheat cream

Heat the olive oil in a heavy-based saucepan, add the buckwheat and leek, and cook until golden brown, stirring constantly to prevent catching. Add the Madeira and reduce for about 3 minutes, until it has disappeared. Add the brown chicken stock and reduce slowly by two-thirds. Strain the stock through a sieve set over a clean pan; discard the barley. Set the pan on the heat, bring the stock to the boil and add the cream. Reduce to the consistency of single cream. Blitzing with a stick blender, slowly drizzle in the hazelnut oil, emulsifying it into the sauce. Season and keep warm.

trompette noire mushrooms

Trim the ends off the mushrooms. Heat the duck fat in a large frying pan, add the mushrooms and cook quickly, tossing them in the pan, until golden. Season and drain. Keep warm.

dandelions

Heat a large frying pan, add the bacon and cook slowly to render the fat and become crisp. Add the dandelion leaves and toss for 1 minute, until wilted. Season and keep warm.

serving

Place a little mound of roasted buckwheat on the left side of each plate. Set a guinea fowl breast to the right, then arrange the mushrooms and dandelions along the buckwheat. Drizzle the buckwheat cream around.

rib eye of dexter beef, smoked bone marrow, hereford snails, watercress purée

Sometimes there is a group of ingredients that just sings together, and this is one such case. It is quite a classical combination and, as the saying goes: If it ain't broke, don't fix it! Dexter beef is ideal for cooking like this because it is a somewhat smaller breed and the rib eyes are the perfect size for 2 as a main dish (or for 4 as a course on a tasting menu, which is how we serve it). Ox-eye daisy leaves, with their wonderful earthy beetroot taste, finish the dish, providing a little texture. Watercress or land cress are alternatives.

Serves 2

for the smoked bone marrow
3 marrow bones

for the hereford snails
50g unsalted butter
1/2 onion, chopped
1 garlic clove, chopped
12 prepared snails
5g dried burdock root
1 bay leaf
100g red wine
200g brown chicken stock (see page 19)
30g chopped watercress

for the watercress purée
300g watercress leaves
25g double cream
25g unsalted butter

for the rib eye of beef
1 rib eye of beef (preferably Dexter),
  trimmed to the 'eye' of meat 5cm thick
10 black peppercorns, cracked
a good pinch thyme leaves
Maldon salt
50g duck fat
25g unsalted butter

for the beef jus
25g olive oil
3 shallots, finely chopped
1 garlic clove, finely chopped
2 sprigs of thyme
100g port
200g red wine
600g brown beef stock (see page 20)
50g unsalted butter

for the liquid potato
500g peeled Desiree potatoes
100g milk
200g double cream
50g unsalted butter

a good handful of ox-eye daisy leaves, to
  serve

smoked bone marrow

Place the bones on an oven tray and heat through in an oven preheated to 220°C/Gas Mark 7 for 3–5 minutes, to loosen the marrow. Remove the marrow from the bones (you should be able to do this by carefully pushing the marrow out with your finger) and place in a bowl of iced water to cool. You need 3 pieces of bone marrow, each about 8cm long.

Soak the bone marrow in cold salted water for 4 hours to remove the blood. Drain in a colander and cut into 10mm slices. Spread out on a small tray.

hereford snails

Melt the butter in a medium saucepan, add the onion and garlic, and cook without colouring for 3–4 minutes, until soft and translucent. Add the snails, burdock root and bay leaf and cook for a further 5 minutes without colouring. Add the red wine and reduce slowly by half. Finally, add the brown chicken stock and bring to the boil, then simmer for 1–1 1/2 hours, until the snails are tender. Drain the snails and set aside.

watercress purée

Set a large pan of salted water on a high heat and bring to the boil. Add the watercress leaves and stir, then immediately drain and refresh. Squeeze all the moisture from the watercress and place in a blender. Put the cream and butter in a small saucepan and bring to the boil. Pour on to the watercress and blend until smooth. Season. Leave to cool.

rib eye of beef

Season the beef with the cracked peppercorns, thyme leaves and a little Maldon salt. Heat the duck fat in a large

frying pan. When hot, place the beef in the pan and sear for about 6 minutes, until golden on all sides. Add the butter, lower the heat and continue cooking for 15–20 minutes, turning the beef over and basting every 5 minutes. If the rib eye is particularly thick, you may need to cook it a little longer. Remove from the pan and leave to rest in a warm place for 10–15 minutes. Add any juices that escape to the beef jus.

beef jus

Heat the olive oil in a saucepan and, when hot, add the shallots and cook until golden. Add the garlic and thyme followed by the port and reduce to a syrup. Add the red wine and reduce by half, then add the beef stock. Cook for 20–25 minutes. Pass through a fine chinois into a clean pan. Whisk in the butter and season. Set aside.

smoking the marrow

Bring a smoker up to full smoke and remove from the heat. Place the tray in the smoker and leave for 2–3 minutes, just until the marrow has softened. Remove from the smoker and sprinkle with Maldon salt. Keep warm.

liquid potato

Cut the potatoes into even pieces and place in a saucepan of salted water. Bring to the boil and cook until tender. Drain, keeping 75g of the cooking liquid. Put this liquid in a small saucepan with the milk and cream and bring to the boil. Place the drained potatoes in a blender, add the cream mixture and blend until smooth, adding the butter bit by bit. Season, then keep warm.

serving

Quickly reheat the jus. Add the snails and warm through, then remove from the jus with a slotted spoon and sprinkle with the chopped watercress. Make a swipe of watercress purée across each plate. Cut the rib eye into 2 across the rib and place on the plates. Add the snails and pieces of smoked bone marrow. Dot with the liquid potato and drizzle the beef jus over. Finish with a scattering of ox-eye daisy leaves.

gressingham duck breast, jerusalem artichoke and apple cream, globe artichokes, confit of gizzards

Gressingham duck, a cross between wild duck and Peking duck, is one of my favourite birds. Fantastic flavour and wonderful crisp skin are its hallmarks. Here, I have put it with some of its own wonderful gizzards, for texture and a slight offal flavour, and teamed this with earthy artichokes and some sweet and acid flesh from an apple. Sometimes I serve this with duck hearts and make a glaze with honey and Chinese spices to cover the crisp skin.

Serves 6

for the globe artichokes
50g olive oil, plus extra for frying
1 onion, finely chopped
1 celery stick, finely chopped
1 garlic clove, finely chopped
200g chicken stock (see page 19)
200g water
100g white wine
1/2 lemon
10 coriander seeds, crushed
5 black peppercorns, crushed
1 bay leaf
9 small poivrade or baby globe artichokes
50g unsalted butter

for the duck juices
50g olive oil
250g duck bones
3 shallots, sliced
1 garlic clove, sliced
25g cider vinegar
100g Madeira
500g brown chicken stock (see page 19)
25g unsalted butter

for the gressingham duck breast
6 Gressingham duck breasts, 220g each

for the jerusalem artichoke and apple cream
400g Jerusalem artichokes
lemon juice

50g unsalted butter
100g double cream
200g milk
100g chopped Granny Smith apple flesh

for the confit of duck gizzards
5 pieces of Duck Gizzard Confit (see page 22)
30g duck fat

for the choy sum
50g unsalted butter
30g water
12 choy sum stems

1 Granny Smith apple, peeled, cored and cut into fine batons, to serve

globe artichokes
Heat the 50g olive oil in a large saucepan, add the onion, celery and garlic, and cook without colouring for 4 minutes. Add all the other ingredients, except the artichokes and butter, and bring to the boil. Lower the heat to a simmer and cook for 20 minutes.

Meanwhile, remove the small bottom leaves from each artichoke, then remove the large leaves. Snap off the bottom of the stem, leaving a stem about 2–3cm long. Peel this stem. Continue removing outer leaves until you are left with the nice tender inner leaves. Cut off the pointed top of the artichoke. Add the artichokes to the simmering stock and cook for 5–10 minutes, until tender. Remove the pan from the heat and leave the artichokes in the stock to cool down until needed.

duck juices
Heat the olive oil in a large saucepan, add the duck bones and brown all over. Add the shallots and garlic and cook until golden, then deglaze with the vinegar and cook until it has evaporated. Add the

Madeira and reduce by half. Add the brown chicken stock and bring to the boil. Skim, then reduce the heat to a simmer and cook for 30–40 minutes, whisking in the butter towards the end. Strain the juices through a fine chinois into a clean pan. Season and set to one side.

gressingham duck breast
Trim the duck breasts, removing any silver skin and sinew from under the breast. Score the skin across the width of the breasts; don't cut too deep, just into the skin. This will help release the fat during cooking. Heat a couple of non-stick frying pans (putting all the duck breasts in one pan would lower the heat too much). When hot, put the duck breasts, skin side down, in the pans. Cook gently so the fat is rendered, keeping an eye on the breasts to be sure that they are not burning. When the skin is golden, turn the breasts over and cook for 2 minutes, then turn back over on to the skin side. Continue cooking for about 10 minutes, spooning some of the juices and fat over the breasts. Remove from the pan and season. Leave to rest in a warm place until needed. Any juices that escape during resting can be added to the duck juices through a sieve.

jerusalem artichoke and apple cream
Peel the artichokes and slice finely, dropping them into a bowl of water mixed with some lemon juice as you go, to prevent discoloration. Drain. Heat half of the butter in a saucepan and cook the artichokes without colouring for 3–4 minutes. Pour in the cream and milk, then add the apple flesh and cook for a further 20–25 minutes on a simmer. The artichokes should be very tender. Transfer to a blender and blend to a fine, smooth purée, adding the remaining butter towards the end. Season and keep warm.

confit of duck gizzards

Slice the gizzards finely. Heat a large frying pan and, when hot, add the duck fat. Sauté the sliced gizzards quickly, then add 3 tablespoons of the duck juices and toss quickly until the gizzards are glazed. Season and keep warm.

finishing the globe artichokes

Drain the artichokes and cut them lengthways in half. Heat the butter with a little olive oil in a frying pan and cook the artichokes until a light golden brown all over. Drain and season. Keep warm.

choy sum

Place the butter and water in a medium sauté pan and heat until the water boils and forms an emulsion. Split the choy sum lengthways and add to the emulsion. Cook quickly until tender. Season and drain. Keep warm.

serving

Quickly reheat the duck juices. Cut the duck breasts in half and place on the left side of each plate. Dress blobs of artichoke and apple cream to the right. Arrange the choy sum, gizzards and Jerusalem and globe artichokes on the plates. Scatter on the apple batons and, finally, drizzle over the duck juices. (This could be served as a mini course in a tasting menu for 12 people, as shown in the photograph.)

brisket of hereford beef, onion and salted orange purée, scorched spring onions

Brisket, which comes from just below the shoulder, is a cut that lends itself to long, slow braising. Here, it is crisped up after braising and served with a roasted orange purée that has salted orange running through it. This could be replaced with salted lemon or just unsalted orange. The spring onions to use are the larger, thicker variety, so they can be scorched or charred, which gives them a wonderful smoked taste. Leeks or even onion petals could replace the spring onions. This is great served with a quenelle of creamed potatoes that have a little anchoiade through them.

Serves 8

for the brisket of beef
1 brisket of beef joint, about 2kg
50g beef dripping
80g unsalted butter
2 onions, chopped
2 celery sticks, chopped
1 carrot, chopped
3 garlic cloves, chopped
300g red wine
1 pig's trotter, split
2 sprigs of thyme
2 pieces of dried orange peel
1 bay leaf
2kg brown beef stock (see page 20)
30g olive oil

for the onion and salted orange purée
4 large onions
30g olive oil
2 sprigs of thyme
soft peel of 1 Salted Orange (see page 14),
  finely diced
50g unsalted butter

for the scorched spring onions
40 thick spring onions (sometimes called
  salad onions)
30g olive oil

brisket of beef
Trim any fat from the brisket. Heat the dripping in a large roasting tray or heavy pan and, when hot, add 50g of the butter and then the brisket. Cook for about 5 minutes, until golden brown all over. Remove from the tray and place in a casserole.

Add the chopped vegetables and garlic to the roasting tray and cook until golden. Deglaze with the red wine and scrape up sediment from the bottom of the tray. Add the rest of the ingredients, except the olive oil, then pour into the casserole. Put a lid on the casserole and place in an oven preheated to 140°C/Gas Mark 1. Braise for 4–4^1/$_2$ hours, until the meat is very tender when pierced with a knife.

Carefully remove the brisket from the stock and place on a tray lined with cling film. Cover with more cling film and place another tray on top. Set a couple of heavy weights on this to press the brisket, then leave in the fridge overnight. Strain the stock and reduce to 400g, then cool and keep until needed.

The next day, trim the brisket to give a neat rectangle (the trimmings can be frozen and used for another occasion). Cut the trimmed brisket into 8 good pieces.

onion and salted orange purée
Place the unpeeled onions on a large sheet of foil, drizzle over the olive oil and add the thyme. Gather the foil up to make a sealed packet. Place on a baking tray and bake in an oven preheated to 180°C/Gas Mark 4 for 1–1^1/$_2$ hours, until very tender.

Remove from the oven and leave to cool a little. While still warm, remove the skins from the onions. Place the onion flesh in a blender, add the salted orange peel and blend until smooth, adding the butter bit by bit. If needed, pass through a sieve. Season and keep warm.

scorched spring onions
Trim the spring onions and toss in the olive oil. Season. Heat a large cast-iron frying pan and, when hot, add the spring onions. Toss until they have wilted and become scorched with patches of dark brown bordering on black. Taste and season again. Keep warm.

finishing the brisket and sauce
Heat a large cast-iron frying pan and add the olive oil. When very hot, place the brisket in the pan and turn the heat down to moderate. Cook until crisp, then turn over and cook for a further 3–4 minutes, until the brisket is hot. Meanwhile, reheat the sauce, then use a stick blender to blend in the remaining 30g butter.

serving
Make a pool of onion purée on each plate, then set a piece of beef on top. Place the scorched spring onions to one side and drizzle over the sauce.

suckling pig with bilberries, bulrushes, wild marjoram flowers

There is just something so scrummy about suckling pig – its lovely tender flesh that is ever so slightly gelatinous and its beautiful crisp skin. Sweet and sour bilberries are just perfect with it. Bulrushes are quite a new thing to me (I was given some by a forager friend). They need a bit of prep work, stripping them down, but when cooked they have a pepperiness that is quite unique. The root can be used as well, providing a starchy sweetness to dishes. Wild marjoram completes this dish, giving it a wonderful fragrance that complements the suckling pig and Jerusalem artichoke.

Serves 12

for the shoulders
2 suckling pig shoulders, boned
2 strips of orange peel
3 garlic cloves, peeled
leaves from 4 sprigs of wild marjoram
50g sel gris (grey sea salt)
1kg duck fat
50g unsalted butter

for the loin
1 loin of suckling pig from the neck to the rear, boned (bones kept for the pork juices)
100g Maldon salt
leaves from a bunch of flat-leaf parsley
leaves from 4 sprigs of wild marjoram, chopped
2 garlic cloves, crushed
50g olive oil
50g unsalted butter

for the bilberry compote
75g light soft brown sugar
30g wine vinegar
100g port
300g bilberries

for the bulrushes
4 bulrushes
50g unsalted butter
40g water

for the pork juices
bones from the suckling pig (see above)
2 shallots, finely sliced
1 garlic clove, finely sliced
100g Madeira
200g white wine
a sprig of wild marjoram
1kg brown chicken stock (see page 19)
30g unsalted butter

for the Jerusalem artichoke cream
500g Jerusalem artichokes
lemon juice
50g unsalted butter
100g double cream
200g milk

for the roasted Jerusalem artichokes
24 small to medium, round Jerusalem artichokes, scrubbed
25g unsalted butter

wild marjoram flowers, to garnish

shoulders
Make sure the shoulders are free from hair and stubble. Chop the orange peel with the garlic and wild marjoram and combine with the salt. Rub this mixture into the shoulders, then cover and leave in the fridge for 24 hours.

Remove the salt and herbs by rubbing the shoulders with kitchen paper or quickly rinsing under cold water and drying. Melt the duck fat in a heavy, deep roasting tray or a flameproof casserole, just large enough to hold the shoulders snugly, over a low heat. Add the shoulders, which should be completely submerged in duck fat. Place in an oven preheated to 140°C/Gas Mark 1 and simmer gently for 3–4 hours, until

tender. To test, prick with a fork: the juices should be clear and there should be absolutely no resistance.

Carefully remove the shoulders from the duck fat (reserve the fat) and place on a tray lined with cling film. Cover with more cling film and place another tray on top. Set a couple of heavy weights on this to press the shoulders. Leave in the fridge overnight. The next day, trim each shoulder to give 2 neat rectangles, then cut each into 6 even pieces. Keep until needed. (This is best done the day before serving.)

loin
Place the boned loin, skin side down, on a tray. Sprinkle with the salt, then massage it into the meat for 2–3 minutes. Cover and leave in the fridge for 2–3 hours.

Rinse off the salt and dry the loin thoroughly. Score the skin every 4–6mm (I use a Stanley knife or scalpel for this as they are both very sharp). Place the loin, skin side down, on the work surface and spread the parsley leaves over, then sprinkle with the marjoram leaves and garlic. Roll up tightly in a cylinder with the skin on the outside and tie with string at 2cm intervals. Set aside in a cool place.

bilberry compote
Heat the sugar and vinegar in a saucepan until a blond caramel is formed. Add the port, being careful as it will splutter. Cook for 2 minutes. Add the bilberries, bring to the boil and cook for a further 3 minutes. Remove the bilberries with a slotted spoon and put to one side. Reduce the liquid to a syrup. Leave to cool, then add the bilberries. Taste the compote. If the bilberries are tart, add a touch more sugar; if they are too sweet, add a dash more vinegar or lemon juice. Set aside. When needed, warm through.

(continued on page 127)

(continued from page 125)

bulrushes

Remove the base of each bulrush, the outer parts of the stems and the top. Cut each stem across into 3, then wash in several changes of water as the bulrushes can be a little slimy. They should now look a little like peeled and cut leeks. Bring a saucepan of salted water to the boil, add the bulrushes and simmer for 4 minutes. Remove and refresh, then drain. Set aside.

pork juices

Heat 50g of the reserved duck fat (from the shoulders) in a large, heavy-based saucepan, add the bones and cook until a deep golden brown. Add the shallots and garlic and cook for 2–3 minutes. Stir in the Madeira, loosening the sediment on the bottom of the pan, and simmer until evaporated, then pour in the white wine and cook until reduced by half. Add the marjoram and brown chicken stock. Simmer gently for 1 hour, skimming off any fat that rises to the surface. Pass through a fine chinois into a clean pan. Reduce to 400g, then whisk in the butter. Keep warm.

roasting the loin

Heat the oil in a roasting tray on the top of the stove, then add the rolled loin, seam side up. Add the butter and colour the skin all around until golden, basting with the fat. Season again, then transfer to an oven preheated to 200°C/Gas Mark 6. Roast for 30–40 minutes, until the skin is crisp and golden and the meat just cooked. Remove from the oven and leave somewhere warm to rest. When needed, remove the string and cut into 12 thick pieces or 24 thin slices.

jerusalem artichoke cream

Peel the artichokes and slice finely, dropping them into some water with lemon juice added as you go, to prevent discoloration. Drain. Heat half of the butter in a saucepan and cook the artichokes without colouring for 3–4 minutes. Pour in the cream and milk and simmer for 20–25 minutes, until very tender. Transfer to a blender and blend to a fine, smooth purée, adding the remaining butter towards the end. Season and keep warm.

roasted jerusalem artichokes

Heat 50g of the reserved duck fat (from the shoulders) in a roasting tray on top of the stove and, when hot, add the Jerusalem artichokes. Turn in the hot duck fat and leave to cook for 1 minute, then turn again. Place in an oven preheated to 180°C/Gas Mark 4 and roast for 5 minutes, then turn and add the butter. Turn again. Roast for a further 10 minutes, until golden and tender (cooking time depends on the size of your artichokes; they are done when a knife pierces them easily). Remove from the tray and drain. Keep warm.

finishing the shoulders

Heat a large cast-iron pan and add a little of the reserved duck fat. When very hot, place half of the pork shoulder pieces, skin side down, in the pan and turn the heat down to moderate. Cook until the skin is crisp, then turn over, add half of the butter and cook for a further 2–3 minutes, until the meat is hot. Place on a tray and keep warm. Repeat with the other pieces of shoulder, first wiping out the pan before adding more duck fat and the rest of the butter. Keep warm.

finishing the bulrushes

Place the butter and water in a sauteuse and bring to the boil, then add the bulrushes and cook in this emulsion for 2–3 minutes (or perhaps a little longer if they are thick: they should give no resistance when pierced with the point of a knife). Season, drain and keep warm.

serving

Place a thick piece of loin (or 2 slices) and a piece of shoulder on each plate. Arrange 2 pieces of bulrush side by side, then add 2 spoons of artichoke cream. Add the roasted artichokes. Place some bilberries and a little of their juices around the plate, sprinkle with marjoram flowers and, finally, drizzle over the pork juices.

fillet of hogget, sweetbreads, cockles and samphire

I am lucky to be living here in the Cotswolds where there is wonderful lamb and, because of that, some of the best hogget (hogget is lamb that is over one year of age but not as old as mutton, which is 2 years old). The flavour of hogget is more defined than lamb and the flesh is slightly firmer. I have paired it here with cockles for their salty and sweet flavour, and a chervil tuber purée, for its honeyed taste. The briny salt of samphire completes the dish. Parsnip or parsley root could replace the chervil tuber, and winkles the cockles, although they wouldn't add the sweetness. The dish is finished with some fat hen stalks.

Serves 6

for the cockles
750g–1kg fresh cockles in shell
50g olive oil
2 large shallots, chopped
4 parsley stalks
a sprig of thyme
300g white wine
100g water

for the hogget
1 fillet from a large saddle of hogget
50g olive oil
20g unsalted butter

for the sweetbreads
6 hogget sweetbreads
50g olive oil
15g unsalted butter

for the hogget juices
50g olive oil
100g chopped red onions
50g button mushrooms, finely sliced
1 garlic clove, sliced
50g Madeira
200g white wine
800g hogget stock (follow the lamb stock recipe on page 20 but use hogget bones)
a sprig of thyme
50g unsalted butter

for the chervil tuber purée
225g chervil tubers, peeled and sliced
150g milk
125g double cream
75g unsalted butter

for the button onions
30 small button onions, peeled
50g unsalted butter

for the fat hen stalks
30g unsalted butter
100g water
12 fat hen stalks

for the samphire
50g unsalted butter
50g water
200g samphire

cockles
Wash the cockles under cold running water to remove any grit. Heat a large saucepan, add the olive oil, shallots, parsley and thyme, and cook for 30 seconds. Add the cockles, then pour in the white wine and water and immediately put the lid on. Shaking the pan from side to side, cook for 1 minute. The cockles should now have opened. Remove from the stock as quickly as possible and leave to cool a little. Pass the stock through a sieve lined with damp muslin, to catch any grit. Put to one side. Remove the cockles from their shells and rinse a few times to remove any grit, then add them to the stock and set aside in a cool place. When needed, drain the cockles, keeping 125g of the stock to add to the hogget juices.

hogget
Trim any bits of fat from the hogget fillet as well as the long sinew running down the side (keep the trimmings for the hogget juices). Season the hogget. Heat the oil in a cast-iron frying pan, add the butter and, when sizzling, add the hogget. Sear quickly to colour, then flip over on to the skin side

and cook quickly until golden. Transfer to an oven preheated to 200°C/Gas Mark 6 and cook for 5–7 minutes, until rare to medium rare. Remove from the pan and leave to rest in a warm place for 5 minutes. When needed, cut into 6 even pieces.

sweetbreads
Place the sweetbreads in a bowl of cold salted water to cover and leave to soak for 2 hours. This will help pull the blood out of them. Drain and dry well with a cloth. Heat the oil in a large, heavy-based frying pan. Season the sweetbreads and add to the pan. Cook for 4–5 minutes, turning often, until golden. Add the butter and turn a few times while the butter foams. Season again, then drain and keep warm.

hogget juices
Heat the oil in a saucepan and, when hot, add the hogget trimmings, red onions, mushrooms and garlic. Cook until golden. Add the Madeira and reduce to a glaze, then add the white wine and reduce to a glaze. Add the hogget stock and thyme and cook at a simmer for 30 minutes. Pass through a fine sieve into a clean saucepan. Reduce to 200g. Set aside.

When needed, add the reserved 125g cockle stock and reduce by half, then whisk in the butter and bring back to the boil. Check the seasoning and keep warm.

chervil tuber purée
Place the chervil tubers in a saucepan with the milk and cream. Bring to the boil, then reduce the heat to a low simmer and cook until tender. Transfer to a blender and blend to a smooth, velvety purée, adding the butter towards the end. Season and keep warm.

button onions
Place the onions in a medium frying pan and half cover them with water. Add the butter. Bring up to the boil, then reduce to

a simmer. As you cook the onions, the water will reduce and evaporate, leaving the butter to colour the onions. When they are tender, season and keep warm.

fat hen stalks

Place the butter and water in a wide saucepan. Bring to the boil, then add the fat hen stalks and cook until wilted. Drain and season. Keep warm.

samphire

Place the butter and water in a wide saucepan. Bring to the boil, then add the samphire and cook for 2 minutes, until just tender. Drain and season. Keep warm.

serving

Warm the cockles in the hogget juices until just hot – do not boil or they will toughen. Place a little of the chervil tuber purée on each plate. Set a piece of hogget on the purée, then place a sweetbread next to it. Dress samphire and fat hen stalks over the meat, then scatter button onions and drained cockles around the plate. Finally, spoon hogget juices over and around.

lamb with chickpea purée, tahini emulsion, sesame powder

I've used chump of lamb for this recipe, which equates to beef rump. When hung well the chump is tender, with a lovely flavour, and has a good ratio of fat to lean. With the lamb I've put chickpeas, cooked with lemon and a little chilli to give a slight zing, as well as a sesame emulsion and powder to add a subtle nutty flavour. This makes for a fine summer dish for any bright evening.

Serves 6

for the sesame powder
50g sesame seeds, toasted until golden brown
2g salt

for the lamb juices
100g olive oil
500g lamb bones from the chumps (see below), chopped into small pieces
1 onion, chopped
1 celery stick, chopped
1 leek, chopped
2 garlic cloves, crushed
a sprig of thyme
50g Madeira
4 tomatoes, skinned, deseeded and chopped
200g white wine
500g lamb stock (see page 20)
500g water

for the lamb
100g olive oil
6 boned chumps of lamb, 225–250g each (keep the bones for the lamb juices)
30g unsalted butter
3 garlic cloves, crushed lightly in their skins
a sprig of thyme

for the roasted red peppers
4 small red peppers
1 garlic clove, sliced
50g olive oil

for the chickpea purée
10g cumin seeds
1/2 dried chilli
150g olive oil
3 garlic cloves, finely chopped
2 strips of lemon zest
300g soaked and cooked chickpeas
75g water
5g tahini
40g Greek yoghurt
juice of 1 lemon
20g chopped coriander

for the tahini emulsion
350g sesame seeds
2g salt
60g groundnut oil
40g olive oil
10g lemon juice
15g water
4g sumac

for the wild rocket
25g olive oil
125g wild rocket
juice of 1/4 lemon

sesame powder
Place the sesame seeds and salt in a spice mill and pulse until a fine powder is obtained. Keep in a lidded container until needed.

lamb juices
Heat the olive oil in a large saucepan. When hot, add the lamb bones and cook until golden brown. Remove the bones from the pan, and discard the fat that has come out of the bones. Return the pan to the heat and add the onion, celery, leek, garlic and thyme. Cook until coloured. Deglaze with the Madeira, then add the tomatoes and cook until the Madeira has disappeared. Return the bones to the pan. Add the white wine and reduce by half. Add the stock and water and bring to the boil, then skim well and simmer gently for 1½ hours. Pass the stock through a fine sieve or muslin into a container. Leave to cool, then keep in the fridge.

When needed, remove any fat that has risen to the surface. Place in a saucepan and reduce to 300g. Season and keep warm.

lamb
Heat the oil in a large cast-iron frying pan, add the lamb chumps, skin side down, and colour quickly. Turn and sear the other side. Season, then add the butter, garlic and thyme. Turn the lamb over on to the skin side again. Transfer to an oven preheated to 200°C/Gas Mark 6 and cook for 10–15 minutes; the meat should be pink, sort of medium rare. Remove from the oven and leave to rest in a warm place for 10–15 minutes. When needed, season again and slice each chump into 3.

roasted red peppers
Remove the stalks from the peppers and carefully remove the seeds. Place a few slices of garlic and a little sesame powder into each pepper. Drizzle the olive oil all over and season, then place in a small baking tray. Roast in an oven preheated to 180°C/Gas Mark 4 for 20 minutes, until well cooked. Remove from the oven, cut each pepper into thirds and keep warm. Season.

chickpea purée
Set a small frying pan on the heat and dry roast the cumin seeds and chilli until fragrant. Tip into a spice grinder and grind to a powder. Put to one side. Heat a little of the olive oil in a medium saucepan, add the garlic and cook for 2 minutes without colouring. Add the cumin seeds, chilli and lemon zest and cook for 1 minute. Add the chickpeas and water and cook until the chickpeas are hot. Pour into a blender and turn on the machine, then drizzle in the

remaining olive oil in a steady stream. Add the tahini and yoghurt and blend until smooth, then squeeze in the lemon juice and season. Keep warm in a covered saucepan until needed. If the purée is a bit stiff, add a little more water and check the seasoning. Add the chopped coriander just before serving.

tahini emulsion
Scatter the sesame seeds over a baking tray and place in an oven preheated to 180°C/Gas Mark 4. Lightly toast for 5 minutes without colouring. Place in a food processor and process for 2 minutes. Add the salt. With the motor running, drizzle in the groundnut oil to obtain a smooth paste.

Place 30g of this tahini in a blender (the rest can be kept in a jar in the fridge for up to a month). With the motor running, slowly drizzle in the olive oil, then the lemon juice and water, and finally the sumac. Remove from the blender and season. The consistency should be like that of thick double cream.

wilted rocket
Heat the olive oil in a large frying pan. Add the rocket, then remove from the heat, stirring. Squeeze the lemon juice over and season. Place on kitchen paper to drain. Keep warm.

serving
Spoon a little chickpea purée on the left side of each plate and place the lamb on top. Divide the roasted peppers among the plates, to the right, together with the wilted rocket and dress with the tahini emulsion. Spoon the sauce over the lamb and drizzle a little around the plate. Finish with a sprinkling of sesame powder.

desserts

vanilla rice pudding, compote of plums, toasted almond foam

This is a great little dish created by Sue Ellis, the newest member of my brigade and a very talented chef with a good palate. When asked to make a pre-dessert based around some Victoria plums that one of our customers had brought in, this was Sue's response. It is a really comforting dish, with just the right balance of sweetness and acidity. The toasted almond foam is perfect with the plums. The recipe can be altered with different flavourings in so many ways – perhaps an Earl Grey or elderflower rice pudding with a rhubarb or gooseberry compote and an orange foam. It is just up to your imagination.

Serves 12 as a pre-dessert or 6 as a dessert

for the rice pudding
65g carnaroli rice
250g double cream
300g milk
2 vanilla pods, split lengthways
2 egg yolks
50g caster sugar

for the plum compote
30g sugar
20g water
10g unsalted butter
500g Victoria plums, quartered and stoned
1/2 vanilla pod, split lengthways

for the toasted almond foam
240g milk
125g double cream
10g caster sugar
55g flaked almonds
5g bronze gelatine leaves

25g toasted flaked almonds, crushed, to finish

rice pudding
Place the rice, cream and milk in a saucepan. Scrape the vanilla seeds from the pods and add to the pan with the empty pods. Bring to the boil, stirring all the time, then reduce the heat to a simmer and cook for 25–30 minutes, until the rice is tender and the mixture is soft and creamy. Remove from the heat and leave to cool for 2–3 minutes.

Whisk the egg yolks and sugar together, then quickly mix into the rice. Place back on a medium heat and stir for 2–3 minutes without letting the mixture boil. Remove from the heat and take out the vanilla pods (keep them for flavouring some sugar, if you like). Leave the rice mixture to cool a little, then spoon it into the serving glasses, carefully knocking them on a cloth-lined surface to level the top. Leave to cool completely, then cover and keep in the fridge to await the compote.

plum compote
Dissolve the sugar in the water in a medium saucepan and caramelise until golden. Add the butter, plums and vanilla pod and cook until soft and unctuous and the juices have been reduced. Remove from the pan and leave to cool. Once cold, discard the vanilla pod, then divide the compote among the glasses, covering the rice pudding. Cover and return to the fridge.

toasted almond foam
Combine the milk, cream and sugar in a saucepan and leave to heat through slowly. Meanwhile, toast the almonds under a preheated grill until a deep golden brown. Add them to the milk and cream mixture and bring to the boil, then remove from the heat. Leave to infuse for 2–3 hours.

Bring back to the boil, then remove from the heat. Soak the gelatine in a little cold water for about 5 minutes, until soft and pliable. Squeeze out the excess water, then add the softened gelatine to the milk mixture and stir until completely melted. Pass through a fine chinois, pushing down to get as much of the liquid out as possible. Leave to cool. Once cold, place in a 500ml iSi foam gun and chill in the fridge for 6–8 hours.

serving
Remove the rice pudding from the fridge about 30 minutes before needed. Give the iSi gun a good shake, then charge with 1–2 cartridges and shake again. Squirt some of the toasted almond foam on top of the plum compote and sprinkle with the crushed toasted almonds.

marinated raspberries, raspberry yoghurt, toasted muesli

This is a perfect pre-dessert in the summer when raspberries are at their best. I have marinated them with vanilla and dessert wine and, just for freshness, have added some shredded mint. Other flavourings, like orange blossom water or rosewater, could be used. The berries are served with a slightly acidic raspberry yoghurt, to balance their sweetness, and finished with a toasted nut muesli to give a little texture.

Serves 8 as a pre-dessert
or 4 as a dessert

for the toasted muesli
20g hazelnuts, roughly chopped
20g walnuts, roughly chopped
20g almonds, roughly chopped
20g peeled pistachios, roughly chopped
100g jumbo oats
15g pumpkin seeds
10g sunflower seeds
50g sunflower oil
60g maple syrup
25g light muscovado sugar

for the marinated raspberries
50g Monbazillac or another sweet wine
40g caster sugar
juice of 1/2 lemon
300g raspberries
10 mint leaves, finely shredded
seeds from 1 vanilla pod

for the raspberry yoghurt
250g thick Greek yoghurt
125g ripe raspberries
50g caster sugar
juice of 1/4 lemon

toasted muesli
Mix everything together well in a bowl, then spread out thinly on a large baking sheet. Bake in an oven preheated to 180°C/Gas Mark 4 for 15–20 minutes, stirring every 5 minutes. When the mixture is golden all over, remove from the oven and leave to cool. Store in an airtight container until required.

marinated raspberries
Place the Monbazillac in a small saucepan with the caster sugar and just warm through to dissolve the sugar. Remove from the heat and leave to cool. Once cold, add the lemon juice and stir. Put the raspberries in a bowl and pour the syrup over. Add the chopped mint and vanilla seeds and gently turn the raspberries around in the syrup. Leave to marinate in the syrup for 1 hour.

raspberry yoghurt
Put the Greek yogurt in a muslin bag and hang overnight to drain off any excess water.

Purée the raspberries in a blender, then pass through a fine chinois. Fold the raspberry purée through the yoghurt, then add the sugar (you may not need all of it: the sweetness of the raspberries will decide that). Add the lemon juice and mix lightly.

serving
Spoon the raspberries into the serving glasses with just a little of the marinating juices and top with the raspberry yoghurt. Sprinkle with the muesli.

apple crumble and custard

Here's a nice little pre-dessert for the autumn and winter, a play on one of my favourite comfort food desserts. The custard in this case is made into a thick cream flavoured with vanilla, almost brûlée-esque. The apple is a little purée laced with a dash of white Calvados from a friend in Normandy, and the topping a little crisp baked crumble spiced with cinnamon. The cream could be flavoured with caramel, orange, walnut leaf or chocolate; the purée could be pears, dates or prunes; and the crumble could be ginger or chocolate. A myriad of flavours could be achieved.

Serves 8 as a pre-dessert
or 4 as a dessert

for the custard
100g milk
300g double cream
2 vanilla pods, split lengthways
1 egg
6 egg yolks
60g caster sugar
3.5g bronze gelatine leaves

for the apple purée
200g peeled and cored Bramley apples
200g peeled and cored Golden Delicious apples
juice of 1/2 lemon
10g unsalted butter
35g caster sugar

for the crumble
125g plain flour
2g salt
3g ground cinnamon
50g ground almonds
125g unsalted butter, softened
75g demerara sugar
15g water

icing sugar, for dusting

custard
Place the milk and cream in a medium saucepan. Scrape the vanilla seeds from the pods and add to the pan with the empty pods. Bring to the boil, then remove from the heat and leave to infuse for 1 hour.

Set the pan back on the heat and bring to the boil again. Whisk together the egg, egg yolks and caster sugar in a bowl until pale. Pour the cream mixture on to the eggs, whisking all the time, then pour back into the saucepan. Cook on a low heat, stirring constantly, until thick, being careful not to boil as this will scramble the mixture. Remove from the heat.

Soak the gelatine in a little cold water for about 5 minutes, until soft and pliable. Squeeze out the excess water, then add the softened gelatine to the custard and stir well until completely melted. Strain through a fine sieve into a jug. Pour into serving glasses. Leave to cool completely, then cover and keep in the fridge to await the apple purée.

apple purée
Slice all the apples finely and mix with the lemon juice. Melt the butter in a saucepan, add the caster sugar and sliced apples, and cook on a medium heat, stirring occasionally, until broken down. Tip into a blender and blend until smooth. Taste to see if you need to add a little more sugar or lemon juice; this will be down to the sweetness of the fruit. Leave to cool. When cold, spoon on top of the custard. Cover and return to the fridge.

crumble
Sift the flour, salt and cinnamon together, then add the ground almonds and mix well. Add the butter and work through with a knife, keeping the lumps that form large. Add the demerara sugar and stir, then add the water and use the knife to mix it in. Sprinkle on to a tray and place in the freezer to set for 2–4 hours.

Remove from the freezer, crumble on to a baking tray and bake in an oven preheated to 180°C/Gas Mark 4 for 10–15 minutes, until golden. Remove from the oven and leave to cool. When cold, break up a little, keeping the lumps as large as possible. Store in an airtight container until needed.

serving
Remove the custards from the fridge 30 minutes before needed to get to room temperature. Sprinkle on the crumble and give a light dusting of icing sugar.

yoghurt mousse, lemon geranium jelly, blackcurrant leaf ice cream

My aunt Pat used to make the most wonderful blackcurrant leaf sorbet from the blackcurrant bushes she had in her back garden. Here I've used this idea for an ice cream. It is important that you use the younger blackcurrant leaves as they have the most perfume and flavour. The ice cream is paired with a lemon geranium jelly, and I've used that scented leaf to flavour the blackcurrant compote too, also adding a light yoghurt mousse. The lemon geranium can be replaced with rose geranium for a different flavour.

Serves 6–8

for the yoghurt mousse
50g white chocolate, roughly chopped
5g bronze gelatine leaves
200g plain yoghurt
100g buttermilk
juice of 1/2 lemon
200g whipping cream

for the blackcurrant leaf ice cream
juice of 1 lemon
750g milk
250g double cream
4 large handfuls of young blackcurrant leaves
6 egg yolks
125g caster sugar
40g skimmed milk powder
50g liquid glucose

for the lemon geranium jelly
9g bronze gelatine leaves
200g lemon juice
finely grated zest of 1 lemon
150g water
200g caster sugar
50g lemon geranium leaves (such as Lady or Mabel Grey)

for the blackcurrant compote
50g water
100g caster sugar
juice of 1/2 lemon
30g lemon geranium leaves
400g blackcurrants
2g bronze gelatine leaves

yoghurt mousse
Melt the white chocolate, then set aside. Soak the gelatine in cold water for about 5 minutes, until soft and pliable. Warm the yoghurt with the buttermilk, but do not boil. Heat the lemon juice in another small pan. Squeeze excess water from the gelatine, then add to the lemon juice and stir until melted. Add to the melted chocolate and stir, then add the yoghurt and buttermilk mixture and mix well. Leave to cool. Whip the cream to the ribbon stage, then fold into the yoghurt mixture. Pour into 6–8 moulds of 80–100g capacity. Place in the fridge to set, then leave in the fridge until needed.

blackcurrant leaf ice cream
Put the lemon juice in a medium, heavy-based saucepan and gently bring to the boil, then add the milk, cream and blackcurrant leaves. Bring to the boil, then immediately remove from the heat. Leave to infuse for 3–4 hours.

Bring the infused milk mixture back to the boil. Meanwhile, whisk the egg yolks with the sugar, milk powder and glucose until pale and creamy. Pour half of the milk mixture on to the egg yolk mixture, whisking to incorporate, then pour this back into the saucepan and mix with the remaining milk. Cook on a gentle heat, stirring all the time with a wooden spoon, until the custard reaches 84°C or it thickens enough to coat the back of the spoon. Remove from the heat and immediately strain through a fine sieve into a large bowl, to help stop the cooking. Leave to cool. When cold, churn in an ice cream machine. Transfer to a container and keep in the freezer until needed. Remove to the fridge 20 minutes before serving.

lemon geranium jelly
Soak the gelatine in cold water for about 5 minutes, until soft and pliable. Put the lemon juice and zest, water and caster sugar in a medium saucepan and bring to the boil. Immediately remove from the heat and add the geranium leaves. Pour into a blender and blend until smooth. Squeeze excess water from the gelatine, then add to the syrup and stir until melted. Pass through a fine strainer into a lipped tray to a depth of 1cm. Place in the fridge immediately and leave to set.

blackcurrant compote
Combine the water, sugar, lemon juice and geranium leaves in a medium saucepan and bring to the boil. Remove from the heat and leave to infuse for 30 minutes. Remove and discard the geranium leaves, then add the blackcurrants to the syrup. Heat through just until the blackcurrants release their juices.

Soak the gelatine in cold water for about 5 minutes, until soft and pliable. Meanwhile, drain the blackcurrants in a sieve set over a bowl. Pour the syrup and 100g of the blackcurrants into a blender and blend until smooth. Strain through a fine sieve into a container, pushing as much of the fruit through as you can. While the strained juice is still hot, squeeze the excess water from the gelatine and add it to the juice, stirring to melt. Leave to cool, then add the remaining blackcurrants. Keep in the fridge until needed.

serving
Remove the yoghurt mousse from the moulds and place on the plates. Top each mousse with a few blackcurrants from the compote, then scatter the remaining blackcurrants on the plates with a little of their juices. Place a scoop of ice cream on one side of each plate and, using a teaspoon, add a couple of scoops of lemon geranium jelly.

bergamot parfait, orange jelly, liquorice cream

The flavour of bergamot is extremely sour with a pepperiness, so you may wonder why on earth anyone would use it in a sweet dish. The reason is that its peel has the most wonderful aroma, which you may recognise as it is the fragrance in Earl Grey tea. It is perfect with liquorice, and also goes well with pineapple and sea buckthorn (although I would use half carrot and half sea buckthorn). If you find it hard to get bergamots, you can use mandarins, clementines or tangerines instead.
The whole dessert is tied together with orange jelly and red-veined sorrel. Lemon balm could be substituted for the sorrel.

Serves 12

for the candied bergamots
750g bergamots (or other citrus fruit, see above)
900g water
1.5kg granulated sugar

for the bergamot parfait
2g bronze gelatine leaves
1¹/₂ candied bergamots (see above)
30g water
200g freshly squeezed orange juice
finely grated zest of 1 orange
100g caster sugar
4 egg yolks
140g double cream, whipped to soft peaks

for the orange and bergamot wrap
350g orange juice (from a carton)
³/₄ bergamot, finely chopped
2.4g agar agar
6g bronze gelatine leaves

for the liquorice set cream
3.5g bronze gelatine leaves
4 egg yolks
40g caster sugar
225g double cream
75g milk
5g liquorice stick, crushed

1¹/₂ vanilla pods, split lengthways
grated zest of ¹/₂ orange
grated zest of ¹/₂ lemon
a small pinch of saffron strands

for the orange jelly
14g bronze gelatine leaves
100g orange juice (from a carton)
250g caster sugar
50g water
5g citric acid
grated zest of 2 oranges
400g freshly squeezed orange juice

for the liquorice purée
100g dark muscovado sugar
125g water
20g orange juice
20g liquorice paste
8g black treacle
grated zest of ¹/₄ orange
juice of ¹/₄ lemon
2g agar agar
1g malic acid

for the liquorice tuiles
80g condensed milk
28g plain flour
7g caster sugar
10g milk
7g liquorice paste
1g liquorice powder
2g squid ink

a small punnet of red-veined sorrel, to serve

candied bergamots

Use a pin or the tip of a roasting fork to prick the bergamots all over. Bring a pan of water to the boil and blanch the bergamots for 2 minutes; drain. In a pan large enough to take all the bergamots in one layer, bring the measured water and 750g of the granulated sugar to the boil. Add the bergamots (they should be covered with syrup) and simmer for 5 minutes. Remove from the heat and set aside in a cool place

for 24 hours, making sure the fruit is covered with the syrup.

The next day, lift the bergamots out of the syrup and put them into a bowl. Remove 110g of the syrup and set aside for the parfait and wrap. (This perfumed syrup can be kept in the fridge for a month.)

Add 150g of the remaining granulated sugar to the syrup remaining in the pan and bring to the boil, then pour on to the bergamots. Leave to steep in the fridge for 24 hours. Repeat this operation for another 4 days, draining the syrup from the fruit into a pan and adding the remaining granulated sugar in four separate 150g quantities. Then leave the fruit to steep for a further 48 hours before using. The bergamots can be kept in the syrup, in a sealed container in the fridge, for up to a month.

bergamot parfait

Soak the gelatine in cold water for about 5 minutes, until soft and pliable. Put the candied bergamots, 75g of the reserved bergamot syrup and the water in a saucepan and bring to the boil. Transfer to a blender. Squeeze excess water from the gelatine, then add it to the blender. Blend to a smooth purée, then pass through a fine chinois.

Place the orange juice and zest in a small saucepan. Reduce by roughly half, then add the sugar and reduce further until the syrup reaches a temperature of 121°C. While this is coming up to temperature, put the egg yolks in the bowl of a freestanding electric mixer and whisk until pale and thick. Then, with the machine running on high, slowly drizzle the syrup on to the egg yolks. Carry on whisking until cold. Fold in the warm bergamot purée and leave to cool, then fold in the whipped cream.

(continued on page 140)

(continued from page 139)

Lay a sheet of cling film on the work surface and spoon a quarter of the parfait mixture on to it. Roll into a long 'sausage' shape, about 26 x 10cm, wrapping tightly in the cling film. Make 3 more rolls in the same way. Freeze for 24 hours.

orange and bergamot wrap

Combine the orange juice, 35g of the reserved bergamot syrup, the chopped bergamot and agar agar in a saucepan and set aside to allow the agar agar to swell. Meanwhile, soak the gelatine in cold water for about 5 minutes, until soft and pliable.

Bring the orange mixture up to the boil, stirring until the agar agar has dissolved. Squeeze excess water from the gelatine, then add it to the orange mixture. Transfer to a blender and blend to a smooth purée. Pass through a fine chinois into a jug. Skim any froth from the surface, then pour the mixture on to an acetate-lined baking sheet, about 53 x 32cm. Leave to set in the fridge.

finishing the bergamot parfait

Remove the rolls of parfait from the freezer and trim off the ends. Peel off the cling film. Remove the set orange and bergamot wrap from the fridge. Cut into 4 rectangles, each 26 x 16cm, cutting through the acetate. Place a roll of parfait on top of one rectangle, then wrap like a cannelloni, keeping it in the acetate, so the edges are together along the roll. Place back in the freezer and repeat with the other 'sausages' of parfait. Freeze for 2 hours, then leave in the freezer until needed.

liquorice set cream

Soak the gelatine in cold water for about 5 minutes, until soft and pliable. Whisk together the egg yolks and caster sugar in a bowl just to break them down. Combine the cream, milk, liquorice, vanilla pods, orange and lemon zests and saffron in a saucepan. Bring to the boil, then remove from the heat. Squeeze excess water from the gelatine, then stir into the hot milk mixture until melted. Whisk in the egg yolk

and sugar mixture. Return to the heat and cook, stirring, until slightly thickened, then pass through a fine chinois.

Pour into a baking tray, about 17 x 13 x 4cm, and set this in a larger baking tray with a clean J-cloth on the bottom. Pour enough hot water into the large baking tray to come a third of the way up the sides of the smaller tray. Carefully place in an oven preheated to 96°C (if your oven will not go this low, then cook at the lowest temperature possible) and cook for 20–30 minutes, until the cream has just set in the middle. Remove from the oven and leave in the tray of water to cool. Once cold, remove from the tray of water, cover and keep in the fridge until needed (preferably 24 hours ahead).

orange jelly

Soak the gelatine in cold water for about 5 minutes, until soft and pliable. Put the orange juice from a carton, the sugar, water, citric acid and orange zest in a pan and bring to the boil. Squeeze excess water from the gelatine, then add to the pan and whisk until melted. Add the fresh orange juice. Pass through a chinois into a plastic container, about 20 x 15 x 6cm, then leave to set in the fridge. Keep in the fridge until needed.

liquorice purée

Put all the ingredients, except the malic acid, in a small saucepan and set aside for about 2 minutes to allow the agar agar to swell. Then bring up to the boil and cook for 3–4 minutes on a simmer, stirring to dissolve the agar agar. Remove from the heat and whisk in the malic acid. Cook for a further 2 minutes. Pass through a fine chinois into a container, then place in the fridge. Chill for at least 4 hours, until set. Transfer to a blender and blend until smooth. Place the purée in a squeezy bottle and keep in the fridge until needed.

liquorice tuiles

Put all the ingredients in a bowl and mix together until smooth. Spread in strips, 6 x 2cm, on a baking sheet lined with baking parchment (you need 36 tuiles).

Bake in an oven preheated to 180°C/ Gas Mark 4 for 5–10 minutes, until crisp and dry. Using a palette knife, carefully remove the tuiles from the parchment to a wire rack and leave to cool. Store in an airtight container until needed.

serving

Cut each of the parfait 'cannelloni' into 3; remove the acetate and place a piece on the left side of each plate. Dot liquorice purée on the plate. Using a teaspoon, scoop 2 spoons of liquorice cream on to the plate, then add 3 scoops of orange jelly. Stud 3 liquorice tuiles at different angles into the cream. Drape red-veined sorrel at different angles.

pistachio financier, cherries, meadowsweet ice cream

Cherries are one of my favourite fruits, and when I am in Turkey I eat kilos of them. Perhaps it's the heat and, of course, the cherries there are so juicy and fresh. For this dessert I've put the cherries with pistachios, because it is such a good pairing. The financiers have a good pistachio and nutty butter flavour, although you could use walnuts or hazelnuts instead. The financiers are also served with a meadowsweet ice cream. The lovely creamy flowers of this herb have a wonderful almond flavour and scent. They make a stunning ice cream or brûlée and can also be used when poaching fish or making a gel to go with a game terrine.

Serves 8

for the cherry compote
750g cherries
100g fresh cherry juice
350g red wine
100g caster sugar
5g Kirsch
juice of ¹/₂ lemon

for the meadowsweet ice cream
600g milk
400g double cream
20–35g fresh meadowsweet flowers
8 egg yolks
125g caster sugar
20g skimmed milk powder
30g liquid glucose

for the pistachio financier
240g unsalted butter
75g plain flour
80g ground pistachios
a pinch of salt
180g egg whites
175g icing sugar, plus extra for dusting
25g good-quality honey

cherry compote
Stone the cherries and set aside. Crack 5 of the cherry stones and remove the kernels. Crush the kernels and place in a pan with the remaining ingredients, apart from the cherries. Bring up to the boil, then cook for 3–4 minutes. Add the cherries and cook for 3–4 minutes. Use a slotted spoon to remove the cherries; place them in a bowl and leave to cool. Reduce the cooking juices by half. Cool, then strain on to the cherries. Leave to macerate in a cool place overnight.

meadowsweet ice cream
Pour the milk and cream into a medium saucepan and slowly bring to the boil. Add the meadowsweet flowers, then remove from the heat and leave to infuse for at least 4 hours (the longer they are in there, the more bitter the ice cream will be).

Strain into a clean pan. Set on the stove and slowly bring up to the boil again. Whisk the egg yolks with the caster sugar in a bowl. Add the milk powder and glucose. Pour half of the hot milk mixture on to the egg mixture, whisking, then pour back into the pan and whisk with the remaining milk mixture. Cook on a low heat, stirring constantly with a wooden spoon, until the custard reaches 84°C, or until it thickens enough to coat the back of the spoon. Immediately strain through a fine sieve into a bowl and leave to cool. Pour into an ice cream machine and churn. Transfer to a container and keep in the freezer until needed. Remove to the fridge 10–15 minutes before serving.

pistachio financier
Melt the butter in a medium frying pan and cook until it turns a golden brown. Pass through a sieve into a bowl and leave to cool. Sift the flour into a bowl, add the ground pistachios and salt, and mix well. Mix the egg whites with the icing sugar in another bowl, stirring well, then mix in the brown butter and honey. Add the flour mixture and mix well. Cover and leave in the fridge overnight.

Butter 8 rectangular moulds, each about 10 x 5cm and 3cm deep, and set them on a baking tray. Spoon the financier mixture into the moulds, filling each one about two-thirds full. Bake in an oven preheated to 180°C/Gas Mark 4 for 10 minutes, until golden brown. Remove from the oven and cool for 2 minutes before removing from the moulds. Dust lightly with icing sugar. Keep warm.

serving
Place a warm pistachio financier on each plate with a quenelle of ice cream, some cherries and some of their juices.

caramel-poached pineapple, coconut gel, pineapple and lemon verbena sorbet

I am a real fan of pineapple, both raw and cooked. It carries so many flavours and stands up to other flavours more powerful than its own. Here, it is poached in a caramel butter and served on a spiced bread base, then served with a pineapple and lemon verbena sorbet and a coconut cream gel. Other flavours that work with pineapple, which can be substituted for the lemon verbena, are basil, angelica, lemongrass and lovage. A palm sugar cream could replace the coconut and a molasses cake could replace the spiced bread, maybe flavoured with ginger.

Serves 12

1 loaf Spiced Bread (see page 15)

for the pineapple and lemon verbena sorbet
1kg ripe pineapple
200g caster sugar
juice of 1/2 lemon
30g lemon verbena

for the caramel-poached pineapple
300g caster sugar
150g water
50g double cream
100g unsalted butter
2g salt
2 ripe pineapples

for the coconut cream gel
250g Sicoly coconut purée
100g coconut milk
50g Malibu
50g double cream
20g palm sugar
5g agar agar

for the molasses gel
50g molasses sugar
65g light muscovado sugar
150g apple juice
2.5g agar agar
20g dark rum

for the pineapple crisps
250g water
250g caster sugar
juice of 1/2 lemon
1/4 ripe pineapple, peeled and cut into the thinnest slices possible

48 small lemon verbena leaves, to decorate

pineapple and lemon verbena sorbet
Peel the pineapple, remove the 'eyes' and core, and cut the flesh into 3–4cm chunks. Place in a bowl and sprinkle with the caster sugar and lemon juice. Shred the lemon verbena finely, add to the pineapple and stir to distribute. Cover and leave to macerate in the fridge overnight.

The next day, blend the mixture until puréed, then push through a fine sieve. Churn in an ice cream machine. Transfer to a lidded container and keep in the freezer until needed. Remove to the fridge about 5 minutes before serving.

caramel-poached pineapple
Dissolve the sugar in 100g of the water in a heavy-based pan, then cook on a low heat to make a rich deep caramel (don't let it get too dark or it will be bitter). Remove from the heat and whisk in the cream and remaining water (take care as it will spit) until the caramel has dissolved. Leave to cool a little, then whisk in the butter and salt. Set aside.

Peel one pineapple, removing the 'eyes', and cut 6 nice lengthways slices of flesh, 3 from each side of the core. Repeat with the other pineapple. You will now have 12 slices and lots of trimmings. Dice the trimmings and reserve for the decoration; you need 48 small pieces. Trim each pineapple slice to make a rectangle about 10 x 4cm and 3mm thick.

At the restaurant we put each slice into a vac pac bag and pour in a little of the caramel, but you can place the slices, side by side, in a heavy baking tray and pour the caramel over. Cook at 65°C on top of the stove for about 30 minutes, until tender. Allow to cool, then keep in the fridge until needed.

coconut cream gel
Combine everything in a saucepan and whisk together. Allow the agar agar to swell for a few minutes, then place the pan on the heat and bring up to the boil, stirring to dissolve the agar agar. Boil for 2 minutes, stirring. Pour into a bowl and leave to cool, then cover and chill for 4 hours.

Tip into a blender and blend until smooth. Pass through a fine chinois. Reserve 100g for the molasses cream and put the rest in a squeezy bottle. Keep in the fridge until needed.

molasses gel
Put both sugars and the apple juice in a saucepan. Place on the heat and stir until the sugar has dissolved, then remove from the heat. Whisk in the agar agar. Allow it to swell for a few minutes, then place back on the heat and bring up to the boil, stirring to dissolve the agar agar. Boil for 2 minutes, stirring. Remove from the heat and leave to cool. When cold, stir in the rum, then cover and chill for 4 hours.

Transfer to a blender and blend until smooth. Pass through a fine chinois and place in a small covered container. Keep in the fridge until needed.

pineapple crisps
Combine the water, sugar and lemon juice in a saucepan and bring to the boil. Remove from the heat and leave to cool. Place the pineapple slices in the syrup and leave to macerate for 3 hours.

Drain the pineapple slices and carefully lay them on a baking tray lined with a silicone mat. Dry out in an oven preheated to its lowest setting, or with the pilot light only, for 4–5 hours, until crisp. Remove from the oven and leave to cool, then break into smaller pieces. Store in an airtight container.

spiced bread

Cut the loaf into 12 slices, each about 10 x 4cm and 3mm thick. Any trimmings can be frozen and used in an ice cream, or as crumbs for another dessert.

molasses cream

Mix together the reserved 100g coconut cream gel and 25g of the molasses gel. Place in a squeezy bottle.

serving

Remove the poached pineapple slices from the bag or tray and drain. Brush the spiced bread slices with the pineapple-caramel juices. Lay a slice of pineapple on top of each slice of bread. Using a brush, make a wide stripe of molasses gel in the centre of each plate. Carefully lift a slice of pineapple-topped spiced bread with a palette knife and place on the gel to one side. Add some cubes of fresh pineapple to decorate, plus some drops of coconut gel. Decorate with pineapple crisps and verbena leaves. Place a scoop of sorbet to the right and a drop of molasses cream on either side.

chocolate and brown butter ganache,
brown butter purée, apricot sorbet

Chocolate and apricots have always been a classic combination of flavours. Here I've used the kernels from the apricots in a purée to give a hint of bitter almonds – another flavour complementary to both chocolate and apricots. Brown butter, used in both the ganache and the purée, gives a slight nuttiness to the dish, and the crumble adds a texture that is needed. The chocolate mint finishes the dish off, giving it a freshness when bitten into.

Serves 12–14

for the chocolate and brown butter ganache
200g unsalted butter
375g double cream
50g liquid glucose
200g bitter dark chocolate (64% cocoa solids), melted
200g milk chocolate, melted
3 egg yolks
3g bitter cocoa powder
4g salt

for the brown butter purée
275g unsalted butter
330g water
80g caster sugar
10g cornflour
6g xanthan gum

for the crumble
125g plain flour
125g ground almonds
125g caster sugar
a good pinch of salt
140g chilled unsalted butter, diced

for the apricot sorbet
1kg fresh apricots
145g caster sugar
300g water
3.5g bronze gelatine leaves
juice of ³/₄ lemon

for the apricot and apricot kernel purée
400g stoned fresh apricots
100g caster sugar
juice of ¹/₂ lemon

for the apricots
6 apricots, stoned and sliced

chocolate mint leaves, to serve

chocolate and brown butter ganache
Melt the butter in a medium frying pan and cook until it turns a golden brown. Pass through a sieve into a bowl and leave to cool.

Pour 125g of the cream into a heavy-based saucepan and bring to the boil. Add the glucose and stir to dissolve in the cream. Remove from the heat. Mix the melted dark and milk chocolates together in a bowl and pour the hot cream on to them, stirring until smooth. Set aside.

Whisk the egg yolks in a mixing bowl until pale and creamy. Whisk in the cocoa powder and salt. Slowly drizzle in the brown butter, whisking constantly, as if making mayonnaise. Fold into the chocolate mixture. Whip the remaining cream to the ribbon stage, then fold in. Pour into a mould (36 x 12 x 4cm) lined with 2 sheets of cling film. Cover and leave in the fridge to set. This will take about 6 hours, but overnight would be better. Once set, keep in the fridge until needed.

brown butter purée
Melt the butter in a medium frying pan and cook until it turns a golden brown colour. Add 300g of the water, being careful as it will splutter, and then the sugar. Stir to mix. Bring to the boil. Mix the cornflour with the remaining 30g water until smooth. Whisk this into the butter mixture and boil again, stirring until it thickens.

Pour into a blender. With the machine running, add the xanthan gum to the vortex in the centre and carry on blending for 1 minute. Pass through a fine chinois into a bowl and chill. When cold, blend again. Pour into a squeezy bottle and keep in the fridge.

crumble
Put all the dry ingredients into a mixing bowl, then add the butter. With your fingertips, rub the butter into the flour mixture until you get nice-sized lumps. Scatter on to a baking sheet lined with baking parchment and place in the fridge to set hard.

When hard, just separate the bits a little. Bake in an oven preheated to 180°C/Gas Mark 4 for 5–8 minutes, until golden. Remove from the oven. If the crumble is not quite cooked, stir and bake for another minute or so. Leave to cool, then keep in an airtight container until needed.

apricot sorbet
Remove the stones from the apricots (reserve 6 stones for the kernel purée). Dissolve the sugar in the water in a medium saucepan, then bring to the boil. Add 250g of the apricots and cook for 3 minutes. Leave to cool. When cold, add the remaining apricots.

Soak the gelatine in cold water for about 5 minutes, until soft and pliable. Heat a little of the apricot syrup in a small pan. Squeeze excess water from the gelatine, then add it to the syrup and stir until melted. Put the gelatine, apricots and remaining syrup in a blender and blend until smooth. Pass through a fine chinois, then add the lemon juice. Pour into an ice cream machine and churn. Transfer to a container and keep in the freezer until needed.

apricot and apricot kernel purée
Crack the reserved 6 apricot stones to remove the kernels. Crush the kernels. Place them in a blender with the apricots, sugar and lemon juice and blend until smooth. Pass through a fine chinois, then keep in a squeezy bottle in the fridge until needed.

serving
Remove the ganache from the fridge and carefully remove from the mould. With a knife dipped in hot water, cut lengthways in half, then cut each half across into 6–7 slices. Drag a few lines of apricot and kernel purée across each plate, then place a slice of ganache in the middle of each plate at an angle. Dot brown butter purée across the plate and over the ganache. Scatter crumble in a line on either side of the ganache. Arrange sliced apricots and chocolate mint leaves on the lines of purée. Add a few blobs of apricot and kernel purée on either side of the ganache. Finally, place a quenelle of sorbet on the ganache.

chausson of elderberry and bramley with vanilla ice cream

These are lovely little turnovers, made with a pastry that contains duck fat for added richness. I've used elderberry and apple for the filling, but blackberries, rhubarb and strawberries could take their place (apple with a hint of strawberry makes a wonderful crumble, by the way). I have included a very small amount of lovage in the filling.
This may sound strange but it does work. You could replace the lovage with some lemon balm, lemon verbena or sweet cicely, if you prefer. The chaussons are served with vanilla ice cream, plain and simple.

Serves 6

for the vanilla ice cream
750g milk
250g double cream
4 vanilla pods, split lengthways
10 egg yolks
75g caster sugar
30g dextrose
75g liquid glucose
30g skimmed milk powder

for the duck fat pastry and the chaussons
275g plain flour
a pinch of salt
¹/₂ orange
75g unsalted butter, diced
50g duck fat, diced
50g caster sugar
85–100g water
35g ground almonds
1 egg, whisked with a little milk, for the egg wash
30g granulated sugar, for sprinkling

for the elderberry filling
300g peeled and cored Bramley apples, coarsely diced
25g unsalted butter
40g water
75–100g caster sugar (depending on the ripeness of the berries)
2 lovage leaves, finely shredded
150g elderberries

vanilla ice cream
Put the milk and cream in a medium saucepan and slowly bring to the boil. Remove from the heat. Scrape the seeds out of the vanilla pods and add to the pan along with the empty vanilla pods. Leave to infuse for at least 2 hours (overnight would be better).

Set the pan back on the stove and slowly bring the milk mixture up to the boil. Whisk the egg yolks, caster sugar, dextrose, glucose and milk powder together in a bowl. Pour half of the milk mixture on to the egg mixture, whisking, then pour back into the pan and stir to mix with the remaining milk mixture. Cook on a low heat, stirring constantly with a wooden spoon, until the custard reaches 84°C or it thickens enough to coat the back of the spoon. Immediately strain through a fine sieve into a bowl and leave to cool. When cold, pour into an ice cream machine and churn. Transfer to a container and keep in the freezer until needed. Remove to the fridge 10–15 minutes before serving.

duck fat pastry
Place the flour and salt in a mixing bowl. Zest the orange directly over the bowl. Add the butter and duck fat and rub together until the mixture is like breadcrumbs. Stir in the caster sugar. Add the water, little by little, until the mixture starts to come together. Turn out on to a floured surface and work the mixture as little as possible until it is smooth. Shape into a ball and flatten, then wrap in cling film and chill for at least 3 hours (preferably overnight).

elderberry filling
Put the apples in a medium saucepan with the butter, water, caster sugar and lovage and cook on a moderate heat until nearly collapsing. Add the elderberries and cook for 1 minute, then remove from the heat and leave to cool. When cold, drain off any excess juices from the fruit. Set the fruit aside.

assembling and baking the chaussons
Remove the chilled pastry from the fridge and divide into 6. Gently roll into 6 balls. On a lightly floured surface, roll out each ball into a disc, about 14cm diameter and 3mm thick. Divide the ground almonds among the discs, placing the almonds in the middle. Brush the edge of each disc with egg wash, then place a small mound of the elderberry filling on top of the almonds. Fold the pastry over to make a half-moon shape, pressing hard on the edges to seal. Brush with egg wash and sprinkle with granulated sugar. Make 2 or 3 little slashes on the top of each chausson, so it doesn't burst during baking. Arrange on a baking tray lined with baking parchment and place in an oven preheated to 180°C/Gas Mark 4. Bake for 30–35 minutes, until golden brown.

serving
Serve each chausson warm with a scoop of ice cream.

note
You could make 12 chaussons half the size, but I prefer them big. After all, you can always cut them in half.

coconut macaroon, iced coconut foam, lotus seed ice cream

The macaroon here is not a little French *macaron* filled with buttercream, but an English-style macaroon – the kind I remember seeing in the pastry shops when I was a young boy, drizzled with chocolate and studded with a cherry, set atop rice paper, with a very gooey, chewy texture. I've teamed my coconut macaroon with an iced foam created by using an iSi gun. The flavouring for the ice cream came about after I had been to a Chinese supermarket. I found lotus seeds there, which I'd never seen before. I wondered what they would be like roasted and then made into an ice cream. The resulting flavour combines light toffee and mocha, which works incredibly well with the coconut.

Serves 12

for the lotus seed ice cream
100g lotus seeds (I use those that are split in half)
1kg milk
150g double cream
3 eggs
3 egg yolks
60g caster sugar
20g dextrose
35g skimmed milk powder
7g ice cream stabiliser

for the iced coconut foam
8.5g bronze gelatine leaves
500g Sicoly coconut purée
125g coconut milk
50g Malibu
100g caster sugar

for the toasted coconut purée
50g desiccated coconut
800g coconut milk
100g double cream
5g agar agar
2g kappa carrageen or bronze gelatine leaves
120g demerara sugar

for the coconut macaroons
175g caster sugar
50g water
110g egg whites
85g marzipan
15g Malibu
170g desiccated coconut

for the coconut craquant
200g liquid glucose
200g caster sugar
50g water
50g desiccated coconut

for the date purée
100g stoned dates
200g water
seeds from 1 vanilla pod
40g dark muscovado sugar

for the coconut chips
white meat from 1/2 fresh coconut
150g caster sugar
50g water
70g Malibu
a squeeze of lime juice

lotus seed ice cream

Scatter the lotus seeds on to a baking tray and roast in an oven preheated to 180°C/Gas Mark 4 for 10–15 minutes, until a deep brown colour. While the seeds are roasting, pour the milk and cream into a large saucepan and bring to the boil. Add the hot browned lotus seeds, then remove from the heat and cool. Leave to infuse overnight.

The next day, set the pan back on the stove and bring to the boil again. While it is coming up to the boil, whisk the eggs, egg yolks, caster sugar, dextrose, milk powder and stabiliser together in a bowl. Pour half of the milk mixture on to the egg mixture, whisking, then pour back into the pan and stir to mix with the remaining milk mixture. Cook on a low heat, stirring

constantly with a wooden spoon, until the custard reaches 84°C, or it thickens enough to coat the back of the spoon. Immediately strain through a fine sieve into a bowl. Leave to cool. When cold, pour into an ice cream machine and churn. Transfer to a container and keep in the freezer until needed. Remove to the fridge 10–15 minutes before serving.

iced coconut foam

Soak the gelatine in a little cold water for about 5 minutes, until soft and pliable. Put the coconut purée, coconut milk, Malibu and caster sugar in a saucepan and bring to the boil, stirring to make sure it doesn't catch. Remove from the heat. Squeeze excess water from the gelatine, then whisk it into the coconut mixture until melted. Strain through a fine chinois into a bowl and leave in the fridge overnight.

The next day, whisk again, then pour into a 1-litre iSi gun and charge with 2 cartridges. Shake well. Place 12 oiled moulds, each about 6cm high and 5cm in diameter, on a tray lined with baking parchment. Fill the moulds with the foam and level off with a palette knife. Immediately place in the freezer and leave for 24 hours. Keep in the freezer until needed.

toasted coconut purée

Toast the desiccated coconut under the grill until a deep golden brown. Put the coconut milk and double cream in a medium saucepan and bring to the boil. Remove from the heat. Add the toasted coconut and stir, then leave to infuse for 4 hours. Pass through a fine chinois into a clean pan, pushing down hard to get as much liquid through as possible.

(continued on page 149)

(continued from page 147)

Add the agar agar and kappa carrageen to the coconut cream in the saucepan and set aside to swell for 5 minutes. (If using gelatine, soak it in a little cold water for about 5 minutes, until soft and pliable.) Add the demerara sugar and set on a medium heat. Bring to the boil and cook, whisking, for about 2 minutes. Remove from the heat. (If using gelatine, squeeze out excess water, then whisk into the coconut mixture, making sure it has melted.) Strain through a fine chinois into a bowl and leave in the fridge overnight. The next day, tip into a blender and blend until smooth. Place in a squeezy bottle and keep in the fridge until needed.

coconut macaroons

Dissolve the sugar in the water, then cook to 121°C. Whisk the egg whites in the bowl of a freestanding electric mixer on high until stiff. Slowly pour the syrup on to the whites, whisking all the time. Set the meringue aside.

Cut the marzipan into small dice. Put the Malibu in a small saucepan, add the diced marzipan and stir over a low heat until the marzipan has dissolved. Remove from the heat. Add a little of the meringue to the marzipan (this will help the marzipan break down a little more), then fold the marzipan mixture into the rest of the meringue. Fold in the desiccated coconut.

Spread the mixture about 4mm thick on a baking sheet lined with baking parchment. Bake in an oven preheated to 180°C/Gas Mark 4 for 10–15 minutes, until golden brown. Leave to cool. When cold, cut into 12 rectangles, each about 14 x 5.5cm. (Have any trimmings with a cup of coffee.) Store the macaroons in an airtight container until needed.

coconut craquant

Put the glucose, caster sugar and water in a heavy-based saucepan and dissolve the sugar on a gentle heat, then bring up to the boil and cook until caramelised to a golden amber colour. Add the desiccated coconut and swirl around in the syrup. Immediately pour on to an oiled lipped tray and set aside until cold and very crisp. Break up the caramel, then place in a food processor and pulse to a coarse powder. Store in an airtight container.

When needed, sprinkle the craquant in an even layer on a parchment-lined lipped baking tray to form a large rectangle about 35 x 20cm. Place in an oven preheated to 200°C/Gas Mark 6 and cook for 3–4 minutes, watching carefully, until the craquant has melted and formed a single sheet of caramel.

Remove from the oven and leave to cool. Just before the caramel sets, cut out discs 5cm in diameter. You will need 12 plus a few extra just in case, as they are very brittle – so cut 18. Leave to cool. If the caramel sets too quickly, remove the discs you have cut and return the tray to the oven to soften for a minute or so, then remove and finish cutting. Keep the trimmings because they can be ground down and used again. Store the discs in an airtight container until needed.

date purée

Combine all the ingredients in a saucepan. Bring to the boil, stirring occasionally, then simmer for 15 minutes. Pour into a blender and blend until smooth. Pass through a fine chinois and leave to cool, then place in a squeezy bottle. Keep in the fridge until needed.

coconut chips

Slice the coconut on a mandolin as finely as possible to get thin crescent shapes. Put the caster sugar, water and Malibu in a saucepan. Bring to the boil, then add the lime juice. Add the coconut and reduce the heat to a very low simmer. Poach for 20 minutes.

Drain the coconut, keeping the syrup for another use. Carefully lay the coconut slices on a baking tray lined with a silicone mat. Place in an oven preheated to 120°C/Gas Mark 1/2 and dry out for 4–5 hours, until crisp. Leave to cool, then break into smaller pieces. Store in an airtight container until needed.

finishing the iced coconut foam

Remove the foam-filled moulds from the freezer and push a deep hole into the middle of each one. Fill with the toasted coconut purée and place a coconut craquant disc on top. Return to the freezer while getting the rest of the dessert ready for plating (do not leave in the freezer any longer than 10 minutes).

serving

Place a macaroon in the centre of each plate. Make 3 blobs of date purée on the macaroon, one in the middle and one at each end. In between the middle blob and the left one, set an iced coconut foam. To the right, in between the middle blob and the right one, place a quenelle of lotus seed ice cream. Arrange some coconut chips on the ice cream and on the foam.

gooseberry cake, elderflower sorbet and granola, poached gooseberries

This started out as an idea from my sous chef, Matthew Worswick. He put it forward for our *du jour* menu. After some work on it together, refining the taste and the presentation, this is what we ended up with. It has a wonderful flavour. The combination of gooseberry and elderflower is a classic one, but we have made it our own with the different textures involved, in particular the lovely crunchy elderflower granola. Rhubarb, damsons and cherries would work in place of the gooseberries.

Serves 12

for the elderflower sorbet
7g bronze gelatine leaves
750g water
300g caster sugar
150g elderflower heads
3g malic acid
peel and juice of 1 lemon
peel and juice of ¹/₂ orange

for the gooseberry cake
250g unsalted butter, softened
250g light muscovado sugar
250g self-raising flour
15g baking powder
50g ground almonds
4 eggs
25g Elderflower Cordial (see page 17)
500g gooseberries

for the syrup
75g caster sugar
100g water
juice of 1 lemon
40g elderflower syrup

for the elderflower granola
75g honey
flowers from 5 elderflower heads
40g unsalted butter, melted
75g caster sugar
1.5g salt
200g jumbo oats

for the poached gooseberries
75g caster sugar
50g water
300g small gooseberries

for the gooseberry purée
200g gooseberries
50g caster sugar
flowers from 1 elderflower head

to decorate
12 small gooseberries, sliced
baby lemon balm leaves

elderflower sorbet
Soak the gelatine in cold water for about 5 minutes, until soft and pliable. Meanwhile, combine all the other ingredients in a saucepan and bring to the boil. Remove from the heat. Squeeze excess water from the gelatine, then whisk it into the syrup until melted. Leave to infuse for 10 minutes, then pass through muslin and leave to cool. Churn in an ice cream machine. Transfer to a lidded container and keep in the freezer until needed.

gooseberry cake
Cream the butter with the sugar until light and fluffy. Sift the flour and baking powder into another bowl, then add the ground almonds. Add one egg to the creamed mixture and beat well until smooth. Add a quarter of the flour mixture and beat well, then repeat with the remaining eggs and flour mixture. Finally, add the elderflower cordial and mix well. You should have a lovely smooth batter.

Place in a buttered and parchment-lined baking tray, about 34 x 18 x 4cm, levelling the surface. Stud evenly with the gooseberries. Bake in an oven preheated to 180°C/Gas Mark 4 for about 40 minutes, until deep golden brown; a knife tip inserted in the centre of the cake should come out clean. While the cake is baking, make the syrup.

syrup
Put the caster sugar, water and lemon juice in a small saucepan and bring to the boil. Leave to cool a little, then add the elderflower syrup.

finishing the gooseberry cake
Remove the baked gooseberry cake from the oven. Prick all over with a fork, then evenly pour on the syrup. Set the tray on a wire rack and leave to cool. When needed, remove the cake from the tray and cut into 12 portions, across the width of the tray.

elderflower granola
Melt the honey in a saucepan, then add two-thirds of the elderflowers. Remove from the heat and leave to macerate for 2–3 hours.

Add the butter, caster sugar and salt to the pan and warm over a low heat until the sugar has dissolved. Pour this mixture over the oats in a bowl and mix well, then spread out on a non-stick baking sheet. Bake in an oven preheated to 160°C/ Gas Mark 3 for 30–35 minutes, until a deep golden brown, stirring every 5 minutes. Remove from the oven and give the mixture a final stir, adding the remaining elderflowers. Leave to cool. When cold, store in an airtight container in a cool place (keep for no longer than a week).

poached gooseberries
Put the caster sugar and water in a saucepan and bring to the boil. Add the gooseberries and remove from the heat. Leave to poach in the residual heat until soft, then remove from the syrup with a slotted spoon and place in a container. Bring the syrup back to the boil and reduce by half. Leave to cool, then pour over the gooseberries. Keep in the fridge until needed.

gooseberry purée
Place all the ingredients in a medium saucepan and stir on a moderate heat until the juices are coming out of the gooseberries. Drain off half of the juices, then pour the remainder of the gooseberry mixture into a blender and blend until smooth. Pass through a fine sieve. Place in a squeezy bottle and keep in the fridge until needed.

serving
Place a slice of gooseberry cake on each plate at an angle. Arrange poached gooseberries and dots of gooseberry purée on the cake. Scatter elderflower granola in a line on either side of the cake, at an angle to it. Set a quenelle of sorbet on the granola on either side of the cake. Decorate the plate with sliced gooseberries and lemon balm leaves plus fine streaks of gooseberry purée.

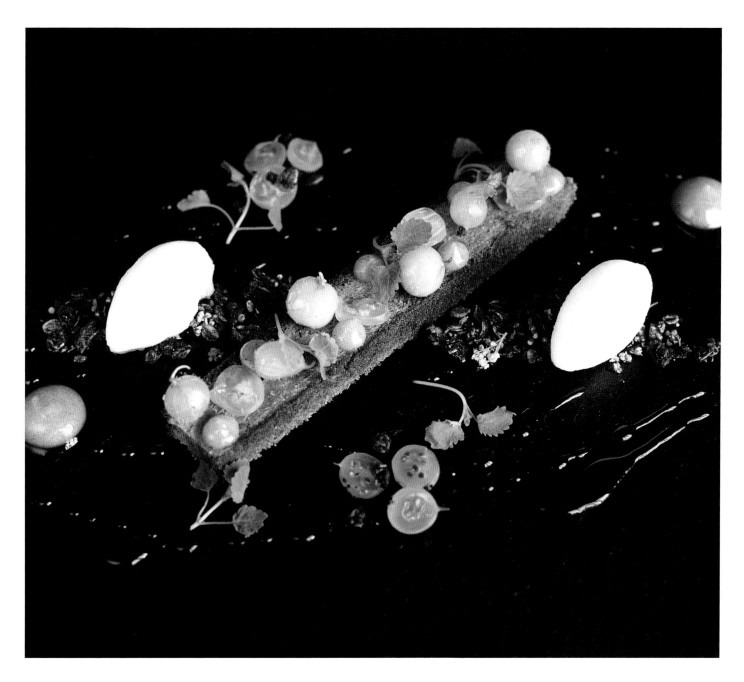

malted milk, roasted dandelion root purée

The taste of this dessert is reminiscent of the favourite nighttime drink Horlicks – I wanted to create something that was not too sweet and that had a playful touch. The roasted dandelion root purée gives a slight bitter caramel note, and the cocoa nibs and toasted barley flakes add the texture that the dish needs. If you can't get dandelion root, you could make a coffee caramel and maybe a latte ice cream instead of the milk.

Serves 12

for the malt cream
30g pearl barley
400g milk
700g double cream
1 vanilla pod, split lengthways
250g egg yolks
90g caster sugar
100g malt extract

for the milk ice cream
1kg milk
7g bronze gelatine leaves
150g condensed milk
200g double cream
75g skimmed milk powder
25g caster sugar

for the milk tuiles
300g condensed milk
30g plain flour

for the milk purée
1.2kg milk
600g double cream
4.5g kappa carrageen
30g caster sugar

for the milk crumble
125g skimmed milk powder
100g plain flour

30g cornflour
50g caster sugar
4g salt
145g unsalted butter, melted

for the roasted dandelion root purée
75g caster sugar
40g water
600g milk
65g double cream
2g iota carrageen
25g ground roasted dandelion root
1g salt
4g agar agar

for the chocolate sauce
200g caster sugar
500g water
150g cocoa powder
50g port
300g red wine

150g bitter dark chocolate (64% cocoa solids), finely chopped

to serve
toasted barley flakes
cocoa nibs (grue de cacao)
icing sugar, for dusting

malt cream

Spread out the pearl barley on a baking tray and toast in an oven preheated to 180°C/Gas Mark 4 until golden brown. Meanwhile, put the milk and cream in a heavy-based pan. Scrape the vanilla seeds from the pod into the pan and add the empty pod too. Add the toasted pearl barley and bring to the boil. Remove from the heat and leave to infuse for 30–40 minutes. Strain through a fine chinois.

Whisk the egg yolks, caster sugar and malt extract together in a bowl. Pour the infused milk on to the egg mixture, whisking well. Pour back into the pan and cook on a low heat, stirring constantly with a wooden spoon, for about 1 minute. Immediately strain through a fine sieve into a jug.

Oil 12 stainless steel rings, each about 10cm in diameter and 3cm deep. Wrap some cling film tightly around the base of each ring, then wrap the ring in foil so it comes halfway up the sides. Make sure the foil is very close fitting, as the object is to make the base airtight. Line a deep baking tray with a clean J-cloth, then set the moulds in the tray.

Pour the malt cream into the moulds, filling each about two-thirds full. Pour enough hot water into the baking tray to come a third of the way up the sides of the moulds. Carefully place in an oven preheated to 96°C (if your oven will not go this low, then bake at the lowest temperature possible) and bake for 30–40 minutes, until the creams have set. Remove from the oven and leave in the tray of water to cool. Carefully lift out of the tray, cover and keep in the fridge until needed (preferably overnight).

milk ice cream

Pour the milk into a large heavy-based saucepan and bring to the boil, then reduce to 750g. Meanwhile, soak the gelatine in cold water for about 5 minutes, until soft and pliable. Add the other ingredients to the reduced milk and bring back to the boil. Squeeze excess water from the gelatine, then add to the pan and whisk until melted. Remove from the heat and pass through a fine chinois. Leave to cool, then leave in the fridge overnight to mature. Churn in an ice cream machine. Transfer to a lidded container and keep in the freezer until needed.

milk tuiles

Put the condensed milk in a bowl and whisk in the flour, mixing until smooth. Chill in the fridge for at least 6 hours.

Using a small palette knife, spread the chilled mixture thinly in rough oblongs, about 8 x 3cm, on a baking sheet lined with baking parchment. You will need 24 tuiles, but make a few extra as they are very brittle. Place in an oven preheated to 180°C/Gas Mark 4 and bake for about 5 minutes to a light golden colour; they will crisp up as they cool. Once cold, carefully slide the palette knife under the tuiles and lift off, then keep in an airtight container, with baking parchment between the layers, until needed.

milk purée

Pour the milk and cream into a large, heavy-based saucepan. Bring to the boil, then lower the heat to a simmer and reduce to 500g, being careful it doesn't scorch on the bottom of the pan. Remove from the heat and whisk in the carrageen and caster sugar. Set aside for 3–4 minutes to allow the carrageen to swell. Place back on the heat, bring to the boil, stirring, and boil for 1 minute. Pass through a fine chinois into a container and leave to cool. Cover and place in the fridge. Leave to set for 6 hours.

Tip into a blender and blend until the mixture has the consistency of clotted cream. Transfer to a lidded container and keep in the fridge until needed.

milk crumble

Combine all the dry ingredients in a bowl and mix together thoroughly. Mix in the melted butter, using a spoon, until lumps form. Scatter on to a baking sheet. Bake in an oven preheated to 120°C/Gas Mark 1/2 for 10 minutes, until dried and crisp with no colour. Leave to cool, then store in an airtight container until needed.

roasted dandelion root purée

Dissolve the sugar in the water in a medium, heavy-based saucepan. Bring to the boil and cook to a deep golden caramel. Add the milk and cream, being careful because it will splutter, and stir until the caramel has dissolved. Remove from the heat and add the remaining ingredients. Leave to infuse for 30 minutes.

Set the pan back on the heat and bring to the boil, whisking all the time. Pass through a fine chinois into a bowl. Allow to cool, then place in the fridge. Leave for 4 hours to set. Once set, transfer to a blender and blend to a thick purée. Pass through a fine sieve again. Place in a squeezy bottle and keep in the fridge until needed.

chocolate sauce

Dissolve the sugar in 100g of the water in a heavy-based pan, then cook until a deep golden caramel. Add the remaining 400g water and the cocoa powder, being careful as the caramel will splutter. Stir to dissolve the caramel, then bring to the boil. Add the port and red wine and return to the boil. Cook for 3 minutes. Remove from the heat and stir in the chocolate until it has all melted. Pass through a fine chinois, then leave to cool. Store in a jar until needed.

serving

Remove the malt creams from the fridge. Make a line of chocolate sauce on the left side of each plate. Remove the cling film from a malt cream, then set it on a plate to the right of the chocolate line; run a small knife around the inside of the ring and carefully it lift off. Place blobs of milk purée and roasted dandelion root purée alternating on the chocolate sauce. Sprinkle with toasted barley flakes, milk crumble and cocoa nibs. Set a milk tuile across the malt cream, top with a quenelle of milk ice cream and set another milk tuile on this. Finish with a dusting of icing sugar.

raspberry cannelloni with anise hyssop cream, raspberry and anise hyssop sorbet

This really is a composition of raspberry and you could add a raspberry mousse or parfait, or even both, if you wished. Raspberry marries well with anise hyssop, which is one of the ingredients that helps to colour absinthe. The herb has a wonderful minty flavour with a slight bitterness, so could be used to replace mint or eucalyptus in other recipes. Raspberries work well with burdock, liquorice root and rose so any of these could replace anise hyssop. You could of course use strawberries, plums or blackberries instead of raspberries.

Serves 8

for the raspberry cannelloni
300g raspberry purée
40g powdered isomalt
5g potato flour
1g citric acid powder

for the anise hyssop cream
5.25g bronze gelatine leaves
400g milk
2 eggs
2 egg yolks
150g caster sugar
50g cornflour
50g anise hyssop
100g unsalted butter
65g double cream, whipped

for the raspberry and anise hyssop sorbet
3g bronze gelatine leaves
125g water
125g caster sugar
40g liquid glucose
500g fresh ripe raspberries
25g anise hyssop
juice of 1/2 lemon

for the raspberry purée
150g fresh ripe raspberries
10g caster sugar
juice of 1/4 lemon

to serve
42 fresh raspberries (freeze 10 of them on a tray)
a punnet of anise hyssop tops

raspberry cannelloni
Put all the ingredients in a blender and blend until smooth. Place in a small saucepan and bring up to 84°C. Remove from the heat. Using a stencil set on a baking tray lined with a silicone mat, spread the raspberry mixture thinly to make 10 x 4cm rectangles. You want to make 18 rectangles, which will give you 2 extra, just in case, as they are brittle (you may have to make them in several batches). Cook in an oven preheated to 120°C/ Gas Mark 1/2 for 10–15 minutes, until dry but still a little pliable.

As the rectangles are cooked, wrap each around a thin piece of dowelling to create a cannelloni, then leave to cool and crisp up. If you have any mixture left over, create one sheet with it and cook, then cool and break up into irregular shapes. Store the cannelloni and broken shapes in an airtight container until needed.

anise hyssop cream
Soak the gelatine in cold water for about 5 minutes, until soft and pliable. Meanwhile, pour the milk into a medium saucepan and bring to the boil. Remove from the heat. Combine the eggs, egg yolks, sugar and cornflour in a bowl and whisk together. Whisk in the hot milk, then return the mixture to the saucepan. Set on a medium heat and cook, stirring all the time, for 4–5 minutes, until thick. Add the anise hyssop halfway through. Remove from the heat and allow to cool a little, then stir in the butter, bit by bit, until it is all melted and incorporated.

Squeeze excess water from the gelatine, then add to the anise hyssop mixture and stir until melted. Transfer to a blender and blend to a smooth purée. Pass through a fine sieve into a bowl. Lay a sheet of cling film on the surface of the mixture and leave to cool. When cold, fold in the whipped cream. Keep in a sealed container in the fridge. When needed, beat well, then spoon into a piping bag fitted with a small plain nozzle.

raspberry and anise hyssop sorbet
Soak the gelatine in cold water for about 5 minutes, until soft and pliable. Meanwhile, combine the water, sugar and glucose in a saucepan and bring to the boil, stirring to dissolve the sugar. Remove from the heat. Squeeze excess water from the gelatine, then add to the syrup and stir until melted. Leave to cool.

Place the raspberries and anise hyssop in a blender with half of the syrup and blend until smooth. Add the remaining syrup and pulse once, then pass through a fine sieve. Add the lemon juice. Pour into an ice cream machine and churn. Keep in a lidded container in the freezer until needed. Remove from the freezer 5 minutes before serving.

raspberry purée
Put all the ingredients in a blender and blend until smooth. Pass through a fine chinois. Place in a squeezy bottle and keep in the fridge until needed.

serving
Fill the cannelloni with the anise hyssop cream. Place 2 at different angles on each plate, then add 2 small scoops of sorbet. Break up the frozen raspberries and scatter the little bits on the plates. Place 4 fresh raspberries at different positions on each plate. Dot with raspberry purée. Finally, rest some broken raspberry shapes against the cannelloni and dress with a few hyssop tops.

rhubarb poached with hibiscus, mascarpone cream, rhubarb and hibiscus sorbet, gin and tonic gel

The rhubarb I use for this is the lovely forced, pale pink champagne rhubarb, which is less fibrous and a touch sweeter than the normal variety. Rhubarb has a natural affinity with hibiscus due to its subtle flavour of rhubarb and raspberry. I have paired the fruit with its own sorbet and a light mascarpone cream, as well as a gin and tonic gel for a touch of sweetness and bitterness.

Serves 10

for the mascarpone cream
5.25g bronze gelatine leaves
200g double cream
150g caster sugar
500g mascarpone
300g cream cheese
seeds from 1 vanilla pod

for the poached rhubarb
25g hibiscus flowers
200g red wine
100g orange juice (from a carton)
150g caster sugar
300g water
10 nice young pink champagne rhubarb
    stalks

for the rhubarb and hibiscus sorbet
500g rhubarb, chopped
150g caster sugar
250g water
5.25g bronze gelatine leaves
50g gin

for the lemonade syrup for the white tapioca
200g lemon juice
grated zest of 1 lemon
150g water
180g caster sugar

for the tapioca pearls
100g tapioca pearls

for the sponge fingers
4 egg whites
150g caster sugar
4 egg yolks
finely grated zest of 1/2 lemon
seeds from 1 vanilla pod
100g plain flour
8g baking powder

for the filo pastry tops
6 sheets of filo pastry
50g unsalted butter, melted
100g icing sugar (50g for dusting the filo
    pastry and 50g for dusting when serving)

for the poached hibiscus petals
75g caster sugar
750g water
75g whole hibiscus flowers

for the gin and tonic fluid gel
400g tonic water
100g water
120g caster sugar
pared zest and juice of 1 lemon
2 lemongrass stems, crushed
6g agar agar
100g gin

mascarpone cream
Soak the gelatine in cold water for about 5 minutes, until soft and pliable. Meanwhile, put the cream and sugar in a saucepan. Squeeze excess water from the gelatine, then add to the pan. Heat, stirring, until the sugar has dissolved and the gelatine has melted. Leave to cool for 3–4 minutes.

Beat together the mascarpone, cream cheese and vanilla seeds in a mixing bowl.

Pour the cream mixture on to the mascarpone mixture and beat until uniform in consistency. Leave to cool, then place in the fridge to set overnight. When needed, transfer to a piping bag fitted with a 2cm plain nozzle.

poached rhubarb
Place all the ingredients, except the rhubarb, in a medium saucepan and bring to the boil. Remove from the heat and leave to infuse for 1 hour. Strain through a fine chinois into a clean pan and set aside.

Lightly peel the rhubarb (keep the peelings for the sorbet) and cut into 11cm lengths. Heat the poaching liquor to 61°C, then add the rhubarb and poach until tender but still keeping its shape. Remove from the syrup and leave to cool. Pour the syrup into a container and cool. Keep the rhubarb in the syrup until needed.

rhubarb and hibiscus sorbet
Combine all the ingredients, except for the gelatine and gin, in a medium saucepan. Add the trimmings from the poached rhubarb and 250g of the hibiscus poaching syrup. Bring to the boil, then cook for about 5 minutes, until the rhubarb is tender. Remove from the heat.

Soak the gelatine in cold water for about 5 minutes, until soft and pliable. Squeeze excess water from the gelatine, then whisk it into the syrup until melted. Measure the syrup and top up with water to make 1kg. Add the gin, then pour into a blender and blend until smooth. Pass through a chinois, then leave to cool. Churn in an ice cream machine. Transfer to a lidded container and keep in the freezer until needed.

(continued on page 158)

(continued from page 157)

lemonade syrup for the white tapioca

Put the lemon juice and zest, water and sugar in a medium saucepan and bring to the boil. Remove from the heat, strain and leave to cool.

tapioca pearls

Place the tapioca pearls in a pan of boiling water and cook until translucent. Rinse in cold water and drain. Divide between 2 bowls. For the red pearls, cover the tapioca pearls in one bowl with some rhubarb poaching syrup and leave to macerate overnight (keep in the syrup until needed). For the white pearls, cover the tapioca pearls in the other bowl with the lemonade syrup, then leave to macerate overnight (keep in the syrup until needed).

sponge fingers

Put the egg whites in a mixing bowl and whisk until frothy, then add the sugar and whisk until soft peaks form. In another bowl, whisk together the egg yolks, lemon zest and vanilla seeds until pale and fluffy. Add a quarter of the whites to the yolk mixture and fold in, then add another quarter and fold in. Sift the flour and baking powder together and fold into the egg yolk mixture. Fold in the rest of the whites.

Spoon into a piping bag fitted with a plain 12mm nozzle. Pipe on to a baking sheet lined with a silicone mat or baking parchment to make strips, each about 11 x 3cm. Make 12 so you have 2 spare. Place in an oven preheated to 200°C/ Gas Mark 6 and bake for 10 minutes, until golden. Transfer to a wire rack to cool. Keep in an airtight container until needed.

filo pastry tops

Brush one sheet of filo pastry with melted butter and dust with icing sugar, then lay another sheet of filo on top. Brush this with butter and dust with sugar, then top with a third filo sheet. Press with a tray. Repeat to make 2 stacked rectangles of filo. Cut each into 6 rectangles, about 15 x 3.5cm, then place on a baking sheet lined with baking parchment. Cover with a sheet of greaseproof or baking parchment and set another baking sheet on top. Place in an oven preheated to 160°C/Gas Mark 3 and bake for 10 minutes, until golden. Leave to cool. Keep in an airtight container until needed.

poached hibiscus petals

Put the sugar and water in a pan and bring to the boil, stirring to dissolve the sugar. Add the hibiscus flowers and poach gently for 30 minutes, until tender. Lift out the flowers and cut into fine strips. Keep them in the poaching syrup until needed.

gin and tonic fluid gel

Combine all the ingredients, apart from the gin, in a medium saucepan. Leave for 3 minutes so the agar agar swells and softens, then bring up to the boil, whisking until the agar agar has dissolved. Remove from the heat, then add the gin and leave to infuse for 10 minutes.

Pass through a fine chinois into a container. Leave in the fridge for 3–4 hours, until set. Transfer to a blender and blend until smooth. Pass through a sieve again. Place in a squeezy bottle and keep in the fridge until needed.

serving

Make a ring of gin and tonic gel on each plate. Trim off the ends of the sponge fingers, then moisten with poached rhubarb syrup. Place one sponge finger on each plate at an angle. Add a line of mascarpone cream along the sponge, followed by a trimmed stick of poached rhubarb. Dust the filo tops with icing sugar and set one on each stick of rhubarb. Top with a few tapioca pearls of each colour and a few poached hibiscus petals. Alternate the different flavoured tapioca pearls and the hibiscus on the gin and tonic gel ring. Finally, add a quenelle of sorbet.

roasted white chocolate iced mousse, roasted strawberries, meadowsweet mascarpone cream

This is a wonderful dessert. Warming the strawberries accentuates their flavour; the meadowsweet gives a slight bitter almond flavour to the mascarpone; and roasting the white chocolate adds a delightful caramel taste. I have decorated the plate with sheep's sorrel, for a sharp bite to offset the richness of the parfait. All these flavours complement each other perfectly. Elderflower could replace the meadowsweet for a more floral taste, and apricots would work very well instead of the strawberries.

Serves 8

for the roasted white chocolate parfait
150g white chocolate, melted
150g double cream
50g water
15g liquid glucose
15g light muscovado sugar
25g caster sugar
75g warm milk
4 egg yolks

for the strawberry sorbet
5g bronze gelatine leaves
80g liquid glucose
75g caster sugar
350g water
100g fresh strawberry juice
500g ripe strawberries
juice of 1/2 lemon

for the meadowsweet mascarpone cream
5g fresh meadowsweet flowers
50g water
1.75g bronze gelatine leaves
250g mascarpone
40g icing sugar
a dash of Amaretto (optional)

for the strawberry powder
150g caster sugar
75g water
juice of 1/4 lemon
500g large strawberries, hulled and sliced

for the strawberry crisps
275g strawberry purée
25g potato flour
75g icing sugar
1g citric acid powder

for the roasted strawberries
24 small strawberries
50g unsalted butter
50g caster sugar

to decorate
32 small sheep's sorrel leaves
8 small strawberries, each sliced into 4

roasted white chocolate parfait
Pour the melted white chocolate on to a non-stick lipped baking tray. Place in an oven preheated to 150°C/Gas Mark 2 and cook for 3–4 minutes. Remove and stir the chocolate, pushing the edges, which should be a little more coloured, into the middle. Repeat this process until all of the chocolate is a rich golden brown. Scrape it into a bowl and stir well, then keep warm.

Whip the cream to the ribbon stage; cover and keep in the fridge until needed. Place the water, glucose and muscovado and caster sugars in a small heavy-based saucepan and heat slowly, stirring to dissolve the sugar, then raise the heat and bring to the boil. Cook the sugar syrup to the soft ball stage (120°C).

Meanwhile, mix the warm milk into the white chocolate, stirring until smooth. In another bowl, whisk the egg yolks using a freestanding electric mixer until thick, airy and white. With the mixer running on high, slowly drizzle the sugar syrup on to the whisked yolks. Carry on whisking until cool. When cold, fold in the white chocolate and milk mixture followed by the whipped cream.

Lay 4 sheets of cling film on the work surface and spoon a quarter of the chocolate mixture on to each. Form into 4 cylinders, each about 20cm long and 4cm in diameter, wrapping them in the cling film. Tie the ends securely. Freeze until firm, then leave in the freezer until needed.

strawberry sorbet
Soak the gelatine in cold water for about 5 minutes, until soft and pliable. Meanwhile, combine the glucose, caster sugar, water and strawberry juice in a saucepan and bring to the boil, stirring to dissolve the sugar. Squeeze excess water from the gelatine, then whisk it into the syrup until melted. Remove from the heat and leave to cool. When cooled, pour the contents of the saucepan into a blender, add the strawberries and lemon juice, and blend until smooth. Pass through a fine sieve, then churn in an ice cream machine. Transfer to a lidded container and keep in the freezer until needed. Remove from the freezer about 4 minutes before serving.

(continued on page 161)

(continued from page 159)

meadowsweet mascarpone cream

Put the meadowsweet flowers in a saucepan with the water and bring to the boil. Cover and remove from the heat, then leave to infuse for 30 minutes. Strain through a fine chinois into a saucepan, pressing on the petals to get as much juice out as you can; discard the flowers. Soak the gelatine in cold water for about 5 minutes, until soft and pliable. Squeeze excess water from the gelatine, then add to the pan and warm through, stirring until the gelatine has melted. Leave to cool.

Add the gelatine mixture to the mascarpone in a mixing bowl and whisk until light and fluffy. Whisk in the icing sugar. Taste, and if you feel the almond flavour has not come through enough add a dash of Amaretto. Cover and keep in the fridge until needed.

strawberry powder

Combine the sugar, water and lemon juice in a saucepan and bring to the boil, stirring to dissolve the sugar. Remove from the heat and leave to cool. Put the sliced strawberries in a bowl and pour the syrup over. Leave to macerate for 3–4 hours.

Remove the strawberries and drain well in a colander. Spread out the strawberry slices in one layer on 1–2 baking sheets lined with silicone mats. Place in an oven preheated to 110°C/Gas Mark ¼ and dry out for 10–12 hours, until crisp. Leave to cool, then place in a spice grinder, a few slices at a time, and grind to a fine powder. Keep the powder in an airtight container until needed.

strawberry crisps

Blend all the ingredients together in a blender. Pour into a small saucepan and bring up to 84°C. Remove from the heat. Spread out thinly on a 30 x 30cm baking sheet lined with a silicone mat and cook in an oven preheated to 150°C/Gas Mark 2 for 10–15 minutes, until crisp. (At the restaurant we use a dehydrator for this, which means we can leave the strawberry mixture in overnight at a lower temperature of 110°C, without the fear of it burning or losing its colour.) Leave to cool, then break up into irregular shapes. Keep in a sealed container in a dry place.

roasted strawberries

Hull the strawberries. Heat the butter in an ovenproof frying pan, then add the strawberries and sprinkle with the sugar. Transfer to an oven preheated to 200°C/Gas Mark 6 and roast until soft but not mushy (this won't take very long). Remove the strawberries from the pan and keep warm. Pour the juices from the pan into a blender and blend until amalgamated; set aside.

serving

Remove the parfaits from the freezer; trim the ends through the cling film, then cut each in half to make 8 pieces. Remove the cling film and roll in some of the strawberry powder. Place back in the freezer to firm up for 5 minutes. Put a spoonful of meadowsweet mascarpone cream in the centre of each plate. Cut each piece of parfait in half at an angle. Set 2 halves on the plate on either side of the cream. Add a quenelle of sorbet, then place a line of strawberry powder along the middle of the plate. Add strawberry crisps, roasted strawberries, sliced strawberries and sheep's sorrel. Finally, drizzle over the juices from the roasted strawberries.

salted chicory mousse, vanilla cheesecake, chocolate sorbet

This is a reworking of a recipe that featured in my book, *Dessert*. It shows that things can be worked on, and that the result of the work is often a more refined dish. This 'adult' combination of flavours, balancing bitterness and sweetness with a touch of salt, is a favourite of mine. The chicory could be omitted from both mousse and glaze, leaving just a salted caramel mousse, and coffee could be your base cheesecake mix. Roasted burdock or dandelion root could be made into an essence and served as well.

Serves 10–12

for the bitter chocolate sorbet
750g water
240g milk
60g caster sugar
60g trimoline
100g cocoa powder
7g bronze gelatine leaves
200g bitter dark chocolate (64% cocoa solids), finely chopped
40g bitter dark chocolate (71% cocoa solids), finely chopped

for the vanilla cheesecake
150g Hobnobs
100g unsalted butter, melted
125g cream cheese
15g plain flour
380g mascarpone
3 eggs
2 egg yolks
125g double cream
100g white chocolate, melted
seeds from 2 vanilla pods
50g caster sugar

for the salted chicory mousse
155g double cream
50g water
150g caster sugar
8.75g bronze gelatine leaves
3 eggs
18g chicory essence
7–10g salt (this is a rough guide as the degree of bitterness of the caramel can alter the saltiness)

for the chicory glaze
50g water
125g caster sugar
3.5g bronze gelatine leaves
135g double cream
17g chicory essence
20g vegetable oil

for the chocolate sauce
200g caster sugar
500g water
150g cocoa powder
50g port
300g red wine
150g bitter dark chocolate (64% cocoa solids), finely chopped

for the walnut crumble
60g icing sugar
120g white bread rolls, diced
120g chopped walnuts
160g demerara sugar
40g cornflour
6g salt
seeds from 2 vanilla pods
150g unsalted butter, melted
40g walnut oil
2 eggs

for the chocolate sticks
100g liquid glucose
100g fondant
100g isomalt
70g bitter dark chocolate (71% cocoa solids), finely chopped

bitter chocolate sorbet
Combine the water, milk, caster sugar and trimoline in a heavy-based pan and bring to the boil. Whisk in the cocoa powder and cook for 2 minutes, whisking occasionally. Remove from the heat. Soak the gelatine in a little cold water for about 5 minutes, until soft and pliable. Squeeze excess water from the gelatine, then whisk it into the cocoa syrup. Leave to cool for 2–3 minutes. Put all the chocolate in a bowl and pour on the cocoa syrup, whisking until thoroughly incorporated and smooth. Strain through a fine sieve, then place in an ice cream machine and churn. Transfer to a container and keep in the freezer until needed. Remove to the fridge about 10 minutes before serving, to soften slightly.

vanilla cheesecake
Carefully wrap foil around the bottom and sides of a metal cooking frame that measures about 36 x 12cm and 4cm deep: the cheesecake is going to be cooked in a water bath so the frame needs to be watertight. Set aside. Put the biscuits in a food processor and grind coarsely. With the machine running, slowly pour in the melted butter. Spoon the mixture over the bottom of the prepared frame to a depth of 5mm. Press down well. Leave to set in the fridge.

Mix the cream cheese with the flour. Add the mascarpone, eggs and egg yolks and mix well. Heat the cream until just below boiling, then remove from the heat and leave to cool for 1 minute. Pour the cream on to the melted white chocolate, stirring to mix. Add to the mascarpone mixture.

(continued on page 164)

(continued from page 162)

Add the vanilla seeds and the sugar to the cheese mixture and stir well. Pour into the prepared frame. Set it in a roasting tin and pour in enough hot water to come halfway up the sides of the frame. Place in an oven preheated to 95°C and bake for 25–30 minutes, until the filling is set. Remove from the oven, cover with cling film and leave to cool in the water bath for 1 hour. Then uncover and remove from the roasting tin. Keep in the fridge while you make the mousse.

salted chicory mousse

Whip 125g of the double cream to the ribbon stage, then cover and place in the fridge. Put the water and 125g of the caster sugar in a small, heavy-based saucepan and heat slowly to dissolve the sugar, then raise the heat and boil to a rich brown caramel. Meanwhile, soak the gelatine in a little cold water for about 5 minutes, until soft and pliable. Whisk the eggs with the remaining 25g caster sugar until thick and white. Whisk the remaining cream into the caramel, then pour on to the eggs in a steady stream, whisking constantly. Squeeze excess water from the gelatine, then add it to the egg mixture and continue whisking until cold. When cold, fold in the chicory essence, whipped cream and salt to taste.

Remove the vanilla cheesecake from the fridge and pour the mousse on top. Replace in the fridge and chill while you make the glaze.

chicory glaze

Put the water and caster sugar in a small, heavy-based saucepan and dissolve the sugar slowly, then raise the heat and boil to a deep, dark caramel. Meanwhile, soak the gelatine in a little cold water for about 5 minutes, until soft and pliable. Remove the caramel from the heat and whisk in the cream and chicory essence, being careful as the mixture will splutter. Squeeze excess water from the gelatine, then whisk it into the caramel mixture. Whisk in the vegetable oil. Bring back to the boil, then pass through a fine chinois. Leave to cool.

When cold, pour over the top of the cheesecake to finish. Leave to set in the fridge.

chocolate sauce

Dissolve the sugar in 100g of the water in a heavy-based pan, then boil to a deep golden caramel. Add the remaining 400g water and the cocoa powder, being careful as the mixture will splutter, and stir to dissolve the caramel. Bring to the boil. Add the port and red wine and return to the boil, then cook for 3 minutes. Remove from the heat, add the chocolate and stir until it has all melted. Pass through a fine chinois and leave to cool. Store in a jar until needed.

walnut crumble

Mix together all the dry ingredients, then mix in the vanilla seeds, melted butter and walnut oil. Whisk the eggs, then add to the walnut mixture and mix well. Scatter on to a baking sheet lined with baking parchment. Place in an oven preheated to 160°C/Gas Mark 3 and bake for about 20 minutes, until golden and dry, stirring every 5 minutes to prevent burning or lumps from forming. Remove from the oven and leave to cool, then break into more even pieces and return to the oven to bake for a further 3 minutes. Leave to cool completely. Keep in an airtight container until needed.

chocolate sticks

Put the glucose, fondant and isomalt in a heavy-based saucepan. Stir well and bring up to the boil, then cook until the sugar is just starting to turn colour, about 160°C. Remove from the heat. Add the chocolate and stir until melted. Pour on to an oiled tray and leave to cool a little. Then, using your fingers, slowly and carefully pull off little pieces of the chocolate mixture, which should form strands (be careful as the mixture is still very warm). When the strands are 100mm long, snip with scissors and gently lay them on a tray – they will be very brittle. You will need 10–12 of these chocolate sticks. If you are keeping them for any length of time, store in an airtight container.

serving

Remove the cheesecake from the frame and cut into 10 or 12 portions with a warm knife. Place one on each plate. Using a pastry brush, draw a line of chocolate sauce on the plate, parallel to the cheesecake. Place a line of walnut crumble on top of the sauce, followed by a scoop of sorbet and a chocolate stick at an angle.

Note: If you have any leftover pieces of chocolate from making the sticks, you can grind to a powder in a food processor, then keep in an airtight container or small jar. When you want some sticks, sprinkle the powder thinly and evenly on a baking tray lined with baking parchment and place in an oven preheated to 180°C/Gas Mark 4 to melt. Then make strands, as above. Or lay a piece of baking parchment on top of the melted mixture and roll out as thinly as possible, then cut into neat shapes (or leave to cool and break into uneven shapes).

semifreddo of jasmine tea and prune, prune kernel ice cream

Tea and prunes are a match made in heaven, with the tannin of the tea balancing the sweetness of the prunes. I have used jasmine tea here for its floral undertones but you could substitute Earl Grey, Lady Grey or even lapsang souchong to give the prunes a smoky taste. It seems logical to use the kernels from the prunes for the ice cream – why waste them? You could make a walnut ice cream instead, or even a citrus ice cream, which would bring out the fruitiness of the prunes. They also go well with liquorice, burdock root and dandelion root.

Serves 12

Marinated Prunes (see page 15: make the full quantity)

for the jasmine tea and prune semifreddo
145g water
30g jasmine tea bags
200g caster sugar
5 egg yolks
120g drained stoned Marinated Prunes (see above), puréed
30g dark rum
2 egg whites
300g double cream

for the prune kernel ice cream
400g milk
600g double cream
45g prune kernels (removed from the stones of Marinated Prunes), crushed
12 egg yolks
25g liquid glucose
200g skimmed milk powder
110g caster sugar
30g Amaretto

for the meringue
30g liquid glucose
50g water
125g caster sugar
100g egg whites

10g powdered burdock root

for the frozen pressed prune
3g bronze gelatine leaves
100g syrup from the Marinated Prunes (see above)
250g stoned Marinated Prunes (see above)

for the sponge
3 eggs
120g icing sugar
75g ground almonds
100g egg whites
15g caster sugar
60g plain flour
25g unsalted butter, melted

to serve
12 Marinated Prunes (see above), stoned and cut in half, then each half formed into a ball

jasmine tea and prune semifreddo
Bring 70g of the water to the boil in a small pan. Remove from the heat, add the jasmine tea and leave to infuse for 20 minutes. Strain this infusion and set aside.

Dissolve 150g of the caster sugar in the remaining 75g water in another saucepan, then bring to the boil and cook to 121°C, which is just when the syrup is changing colour. Meanwhile, put the egg yolks in the bowl of a freestanding electric mixer and whisk on high speed until thick and white. Pour the hot syrup on to the whisked yolks in a slow steady stream, whisking all the time. Keep whisking until the mixture is cool; it should be creamy white and very thick. Fold in the puréed marinated prunes, the tea infusion and the rum.

Whisk the egg whites until frothy, then add the remaining 50g caster sugar and whisk until medium peaks form. Whip the cream to a light ribbon stage (this is when the cream will hold its shape and make a

ribbon trail on the surface when the whisk is lifted out). Fold the cream into the egg yolk mixture, followed by the whisked egg whites.

Lay 4 sheets of cling film on the work surface. Spoon a quarter of the mixture on to each and form into 4 'sausages', each about 4cm in diameter and 32cm long, wrapping them in the cling film. Tie the ends securely. Freeze for 24 hours, then keep in the freezer until needed.

prune kernel ice cream
Pour the milk and cream into a medium saucepan and slowly bring to the boil. Add the crushed prune kernels, then remove from the heat, cover and leave to infuse overnight.

Set the pan back on the stove and slowly bring up to the boil again. Whisk the egg yolks, glucose, milk powder and caster sugar together in a bowl. Pour half of the hot milk mixture on to the egg mixture, whisking constantly. Pour back into the pan and mix with the remaining milk mixture. Cook on a low heat, stirring constantly with a wooden spoon, until the custard reaches about 84°C, or until it thickens enough to coat the back of the spoon. Immediately strain through a fine sieve into a bowl. Leave to cool, then stir in the Amaretto. Pour into an ice cream machine and churn. Transfer to a container and keep in the freezer until needed. Remove to the fridge 10–15 minutes before serving.

meringue
Combine the glucose, water and 100g of the caster sugar in a saucepan. Heat until the sugar has dissolved, then bring to the boil and cook to 120°C.

(continued on page 167)

(continued from page 165)

When the syrup reaches 110°C, start whisking the egg whites with the remaining caster sugar in a freestanding electric mixer. Once the whites are at soft peak stage and the syrup is at 120°C, turn the machine speed down to medium and slowly pour the syrup down the side of the bowl in a steady thin stream. Continue whisking the meringue until cold.

Spread the meringue to a thickness of 2mm on 2 baking trays lined with baking parchment. Dust with the powdered burdock. Cook in an oven preheated to 100°C (or the lowest gas setting) for 50–60 minutes, with the oven door slightly ajar or the vent open, until the meringues are dry and crisp. Leave to cool, then store in an airtight container. When needed, break into uneven pieces.

frozen pressed prune
Soak the gelatine in a little cold water for about 5 minutes, until soft and pliable. Bring the prune syrup to the boil in a small saucepan. Squeeze excess water from the gelatine, then whisk it into the syrup, making sure it has melted. Remove from the heat. Chop the prunes roughly and add to the syrup.

Line a 22 x 17.5cm baking sheet with acetate. Spoon the prune mixture on to the acetate and cover with another sheet of acetate. Using a palette knife on the top sheet of acetate, spread and push out the prune mixture to form an even layer. Freeze until firm. When frozen, cut out 12 rectangles, each about 9 x 3cm. Keep in the freezer until needed.

sponge
Line a baking tray, about 45 x 30cm, with greaseproof paper. Put the eggs in a mixing bowl with the icing sugar and ground almonds and whisk together until light and fluffy. In another bowl, whisk the egg whites with the caster sugar to stiff peaks. Gently fold the whites into the egg mixture. Fold in the flour, then carefully fold in the melted butter.

Spread out the sponge mixture on the prepared baking sheet and bake in an oven preheated to 220°C/Gas Mark 7 for 5–7 minutes, until golden. Remove from the oven, cover with another sheet of greaseproof paper and invert the sponge on to it. Peel off the lining paper from the base. Leave to cool. Once cool, cut the baked sponge into 12 rectangles just slightly smaller than 10 x 3cm, for the semifreddo to sit on.

serving
Brush the sponge rectangles with a little syrup from the marinated prunes, to moisten. Place one at the top of each plate. Set a frozen pressed prune rectangle at the front of each plate, then put a prune ball on each side and dot with some marinated prune syrup. Remove the semifreddo from the freezer. Trim the ends of the 'sausages' through the cling film, then cut each into 3 even cylinders; remove the cling film and place on the soaked sponge. Arrange the meringue over the semifreddo. Finally, set a quenelle of ice cream on the frozen pressed prune, which should have thawed by now but kept its shape.

coffee ice cream, espresso granita, milk foam, cocoa nib tuile

One of my favourite things is coffee. I am a real fan of espresso, often having a triple cappuccino from my friend Vlad's coffee shop, just down the road. Coffee is wonderful in desserts too and here we have a superb mixture of textures and flavours featuring the drink I love: the espresso in the form of a granita and the coffee ice cream and milk foam representing the cappuccino top, with the cocoa sprinkle in the form of a cocoa nib tuile. You could adapt the recipe to use chicory coffee, if you wish. Spices like cardamom or cinnamon could be added to the coffee ice cream to give it an Arabic feel; liquorice would also work well.

Serves 8

for the coffee ice cream
500g milk
400g double cream
8 egg yolks
100g light muscovado sugar
10g liquid glucose
75g ground fresh coffee
30g Tia Maria or Kahlua

for the espresso granita
125g light muscovado sugar
100g water
600g brewed strong espresso coffee
30g Tia Maria or Kahlua

for the milk foam
5.25g bronze gelatine leaves
350g milk
150g double cream
60g caster sugar

for the cocoa nib tuiles
100g liquid glucose
100g fondant
50g light muscovado sugar
50g bitter dark chocolate (64% cocoa solids), roughly chopped
35g cocoa nibs (grue de cacao)

coffee ice cream
Pour the milk and cream into a medium, heavy-based saucepan and gently bring to the boil. Meanwhile, whisk the egg yolks with the sugar and glucose in a bowl until pale and creamy. Pour half of the milk mixture on to the eggs, whisking to incorporate, then pour this back into the saucepan and stir with the remaining milk mixture. Cook on a gentle heat, stirring all the time with a wooden spoon, until the custard reaches 84°C, or it thickens enough to coat the back of the spoon. Remove from the heat and stir in the ground coffee. Pour into a large bowl and leave to infuse for 45 minutes.

Strain through a fine sieve, then add the coffee liqueur. Churn in an ice cream machine. Transfer to a lidded container and keep in the freezer until needed.

espresso granita
Chill a 1-litre capacity baking dish in the freezer. Meanwhile, combine the sugar and water in a small saucepan and bring to the boil. When the sugar has dissolved, add to the espresso. Leave to cool, then stir in the coffee liqueur. Pour into the chilled baking dish and freeze for 2 hours. Remove from the freezer and stir with a fork to bring the ice crystals that have formed around the edges into the centre. Return to the freezer. Every 30 minutes stir with a fork as before, until all of the mixture is fine crystals. Place the granita in an airtight container and keep in the freezer until needed.

milk foam
Soak the gelatine in a little cold water for about 5 minutes, until soft and pliable. Meanwhile, bring the milk, cream and caster sugar up to the boil in a saucepan. Remove from the heat. Squeeze excess water from the gelatine, then whisk it into the milk mixture, making sure it has melted. Leave to cool. When cold pass through a fine sieve and place in an iSi

cream cylinder. Put the lid on and charge with 1 cartridge. Leave to set in the fridge overnight. Remove from the fridge 20 minutes before needed.

cocoa nib tuiles
Put the glucose, fondant and light muscovado sugar in a small heavy-based saucepan and stir well. Bring up to the boil, then cook until just starting to turn colour, about 150–160°C. Remove from the heat. Add the chocolate and stir until melted, then add the cocoa nibs. Pour on to an oiled tray and leave to cool completely. Smash into small pieces with a rolling pin, then place in a food processor and grind to a powder. Keep in an airtight container, such as a small jar, until needed.

To make the tuiles, sprinkle the powder thinly and evenly on a baking tray lined with baking parchment and place it in an oven preheated to 180°C/Gas Mark 4. Cook for 3–4 minutes to melt. Remove from the oven and lay a sheet of baking parchment on top. Roll out the melted mixture as thinly as possible, then cut into neat shapes (or leave to cool and then break into uneven shapes). While still warm the tuiles will be pliable, so the pieces can be draped over something; however, they cool and harden very quickly. Leave to cool before serving.

serving
You can either divide the ice cream among 8 metal rings set on the plates (then lift off the rings) or make 8 scoops. Top each with granita, forming a little pyramid. Give the milk foam a good shake, then squirt on top and finish each with a cocoa nib tuile. The idea is to eat through the layers, experiencing the different textures.

bilberry fool, *buttermilk ice cream, lemon verbena shortbread*

Bilberries are known by many other names including blaeberry, winberry and whortleberry, to name but three. In season in August and September, they benefit from the sun shining on them, making them sweeter. If you cannot find them, you could use blueberries instead. Bilberries have quite a deep flavour, so I have teamed them with a buttermilk ice cream to give a slight acidity to the dish, and lemon verbena shortbread to add some texture. You could replace the shortbread crumble with some violet meringue pieces or maybe a liquorice granola.

Serves 8

for the buttermilk ice cream
grated zest of 1 lemon
25g lemon juice
250g milk
300g double cream
4 egg yolks
10g liquid glucose
150g caster sugar
500g buttermilk

for the bilberry fool
¹/₂ vanilla pod, split lengthways
750g picked-over bilberries
juice of ¹/₂ lemon
about 225g caster sugar
700g double cream

for the shortbread
300g plain flour
125g rice flour (or cornflour)
20 large lemon verbena leaves, chopped
150g caster sugar
300g chilled unsalted butter, diced
1 egg
1 egg yolk

40g bilberries, to serve
sheep's sorrel or lemon balm leaves, to decorate

buttermilk ice cream
Put the lemon zest and juice in a heavy-based pan and bring to the boil. Add the milk and then the cream and return to the boil. Remove from the heat. Whisk the egg yolks, glucose and caster sugar together in a bowl. Pour half of the milk mixture on to the egg mixture, whisking continuously, then pour back into the pan and stir to mix with the remaining milk mixture. Cook on a low heat, stirring constantly with a wooden spoon, until the custard reaches 84°C or until it thickens enough to coat the back of the spoon. Immediately strain through a fine sieve into a bowl. Leave to cool, then whisk in the buttermilk. Cover and leave to mature in the fridge overnight. Pour into an ice cream machine and churn. Transfer to a container and keep in the freezer until needed. Remove to the fridge 10–15 minutes before serving.

bilberry fool
Scrape the seeds from the vanilla pod and set them aside. Put the empty pod in a small saucepan with the bilberries, lemon juice and 200g of the caster sugar. Bring to the boil, stirring frequently, then cook on a moderate heat for about 5 minutes, until the bilberries begin to break down and the juices boil and thicken. Remove from the heat. Now you need to decide if you want a smooth fool. If so, pass the mixture through a fine sieve, pushing the pulp through to get a purée. If you want texture in the fool, then do not sieve (discard the vanilla pod once the fool is cold). Leave to cool.

Combine the cream, remaining caster sugar and the vanilla seeds in a mixing bowl and whisk until a little stiffer than ribbon stage. Add the bilberry purée (or mixture) in 3 stages, folding well after each addition. Taste and add a little more sugar if the fool is not sweet enough, or a little extra lemon juice if it is too sweet. Divide equally among 8 serving bowls or glasses. Keep in the fridge until needed.

shortbread
Put the flour, rice flour, chopped verbena and sugar in a mixing bowl. Add the butter and rub in until a breadcrumb-like texture is obtained. Add the egg and egg yolk and gently mix together to make a cohesive mass. Cover and chill for 6 hours.

Break the mixture into little 'rocks' and place on a baking sheet lined with baking parchment. Bake in an oven preheated to 180°C/Gas Mark 4 until golden. Remove from the oven and leave to cool on the baking sheet. Break up again and keep in an airtight container until needed.

serving
Scatter some broken lemon verbena shortbread over each serving of fool, followed by some bilberries. Carefully place a scoop of buttermilk ice cream in the middle of each bowl and decorate with a few sheep's sorrel or lemon balm leaves.

wild plum blossom cream, roasted pear, hibiscus meringue

One of the boys brought some plum blossom in one day and asked if we could use it for a dessert. I decided to try to come up with a recipe. Plum blossom has a distinct perfume and a flavour somewhat like bitter almonds. I thought it would go well with roasted pear and to complement this added a meringue flavoured with hibiscus, for a bit of 'crunch' and a slight acidic note to balance the sweetness of the pears. The freshness from raw pear and pear sorbet provides the depth that the dish requires. Here is the result of my experiments. It tastes amazing.

Serves 6

for the wild plum blossom cream
675g double cream
225g milk
45g wild plum blossom
10.5g bronze gelatine leaves
12 egg yolks
100g caster sugar

for the hibiscus meringue
320g caster sugar
100g water
20g ground dried hibiscus flowers
150g egg whites

for the pear purée
3 ripe Williams pears
25g unsalted butter
seeds from 1 vanilla pod
juice of 1/2 lemon
30g caster sugar

for the roasted pears
3 large, ripe Williams pears
100g unsalted butter
75g soft light brown sugar
50g caster sugar
50g water
1 vanilla pod, split lengthways

to serve
2 Williams pears, peeled, finely sliced and
   cut into 2.5cm discs
a small handful of wild plum blossom

wild plum blossom cream
Put the cream, milk and plum blossom in a medium saucepan and bring to the boil. Remove from the heat, cover and leave to infuse for 10–30 minutes. During this time, taste the cream now and again. When you think it has enough flavour (this depends on how bitter the blossom is), strain through a fine chinois into a clean pan, pressing to extract as much liquid from the blossom as you can.

Soak the gelatine in a little cold water for about 5 minutes, until soft and pliable. Set the pan back on the stove and bring the infusion back to the boil. Meanwhile, whisk the egg yolks with the sugar until pale and creamy. Pour half of the infusion on to the eggs, whisking to incorporate, then pour this back into the saucepan and mix with the remaining infusion. Cook on a gentle heat, stirring all the time with a wooden spoon, until the cream starts to thicken and coats the back of the spoon. Remove from the heat. Squeeze excess water from the gelatine, then whisk it into the cream until melted.

Pour into a baking tray, about 26 x 20 x 4cm. Lay a clean J-cloth on the bottom of a large, deep baking tray and set the smaller tray in it. Pour enough hot water into the large baking tray to come a third of the way up the sides of the smaller tray. Carefully place in an oven preheated to 96°C (if your oven will not go this low, then cook at the lowest setting possible) and cook for 20–30 minutes, until the cream has just set in the middle. Remove from the oven and leave in the tray of water to cool. When cold, remove from the water, cover and keep in the fridge until needed (preferably make this the day before).

hibiscus meringue
Put 300g of the caster sugar, the water and ground hibiscus in a small saucepan and heat to dissolve the sugar, then bring to the boil. Cook to 121°C. When the syrup reaches 110°C, start whisking the egg whites with the remaining caster sugar in a freestanding electric mixer. Once the egg whites are at soft peak stage and the syrup is at 121°C, slowly pour the syrup down the side of the bowl in a steady, thin stream, whisking on high.

Drizzle the hibiscus syrup on to the egg whites in a steady stream, then continue whisking the meringue until cold.

Spoon the meringue into a piping bag fitted with a small plain nozzle. Pipe 5–6cm spikes with a bulbous end on to a baking tray lined with baking parchment. (You will need 24 perfect spikes; any that are not so perfect can be crumbled on to the dessert.) Place in an oven preheated to 100°C (or the lowest gas setting) and bake for 50–60 minutes, with the oven door slightly ajar or the vent open, until the meringues are dry and crisp. Leave to cool, then store in an airtight container until needed.

pear purée
Peel, core and dice the pears. Melt the butter in a saucepan, add the pears and sweat without colouring for 2 minutes. Add the vanilla seeds, lemon juice and sugar, then cook on a gentle heat until the pears are tender. Pour into a blender and blend until smooth. Pass through a fine chinois and leave to cool. Store in a squeezy bottle in the fridge until needed.

roasted pears
Peel the pears. Cut each into 6 wedges and remove the cores. Heat the butter in a large ovenproof frying pan and, when frothing, add the pears. Cook for 3–4 minutes, until they are golden brown on all sides. Add the brown and caster sugars and cook until they have dissolved, then add the water and split vanilla pod. Place the pan in an oven preheated to 180°C/Gas Mark 4 and cook for 5–6 minutes, basting with the pan juices halfway through, until a deep golden brown. Remove the pears from the juices and keep warm until needed; discard the juices.

serving
Remove the wild plum blossom cream from the fridge and scoop 4 quenelles on to each plate, placing them down the middle at different angles. Lay 3 wedges of roasted pear in between the quenelles. Angle 4 meringue spikes along the plate. Add pear discs, dot with pear purée and scatter over some crushed meringue. Finally, sprinkle with plum blossom.

yeast parfait, lemon and toasted brioche ice cream

This wonderful parfait has the lovely yeasty flavour that you get in sweet yeast pastries. It seemed obvious to marry it with some sort of bread, and brioche, with its buttery note, was a natural choice. I have added lemon to the ice cream, because of the slight natural acidity of the yeast. You could of course replace the lemon with orange, and maybe serve the parfait with a beer ice cream, another yeasty product.

Serves 12

for the yeast parfait
50g milk
30g fresh yeast
125g caster sugar
400g double cream
100g water
8 egg yolks
a pinch of salt

for the lemon and toasted brioche ice cream
150g Brioche (see page 23), made into
  crumbs
75g soft light brown sugar
grated zest and juice of 3 lemons
600g milk
400g double cream
8 egg yolks
150g caster sugar
25g liquid glucose
10g ice cream stabiliser

for the brioche craquant
200g caster sugar
200g liquid glucose
50g water
200g Brioche (see page 23), made into
  crumbs

for the caramelised apple syrup
25g water
100g caster sugar
500g apple juice

for the caramelised apple purée
50g caster sugar
250g peeled and cored Granny Smith apples
40g unsalted butter
seeds from 1 vanilla pod
a pinch of salt
juice of ¹/₂ lemon

yeast parfait
You will need a metal cooking frame about 36 x 12cm and 4cm deep. Place it on a tray and brush the interior and the tray with a little water or oil. Line with a double layer of cling film – it should be very smooth with no creases.

Warm the milk in a small saucepan, to just a little higher than blood heat. Remove from the heat. Add the yeast and whisk to break it up until smooth, then add 5g of the caster sugar and mix. Leave in a warm place for about 15 minutes, until frothy. Set the pan back on the heat and bring to just under boiling point. Leave to cool.

Whip the cream to the ribbon stage, then place in the fridge. Put the remaining 120g caster sugar and the water in a small saucepan and heat to dissolve the sugar, then bring to the boil. Meanwhile, place the egg yolks in the bowl of a freestanding electric mixer and whisk until thick, airy and white. Cook the sugar syrup to the soft ball stage (121°C). Then with the mixer on high, slowly drizzle the syrup on to the egg yolks. Carry on whisking until cold. Fold in the yeast mixture and the salt, using a light and airy folding motion. Finally, fold in the whipped cream. Pour into the lined frame and freeze for 24 hours, then keep in the freezer until needed.

lemon and toasted brioche ice cream
Mix together the brioche crumbs and soft brown sugar, then scatter on to a greased baking sheet. Bake in an oven preheated to 200°C/Gas Mark 6 for 9–12 minutes, stirring every 3 minutes, until the sugared crumbs are evenly golden; be careful not to let them burn. Remove from the oven and leave to cool, then break up into crumbs again.

Put the lemon zest and juice in a medium, heavy-based saucepan and gently bring to the boil, then add the milk and cream. Remove from the heat and leave to infuse for 2 hours. After this time, set the pan back on the heat and bring to the boil. Meanwhile, whisk the egg yolks with the caster sugar, glucose and stabiliser until pale and creamy. Pour half of the milk mixture on to the egg yolk mixture, whisking to incorporate, then pour this back into the saucepan and mix with the remaining milk mixture. Cook on a gentle heat, stirring all the time with a wooden spoon, until the custard reaches 84°C, or it thickens enough to coat the back of the spoon. Remove from the heat and immediately strain through a fine sieve into a large bowl, to help stop the cooking. Leave to cool.

Once cold, churn in an ice cream machine; when nearly churned, fold in the toasted brioche crumbs, then finish churning. Transfer to a container and keep in the freezer until needed. Remove to the fridge 5–10 minutes before serving.

brioche craquant
Combine the caster sugar, glucose and water in a heavy-based saucepan. Dissolve the sugar on a gentle heat, then bring up to the boil and cook until caramelised to a golden amber colour. Add the brioche crumbs and swirl around in the caramel. Immediately pour on to an oiled lipped baking tray. Leave until cold and very crisp. Break up the caramel, then place in a food processor and pulse to a coarse powder. Store in an airtight container.

When needed, sprinkle the powder in a thin, even layer on a lipped baking tray lined with baking parchment to form a large rectangle. Place in an oven preheated to 200°C/Gas Mark 6 and cook until the craquant has melted and formed a single sheet of caramel. Remove from the oven and leave to cool. Just before it sets, cut into 24mm x 4cm strips. You will need 24 but cut a few more just in case as they are very brittle – say 30 altogether. Leave to cool completely. (Keep the trimmings in an airtight container: they can be ground down and used again.)

caramelised apple syrup
Dissolve the sugar in the water in a saucepan, then cook to a deep golden brown caramel – you want to catch it just before it burns. Whisk in the apple juice, then slowly bring to the boil again and reduce to a syrup-like consistency. Leave to cool. If the cold syrup is too thick, add a little water and re-boil. Place in a squeezy bottle.

caramelised apple purée
Melt the sugar in a heavy-based frying pan, then cook to a golden caramel. Roughly dice the apples, add to the caramel with the butter and vanilla seeds, and stir. Cook until the apples have broken down and become golden. Stir in the salt and lemon juice.

Blend until smooth, then pass through a fine chinois. Leave to cool. Keep in a squeezy bottle in the fridge until needed.

serving
Remove the parfait from the freezer. Cut it lengthways down the middle, then cut across 6 times to give 12 cubes. Sandwich each cube between 2 strips of craquant. Draw 2 lines of caramelised apple syrup on each plate. Set a parfait 'sandwich' in the centre at an angle. Top with a quenelle of lemon and toasted brioche ice cream. Finish with blobs of caramelised apple purée.

acorn tart, chestnut ice cream, beech nut crumble

The flavour of roasted acorns is a complex mixture of caramel, mocha and chocolate with a light spice note. There is a slight similarity to wattle seeds and these could be substituted, as could chicory root. We gather the acorns in autumn when we walk the dogs in the forest. This is a good time to pick up some chestnuts and beech nuts too. The result is a truly autumnal feast of foraged ingredients.

Serves 12–14

for the chestnut ice cream
250g double cream
750g milk
275g peeled cooked chestnuts
8 egg yolks
100g caster sugar
100g liquid glucose
30g single malt whisky (as peaty as
    possible)

for the acorn tart
450g Sweet Pastry (see page 21)
1.1kg double cream
125g ground roasted acorns, plus a little
    extra for sprinkling
12 egg yolks
125g caster sugar

for the beech nut crumble
50g caster sugar
75g plain flour
a pinch of salt
50g ground shelled beech nuts
25g ground almonds
75g unsalted butter, melted
25g shelled beech nuts, toasted and roughly
    chopped

chestnut ice cream

Place the cream, milk and chestnuts in a medium saucepan. Bring to the boil, then simmer for about 5 minutes. Remove from the heat and tip into a blender. Purée until smooth. Whisk together the egg yolks, sugar and glucose in a bowl. Gradually add half of the milk mixture to the egg mixture, whisking constantly. Pour back into the pan and stir to mix with the other half of the milk mixture. Cook on a low heat, stirring constantly with a wooden spoon, until the custard reaches 84°C, or until it thickens enough to coat the back of the spoon. Immediately strain through a fine sieve into a bowl. Leave to cool before stirring in the whisky. Churn in an ice cream machine, then transfer to a sealed container and keep in the freezer until needed. Remove the ice cream to the fridge 20 minutes before serving.

acorn tart

Roll out the pastry and use to line a buttered loose-based tart tin that is 29cm in diameter and 3–3.5cm deep. Chill for 40–50 minutes.

Prick the base of the pastry case with a fork, then line with baking parchment and fill with dried rice or baking beans. Set the tin on a baking sheet and bake blind in an oven preheated to 160°C/Gas Mark 3 for 10–15 minutes, until the pastry is set and golden. Carefully remove the paper and beans. Set the pastry case aside.

Pour the cream into a saucepan, add the ground acorns and bring to the boil. Remove from the heat and leave to infuse for 30 minutes. Place back on the heat and bring to the boil again. Put the egg yolks and sugar in a bowl and whisk lightly to combine. Pour the hot cream on to this mixture, whisking all the time, then pour back into the saucepan and heat through gently for about 2 minutes, stirring

constantly. You do not want to cook the custard, just raise the temperature so the tart will cook more quickly and evenly.

Strain the custard through a fine sieve and carefully pour into the pastry case. Sprinkle with a little extra ground acorns. Place in the oven and bake for 20–30 minutes, until the filling has just set. Remove from the oven and set the tart, still on the baking sheet, on a heatproof work surface. Cover with another baking sheet and leave for 10 minutes so the tart can finish its cooking. Then uncover and leave to cool thoroughly. Keep in a cool place, not the fridge, until needed.

beech nut crumble

Mix together the sugar, flour, salt and ground nuts. Add the melted butter and mix well. Scatter over a baking sheet lined with baking parchment and bake in an oven preheated to 160°C/Gas Mark 3 for 40–50 minutes, until dry and crisp. Leave to cool, then add the chopped beech nuts. Store in an airtight container until needed.

serving

Cut the acorn tart into slices and place on the plates. Add a scoop of ice cream sitting on some beech nut crumble alongside.

amaretto blancmange, roasted damsons, damson and liquorice sorbet

Those of you who have read my other two books know I have something of a liking for liquorice, probably because I was given root liquorice to chew on when I was a child rather than sweets. Liquorice has a masculine flavour that goes well with many other strong flavours, but it can also be quite subtle. Here it complements damsons, a rich, fruity tangy plum that we are lucky enough to pick from a friend's allotment. The Amaretto blancmange pays homage to the classic almond blancmange, the almonds appearing in a toasted form to add texture. The blancmange was originally set with something called isinglass, but nowadays gelatine or carrageen is used.

Serves 8

for the damson and liquorice sorbet
7g bronze gelatine leaves
300g water
75g caster sugar
50g liquid glucose
4g ground liquorice root
500g damson purée
juice of ¹/₂ lemon

for the amaretto blancmange
9g bronze gelatine leaves
650g double cream
150g milk
100g caster sugar
2g cornflour
40g Amaretto

for the roasted damsons
350g damsons
120g caster sugar
50g unsalted butter
a pinch of ground liquorice root

30g toasted flaked almonds, to serve

damson and liquorice sorbet
Soak the gelatine in a little cold water for about 5 minutes, until soft and pliable. Put the water, sugar, glucose and liquorice powder in a large saucepan. Bring to the boil, then remove from the heat. Squeeze excess water from the gelatine, then whisk it into the syrup, making sure it has melted. Add the damson purée and whisk in, then pass through a fine chinois and leave to cool. Pour into a container and add the lemon juice. Cover and leave in the fridge overnight. The next day, strain into an ice cream machine and churn. Transfer to a container and keep in the freezer until needed.

amaretto blancmange
Soak the gelatine in a little cold water for about 5 minutes, until soft and pliable. Put the cream, milk and sugar in a heavy-based saucepan and gently bring to the boil. Mix the cornflour with the Amaretto and add to the cream mixture, then whisk until it thickens slightly. Remove from the heat. Squeeze excess water from the gelatine, then whisk it into the cream mixture until completely melted. Strain through a coarse sieve and leave to cool. Pour into 8 lightly oiled dariole moulds, each about 120g capacity (we use a large canelé mould). Cover and chill until set, then keep in the fridge until needed.

roasted damsons
Remove the stones from the damsons, then put them in a bowl. Sprinkle with half of the sugar and leave to macerate for 2–3 hours. Drain, keeping the juices. Heat the butter in an ovenproof frying pan. When foaming, add the damsons and the remaining sugar. Transfer to an oven preheated to 200°C/Gas Mark 6 and roast for 2 minutes, stirring halfway through. Remove from the oven and set the pan on a high heat. Cook until the damsons are just soft.

Remove the damsons from the pan and set aside. Add the juices from macerating the damsons to the pan, stir in the liquorice powder and cook until reduced to a syrup. Strain and leave to cool.

serving
Dip the moulds in hot water for 2–3 seconds to loosen the blancmanges, then dry. Gently pull each blancmange away from the side of its mould. Quickly turn out on to a serving plate (you must be quick to prevent any weeping). Arrange the roasted damsons on the plate in a line and stud with some toasted almonds. Drizzle with damson syrup and, finally, add a quenelle of damson sorbet.

sea buckthorn and orange pastilles

Sea buckthorn is a wonderful little berry that usually grows in coastal areas, although I have also seen it alongside the motorways of Calais. It has a very sour flavour with a pronounced tang, and I equate it to passion fruit and mandarin. I have combined it here with orange so it isn't too powerful. Carrot juice can replace the orange. If you can't get sea buckthorn juice, or the berries to make your own juice, then use passion fruit instead. To give the pastilles an added zing, you could add 30g of citric acid to the coating of granulated sugar.

350g orange juice
250g sea buckthorn juice
500g caster sugar
100g liquid glucose
20g pectin powder
7g tartaric acid
200g granulated sugar

Combine the orange juice, sea buckthorn juice, 450g of the caster sugar and the glucose in a large saucepan and bring to the boil, stirring all the time. Cook to 102°C, stirring occasionally so the syrup doesn't catch on the bottom of the pan.

Mix the remaining 50g caster sugar with the pectin powder, thoroughly combining them. When the syrup reaches 102°C, whisk in the pectin mixture until dissolved, taking care as the mixture will be getting extremely hot. Continue cooking on a high heat to 110°C, stirring occasionally. Then

whisk in the tartaric acid. Strain through a conical sieve into a 50 x 15cm lipped baking tray lined with baking parchment, to a depth of 1cm. Leave to cool.

Once cool, cut into pastille shapes using a 20mm cutter, or into squares, strips or rectangles (at the restaurant we use a silicone mould for the pastilles, which cuts down on wastage). Toss the pastilles in the granulated sugar, then place on a wire rack to air-dry for 6 hours. Keep in an airtight container in single layers, interleaved with baking parchment, in a cool dry place.

salted caramel and peanut truffles

I have to admit to being partial to the odd Snickers bar now and again. What's not to like? I mean, caramel, peanuts and chocolate. Well, this is my little version of them. The peanuts can be replaced with pistachios or walnuts, and you could add a little ground coffee to the caramel, or a few cumin or fennel seeds. This makes quite a few truffles, so why not give some as a surprise gift to someone? They are rather moreish, though, and you may want to keep them for yourself!

Makes about 90 truffles

400g caster sugar
400g liquid glucose
500g double cream
300g chilled unsalted butter, finely diced
100g crunchy peanut butter
14g salt
400g peanuts, roasted, skinned and roughly
  chopped
475g milk chocolate, melted
100g cocoa powder

Put the caster sugar and glucose in a heavy-based saucepan. Set on a medium high heat and stir until the sugar has dissolved, then raise the heat and cook to a deep golden brown caramel. Add the cream and butter, being careful as it will splatter, then cook to 115°C, stirring all the time.

Remove from the heat and leave to cool for 2–3 minutes, then stir in the peanut butter. Add the salt and mix well. Pour into a parchment-lined tray. Cover and leave to set in the fridge (overnight would be perfect).

Roll the chilled mixture into 15g balls, then roll the balls in the chopped peanuts. Place on the tray and return to the fridge to set.

When the balls are firm, one by one roll them in the melted chocolate, removing a little of the excess with your hands, then drop into the cocoa powder. Shake the balls in the cocoa powder until covered, then carefully remove to another tray lined with baking parchment. Once the chocolate has set, transfer to an airtight container and keep in the fridge until needed (they can be kept for 2 weeks – if you can resist them). Remove from the fridge 15 minutes before serving.

beetroot and tangerine nougat

I love the earthiness of beetroot and its natural sweetness means it is great for desserts, chocolates and these petits fours. The flavour of beetroot is a perfect match for orange, so here I have added a little tangerine into the equation.

Makes 81–90 pieces

900g fresh beetroot juice (1kg pressed raw beetroot will yield 400g juice, so you will need about 2.25kg beetroot)
400g caster sugar
175g liquid glucose
300g roasted walnut halves
300g roasted blanched almonds
200g shelled Sicilian pistachios
125g jasmine honey
finely grated zest of 2 tangerines
75g egg whites

Put the beetroot juice in a heavy-based saucepan and gently bring to the boil. Skim off any scum using a slotted spoon, then strain through a chinois into a clean pan. Bring to the boil again, then simmer until reduced to 200g. Add the sugar and glucose and bring to the boil, stirring occasionally to dissolve the sugar. Cook to 155°C.

Meanwhile, spread all the nuts on a baking tray and warm them in an oven preheated to 120°C/Gas Mark ½. Keep warm.

In another saucepan, heat the honey with the tangerine zest to 140°C.

When the honey and the beetroot syrup are nearly at the right temperature, start whisking the egg whites in a freestanding electric mixer. When they will form soft peaks, add the honey, pouring it in in a steady stream, whisking on high speed. Then slowly pour in the syrup, still whisking. Add the warm nuts and fold in quickly but gently.

Line a 42 x 16 x 1.5cm tray with rice paper. Spoon the nut mixture on to the paper and spread out evenly with a wet palette knife, then lay another sheet of rice paper on top. Roll over with a rolling pin to flatten and smooth the surface. Wrap the tray in cling film, then leave to set in the fridge. When the nougat is firmly set, cut into 3 blocks and vacuum pack, or wrap tightly in cling film and place in an airtight container. Store in the fridge until needed (the nougat can be kept for 2–3 weeks). To serve, cut each block into 3 and then each of these into 9 or 10 pieces.

calissons

I first tasted these wonderful little cakes when one of my old second chefs, Laurent, brought them back from Montpellier in the south of France. Here I have put my own stamp on them, with a little Amaretto and some dried apricots. This recipe would work with most glacé or dried fruits – for example, dried figs work well with glacé ginger.

Makes about 60

for the cakes
400g dried apricots
200g glacé melon
125g Amaretto di Saronno
425g ground almonds, plus extra for dusting
300g caster sugar
finely grated zest of 1 orange
finely grated zest of 1 lemon

for the icing
50g egg whites
275g icing sugar

cakes
Roughly chop the apricots and melon and place in a saucepan with the Amaretto. Bring to the boil, then simmer for 1 minute, stirring all the time. Remove from the heat, cover and leave to soften for 2 hours. Transfer the apricot mixture to a food processor and blitz to a fine, sticky paste. Remove to a bowl and leave to cool.

Add the ground almonds, caster sugar and zests to the paste and mix well. Turn out on to a work surface and knead well until the mixture comes together. Dust the surface with a little ground almonds, then roll out the mixture to a near square measuring 20 x 21cm and 1.5cm thick.

Lay this on a tray and keep in the fridge while you make the icing.

icing

Put the egg whites in a bowl and sift in the icing sugar. Mix well with a wooden spoon or spatula. Spread the icing evenly on top of the fruit mixture. Cut into 20 x 35mm rectangles. Place on a baking sheet lined with baking parchment. Leave somewhere warm, such as the oven with just the pilot light on, to dry for 6–8 hours – they are ready when they are dry to the touch. Alternatively, cook in an oven preheated to 120°C/Gas Mark 1/2 for 15 minutes, just to dry a little, then leave to cool. Store in an airtight container, with baking parchment between the layers of calissons (they can be kept for a week).

The team and me out foraging for ingredients.

The brilliant team who have been with me during the creation
of this book:
Left to right: Matthew Worswick, Sue Ellis, me, Keiron Stevens
and Mark Stinchcombe.

my suppliers

food

flying fish seafoods

Units 9 and 10
Indian Queens Workshops
Indian Queens
Cornwall TR9 6JP
www.flyingfishseafoods.co.uk
01726 862876

Johnny, the best fishmonger I have ever
had, without a doubt. Thank you for all
your help and advice when needed. If only
all suppliers could be as passionate about
their products as you are about your fish.
Are you sure you aren't a chef?!

m.j. & j.a. watts

5 Suffolk Parade
Cheltenham
Gloucestershire GL50 2AB
01242 522151

My butchers, who have been with me for
25 years now. Thanks for teaching me and
allowing me to teach you.

carroll's heritage potatoes

Tiptoe Farm,
Cornhill-on-Tweed
Northumberland TD12 4XD
www.heritage-potatoes.co.uk
01890 883833
01890 882205 (**phone and fax**)

Wonderful selection of seasonal British
potatoes grown with care. We use several
varieties for our dishes, each potato
displaying its own characteristics.

island divers

Unit 26, F3, Kyle Industrial Estate
Kyle of Lochalsh
Ross Shire IV40 8AX
01599 530300

My amazing scallop and langoustine
supplier. Madeleine, some of the best
shellfish around.

hereford snails

L'Escargot Anglaise
Credenhill Snail Farm
Credenhill
Hereford
Herefordshire HR4 7DN
01432 760750 / 01432 760218

campbell environmental oils

Swell Buildings Farm
Lower Swell
Stow-on-the-Wold
Cheltenham
Gloucestershire GL54 1HG
www.r-oil.co.uk
01451 870387

I use Hamish Campbell's rapeseed oil
for many of our dressings, a wonderful
product from a man who cares as much
about his oil as we do about our food.

the forager

Unit 1, Deanery Farm
Bolts Hill
Chartham, Canterbury
Kent CT4 7LD
01227 738826

Wild food and spices from Miles and Ezra.
Thank you for introducing me to some new
experiences!! A wealth of knowledge by
some great guys.

the mountain food company

Banc Y Ddol Isaf
Whitland
Dyfed SA34 0YR
www. mountainfood.org
01994 419555

Yun helps supply us with some of the wild
foods, when I am either too busy to be able
to get out, or when I need foods from the
sea. Thank you for sharing your
knowledge.

g. baldwin and co.

171–3 Walworth Road
London SE17 1RW
www.baldwins.co.uk
020 7703 5550

Suppliers of a huge range of dried herbs,
roots and flowers, including burdock root.

msk

PO Box 1592
Dronfield
Sheffield S18 8BR
www.msk-ingredients.com
01246 412211

MSK supplies us with some of the gums,
agar and pralines that we use, and has
all the ingredients the modern chef needs.
Have a good look at the website; it's very
interesting.

china and tableware

bodo sperlein

Unit 2.05 Oxo Tower Wharf
Barge House Street
London SE1 9PH
www.bodosperlein.com
020 7633 9413

A big thank you to Bodo for some of the
china supplied in the book. An artistic genius.

goodfellow & goodfellow

7–8 Burdon Drive
North West Industrial Estate
Peterlee
County Durham SR8 2JH
www.goodf.co.uk
0844 334 5232

Paul Goodfellow's latest venture supplying
some of the most cutting edge china and
equipment out there. The fantastic team is
always willing to help out and find things
to your exact requirements.

table concepts

Crest House
102–104 Church Road
Teddington
Middlesex TW11 8PY
www.tableconcepts.co.uk
020 8977 8820

A wide range of china and glasses.
Only too keen to help find what we need.

art for glass

12 Victoria Terrace
London N4 4DA
www.artforglass.co.uk
020 7272 9341

Steven Newell makes some of the most
interesting glass plates and is keen to listen
to what designs you want.

chef's knives and kitchenware

robert welch

Robert Welch Customer Services
Lower High Street
Chipping Campden
Gloucestershire GL55 6DY
www.robertwelch.com
01386 840522

Currently all my chefs and I use Robert
Welch knives. Surely you can't get a better
endorsement? British Design at its best.

cheltenham kitchener

4 Queens Circus
Cheltenham
Gloucestershire GL50 1RX
www.kitchenercookware.com
01242 235688

It's great to have this equipment supplier
just around the corner. If Ed can't get it,
I don't know who can.

Foraging for ingredients in the beautiful Cotswold countryside.

glossary

agar agar
Derived from red dulse, a form of seaweed, this is a good setting agent, suitable for vegetarians. It allows you to make warm mousses as it doesn't start to melt until approximately 83°C. If too much is used it can be very brittle with a horrid texture.

bucks horn plantain (*plantago coronopus*)
An attractive little plant with pronged leaves and an earthy flavour, use it raw as a garnish – it's good with beetroot and root vegetables. Wilt the large leaves.

burdock (*arctium lappa*)
A wonderful plant that you can use in its entirety – seeds, leaves, roots and stalks. It is relatively easy to find dried, which is a good job because the roots are a real pain to dig up. The Japanese use the fresh root as a vegetable.

carrageen moss (*chondrus crispus*)
A form of red algae, this setting agent is available dried or powdered. You should be able to find it in healthfood shops.

cleavers (*galium aparine*)
Cleavers grow all over the place – in hedges, gardens, fields, etc – during spring and summer. The young tips have a clean taste like freshly podded peas. We use them raw in salads and dishes that need a little texture. Pea shoots could be substituted.

dandelion root (*taraxacum officinale*)
We know about the culinary use for the flowers and leaves, but the root is edible too. Dried and roasted, we use it for ice creams and brûlées and to add bitterness to dishes.

fat hen (*chenopodium album*)
Related to quinoa, the leaves and young shoots of this plant are eaten as a vegetable. The black seeds are edible too. Fat hen does have oxalic acid present; cooking destroys most of this, but you shouldn't eat too much of it raw.

good king henry
(*chenopodium bonus-henricus*)
This produces leaves and shoots (young shoots are also called 'poor man's asparagus'). The young leaves can be used as you would spinach.

green aniseed
This is one of my favourite spices. I love aniseed drinks, such as pastis, ouzo and raki, and have paired it with chocolate on many occasions. It is traditionally used in cakes and pastries in the Mediterranean and is very good for the digestion.

hairy bittercress (*cardamine hirsuta*)
This grows almost everywhere, and both stems and leaves are used. It has a real fiery bite to it, especially before it flowers.

hedge bedstraw (*galium mollugo*)
Very prolific in rough grassland, hedge banks and so on, this plant has a slight almond flavour. It is good as a garnish for fish and cold dishes that need a lift.

hogweed
At its best from April to July, hogweed is very common in woods, hedges and grassy areas. The leaves are good for soups and purées; the young stalks should be lightly peeled and cooked with a little butter and water.

isomalt
A derivative of sucrose obtained from sugar beet, this is used a lot in pastry kitchens. It takes longer to crystallise than sugar.

kecap manis
This is basically Indonesian sweet soy sauce (*manis* means sweet in Indonesian). It's a good ingredient to have in your storecupboard for stir-fries and for the stock base for the Chicken Mushi.

kuzu
This is the Japanese name for the natural thickener and gelling agent extracted from the root of the kudzu vine.

lecithin powder
I get lecithin granules and grind them to a powder in a spice grinder, then keep in a jar with an airtight lid.

lotus seed
Used in Asian cuisine, the seeds may be brown or white (I use the brown split seeds, that is to say seeds that have been dried with their membrane on). Interestingly, in the areas where lotus root is harvested, the seeds are sold fresh as a snack.

meadowsweet
(*filipendula ulmaria/spiraea ulmaria*)
Meadowsweet can be found in damp woods, fields and marshy areas. It flowers from early May until October in warm summers, and the sweet-scented blossoms are ideal for infusing in cream to make ice creams, parfaits and syllabubs.

orpine (*sedum telephium*)
A flashy leaf, this can add a welcome blast of moisture to rich foods and salads.

ox eye daisy (*leucanthemum vulgare*)
I love this plant for its leaves that taste of raw beetroot. The petals make a nice addition to amuse bouche.

sashimi togarashi
A wonderful Japanese spice mix, sometimes called 7 spice, this contains chilli, sansho, dried tangerine peel, seaweed, ginger and sesame seeds, and may also include mustard, poppy or hemp seeds. It can spice up anything. I like it with shellfish.

sea aster (*aster tripolium*)
Normally found near salt marshes, this perennial grows up to 50cm in height, with

fleshy leaves. Young small leaves are lovely raw; the large leaves can be wilted like spinach.

sea lettuce (*ulva lactuca*)
Try this raw in salads or cooked in soups and stews. I have used it for a jelly in this book.

sea purslane
Sea purslane, with its lovely salty flavour, can be found on salt marshes all year round. We prefer to use the young leaves raw for their crisp texture. The larger leaves can be quickly wilted and, with a little cream to bind, make a good accompaniment to fish dishes.

sheep's sorrel (*rumex acetosella*)
These wonderful, arrowhead-shaped leaves grow in fields and pastures. As with all sorrels, they have a pleasing lemony bite and make a great ice cream.

stonecrop (*sedum album*)
This can be found in dry places, in between rocks or stone walls. When eaten raw it provides a crunch and a burst of moisture. If cooking, cook very quickly in a butter emulsion.

trimoline
This is an invert sugar that prevents the re-crystallisation of sugar. It is particularly good to use in sorbets.

ultratex
A flavourless starch modified from tapioca, this is used to prevent things like a parsley purée from bleeding. It also thickens liquids without heat.

xanthan gum
Produced by the fermentation of corn syrup, this is used in a powder form as a thickening or gelling agent.

yarrow (*achillea millefolium*)
This has a very bitter taste and I use it in small doses when I want to add bitterness.

index

acknowledgements

Thank you to my kitchen brigade for their relentless hard work, both on work days and for coming in on your days of rest; your dedication is appreciated so much. To Matt, my sous chef, for his willingness to grasp new ideas, provide stability and 'your music choice' – thank God. To Mark, for his creativity and sheer talent. To Keiron, our apprentice, now a commis – you have grown up in the kitchen; thank you for your enthusiasm. To Sue, our new arrival, for her level head and sheer organisation, and that big smile. Thank you to George Blogg, my last sous chef, for all his help, wisdom and loyalty. And to the chefs that have worked here, I am proud of you all.

To our front of house girls, Eva, Matt's wife, thank you for your hard work. We were delighted when you joined us at the beginning of the year. And a very special thank you to Justyna, our longest serving member of staff; you have proved to be a great asset to the restaurant and your thirst for knowledge is inspiring!

To Lisa Barber for her work on this third book; your work is better than ever, hard when it is always brilliant. To my publisher Jon Croft, thank you for sticking with me through Beyond Essence. To Matt Inwood for your artistic eye in designing the book. To Norma MacMillan for all the help and suggestions to make me a better writer.

And last but not least, our customers: thank you for your support and here's to the next 25 years!

With our white Boxer, Alba and Brindle Boxer, Truffle.